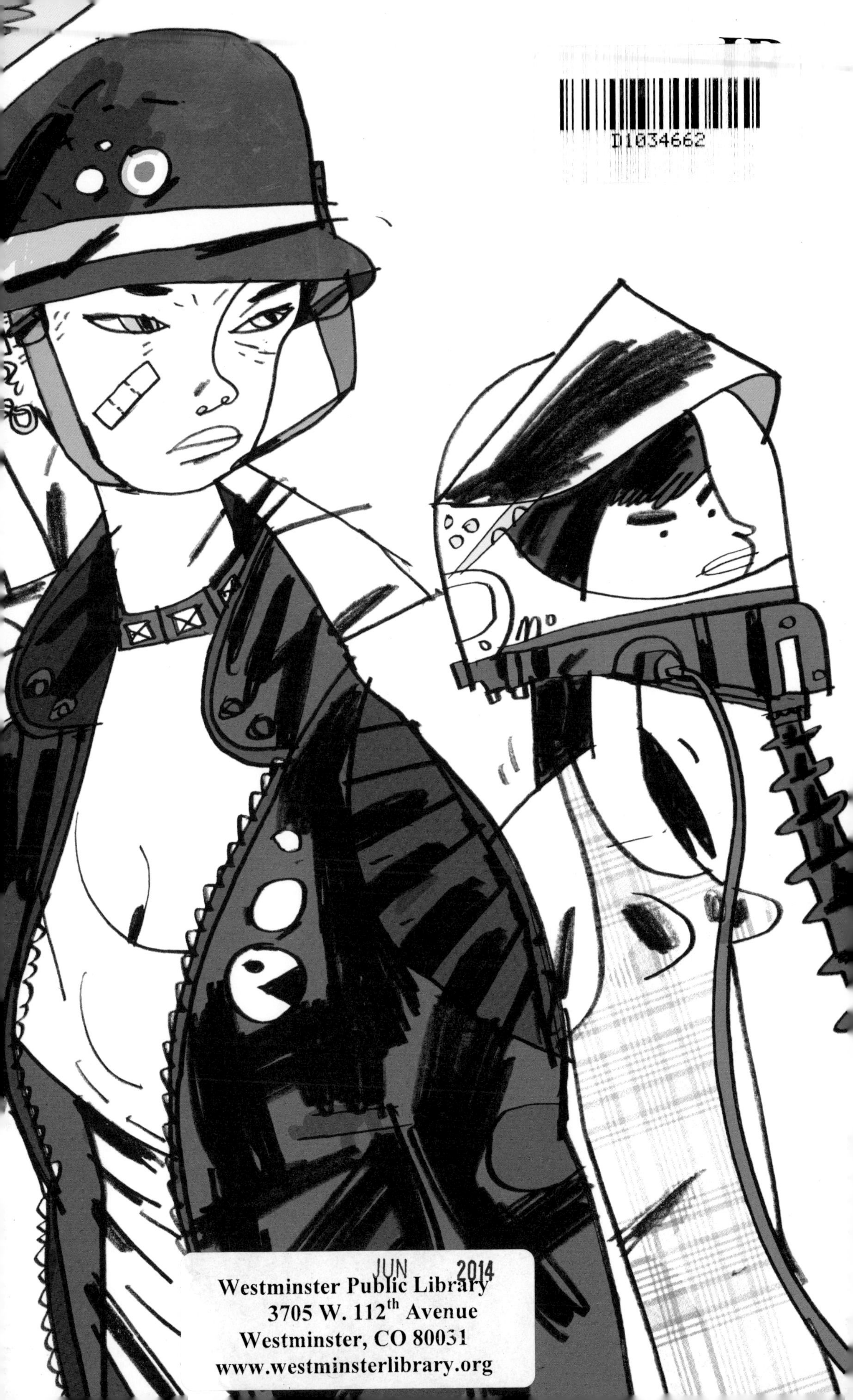

Solid State
TANK ★ GiRL

ALAN MARTIN

WARWICK
JOHNSON-CADWELL

Titan
COMICS

Solid State
TANK ★ GiRL

EDITOR
Steve White

DESIGNER
Tom Hunt

TITAN COMICS EDITORIAL
Andrew James, Jon Chapple,
Gabriela Houston

PRODUCTION SUPERVISORS
Kelly Fenlon, Jackie Flook

INTERIM PRODUCTION ASSISTANT
Peter James

ART DIRECTOR
Oz Browne

STUDIO MANAGER
Selina Juneja

CIRCULATION MANAGER
Steve Tothill

MARKETING MANAGER
Ricky Claydon

MARKTING ASSISTANT
Tara Felton

PUBLISHING MANAGER
Darryl Tothill

PUBLISHING DIRECTOR
Chris Teather

OPERATIONS DIRECTOR
Leigh Baulch

EXECUTIVE DIRECTOR
Vivian Cheung

PUBLISHER
Nick Landau

To receive news, competitions, and
exclusive offers online, please sign up for
the Titan Comics newsletter on our website:
WWW.TITAN-COMICS.COM

SOLID STATE TANK GIRL
ISBN: 9781782760030

Published by Titan Comics
A division of Titan Publishing
Group Ltd
144 Southwark St
London
SE1 0UP

A CIP catalogue record for this
title is available from the British
Library.

First edition: January 2014

10 9 8 7 6 5 4 3 2

Printed in China.
Titan Comics. TC006

What did you think of this book? We love to hear from
our readers. Please email us at:
READERCOMMENTS@TITANEMAIL.COM
or write to us at the above address.

Solid State

WRITER
ALAN C MARTIN

ARTIST
WARWICK JOHNSON-CADWELL

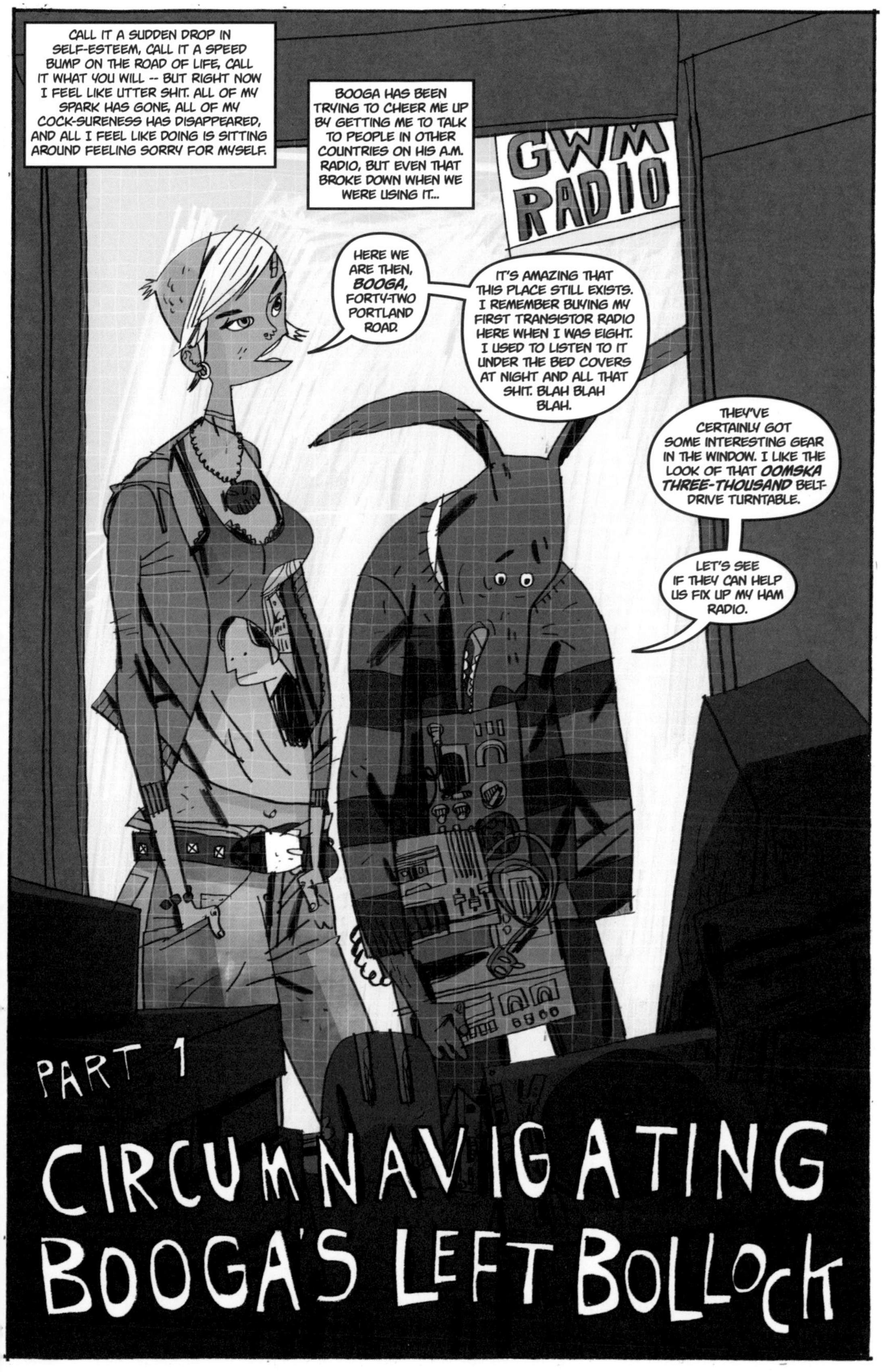

CALL IT A SUDDEN DROP IN SELF-ESTEEM, CALL IT A SPEED BUMP ON THE ROAD OF LIFE, CALL IT WHAT YOU WILL -- BUT RIGHT NOW I FEEL LIKE UTTER SHIT. ALL OF MY SPARK HAS GONE, ALL OF MY COCK-SURENESS HAS DISAPPEARED, AND ALL I FEEL LIKE DOING IS SITTING AROUND FEELING SORRY FOR MYSELF.
BOOGA HAS BEEN TRYING TO CHEER ME UP BY GETTING ME TO TALK TO PEOPLE IN OTHER COUNTRIES ON HIS A.M. RADIO, BUT EVEN THAT BROKE DOWN WHEN WE WERE USING IT...
GWM RADIO
HERE WE ARE THEN, *BOOGA,* FORTY-TWO PORTLAND ROAD.
IT'S AMAZING THAT THIS PLACE STILL EXISTS. I REMEMBER BUYING MY FIRST TRANSISTOR RADIO HERE WHEN I WAS EIGHT. I USED TO LISTEN TO IT UNDER THE BED COVERS AT NIGHT AND ALL THAT SHIT. BLAH BLAH BLAH.
THEY'VE CERTAINLY GOT SOME INTERESTING GEAR IN THE WINDOW. I LIKE THE LOOK OF THAT *OOMSKA THREE-THOUSAND* BELT-DRIVE TURNTABLE.
LET'S SEE IF THEY CAN HELP US FIX UP MY HAM RADIO.
PART 1
CIRCUMNAVIGATING BOOGA'S LEFT BOLLOCK

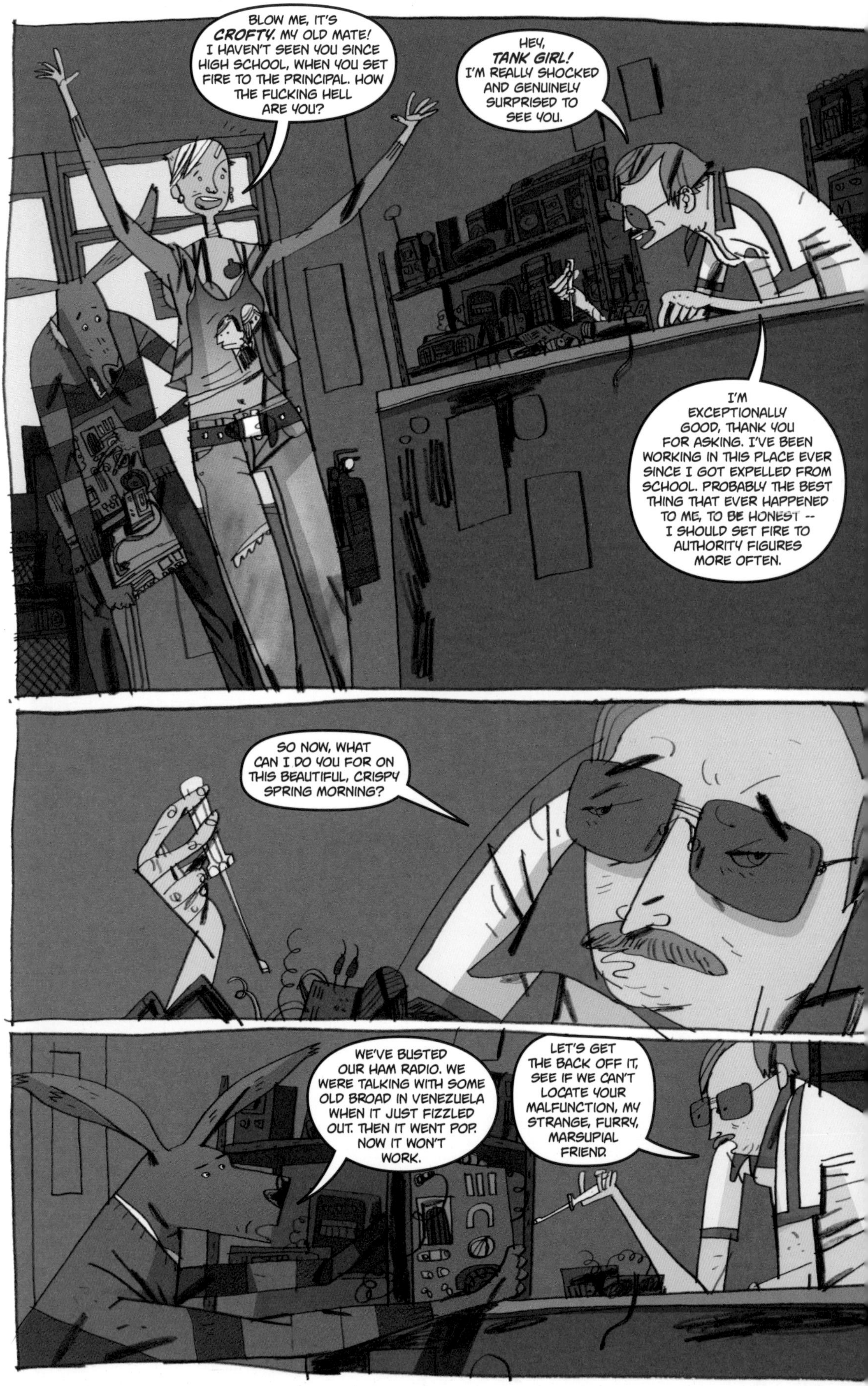
BLOW ME, IT'S CROFTY. MY OLD MATE! I HAVEN'T SEEN YOU SINCE HIGH SCHOOL, WHEN YOU SET FIRE TO THE PRINCIPAL. HOW THE FUCKING HELL ARE YOU?
HEY, TANK GIRL! I'M REALLY SHOCKED AND GENUINELY SURPRISED TO SEE YOU.
I'M EXCEPTIONALLY GOOD, THANK YOU FOR ASKING. I'VE BEEN WORKING IN THIS PLACE EVER SINCE I GOT EXPELLED FROM SCHOOL. PROBABLY THE BEST THING THAT EVER HAPPENED TO ME, TO BE HONEST -- I SHOULD SET FIRE TO AUTHORITY FIGURES MORE OFTEN.
SO NOW, WHAT CAN I DO YOU FOR ON THIS BEAUTIFUL, CRISPY SPRING MORNING?
WE'VE BUSTED OUR HAM RADIO. WE WERE TALKING WITH SOME OLD BROAD IN VENEZUELA WHEN IT JUST FIZZLED OUT. THEN IT WENT POP. NOW IT WON'T WORK.
LET'S GET THE BACK OFF IT, SEE IF WE CAN'T LOCATE YOUR MALFUNCTION, MY STRANGE, FURRY, MARSUPIAL FRIEND.

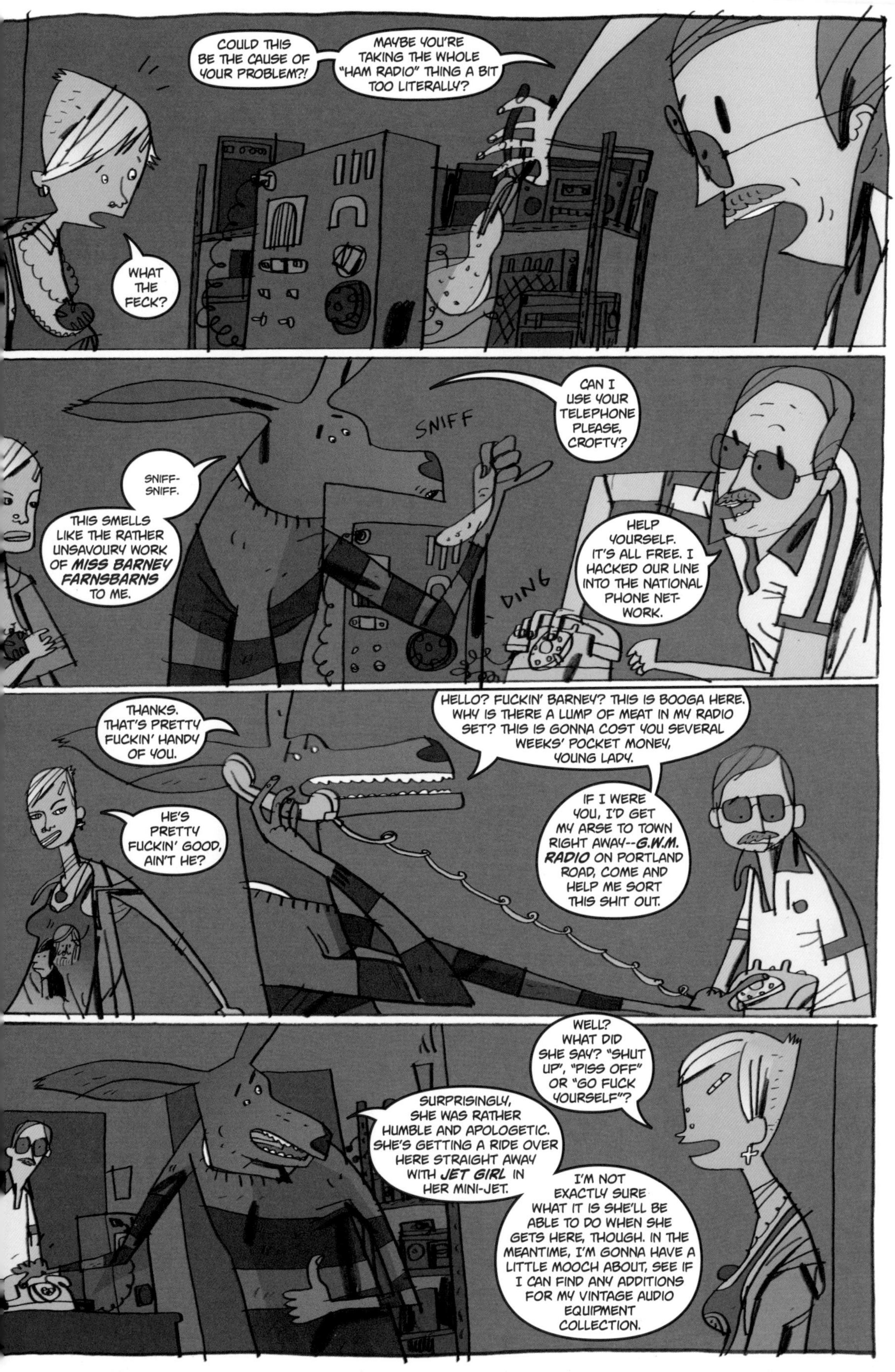
COULD THIS BE THE CAUSE OF YOUR PROBLEM?!
MAYBE YOU'RE TAKING THE WHOLE "HAM RADIO" THING A BIT TOO LITERALLY?
WHAT THE FECK?
CAN I USE YOUR TELEPHONE PLEASE, CROFTY?
SNIFF
SNIFF-SNIFF.
THIS SMELLS LIKE THE RATHER UNSAVOURY WORK OF MISS BARNEY FARNSBARNS TO ME.
HELP YOURSELF. IT'S ALL FREE. I HACKED OUR LINE INTO THE NATIONAL PHONE NET-WORK.
DING
THANKS. THAT'S PRETTY FUCKIN' HANDY OF YOU.
HELLO? FUCKIN' BARNEY? THIS IS BOOGA HERE. WHY IS THERE A LUMP OF MEAT IN MY RADIO SET? THIS IS GONNA COST YOU SEVERAL WEEKS' POCKET MONEY, YOUNG LADY.
HE'S PRETTY FUCKIN' GOOD, AIN'T HE?
IF I WERE YOU, I'D GET MY ARSE TO TOWN RIGHT AWAY--G.W.M. RADIO ON PORTLAND ROAD, COME AND HELP ME SORT THIS SHIT OUT.
WELL? WHAT DID SHE SAY? "SHUT UP", "PISS OFF" OR "GO FUCK YOURSELF"?
SURPRISINGLY, SHE WAS RATHER HUMBLE AND APOLOGETIC. SHE'S GETTING A RIDE OVER HERE STRAIGHT AWAY WITH JET GIRL IN HER MINI-JET.
I'M NOT EXACTLY SURE WHAT IT IS SHE'LL BE ABLE TO DO WHEN SHE GETS HERE, THOUGH. IN THE MEANTIME, I'M GONNA HAVE A LITTLE MOOCH ABOUT, SEE IF I CAN FIND ANY ADDITIONS FOR MY VINTAGE AUDIO EQUIPMENT COLLECTION.

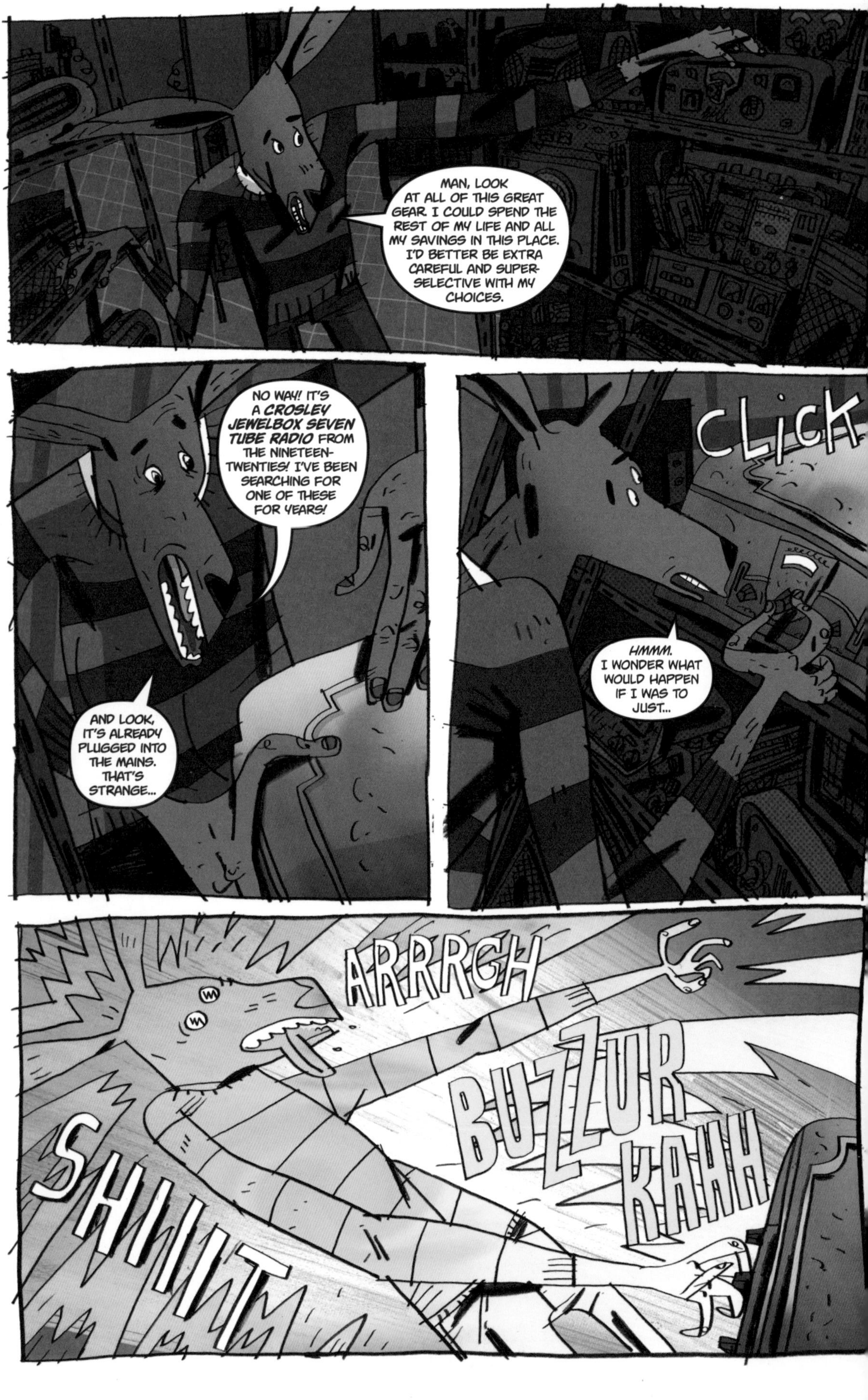
MAN, LOOK AT ALL OF THIS GREAT GEAR. I COULD SPEND THE REST OF MY LIFE AND ALL MY SAVINGS IN THIS PLACE. I'D BETTER BE EXTRA CAREFUL AND SUPER-SELECTIVE WITH MY CHOICES.
NO WAY! IT'S A CROSLEY JEWELBOX SEVEN TUBE RADIO FROM THE NINETEEN-TWENTIES! I'VE BEEN SEARCHING FOR ONE OF THESE FOR YEARS!
AND LOOK, IT'S ALREADY PLUGGED INTO THE MAINS. THAT'S STRANGE...
CLICK
HMMM. I WONDER WHAT WOULD HAPPEN IF I WAS TO JUST...
ARRRGH
BUZZUR
KAHH
SHIIIT

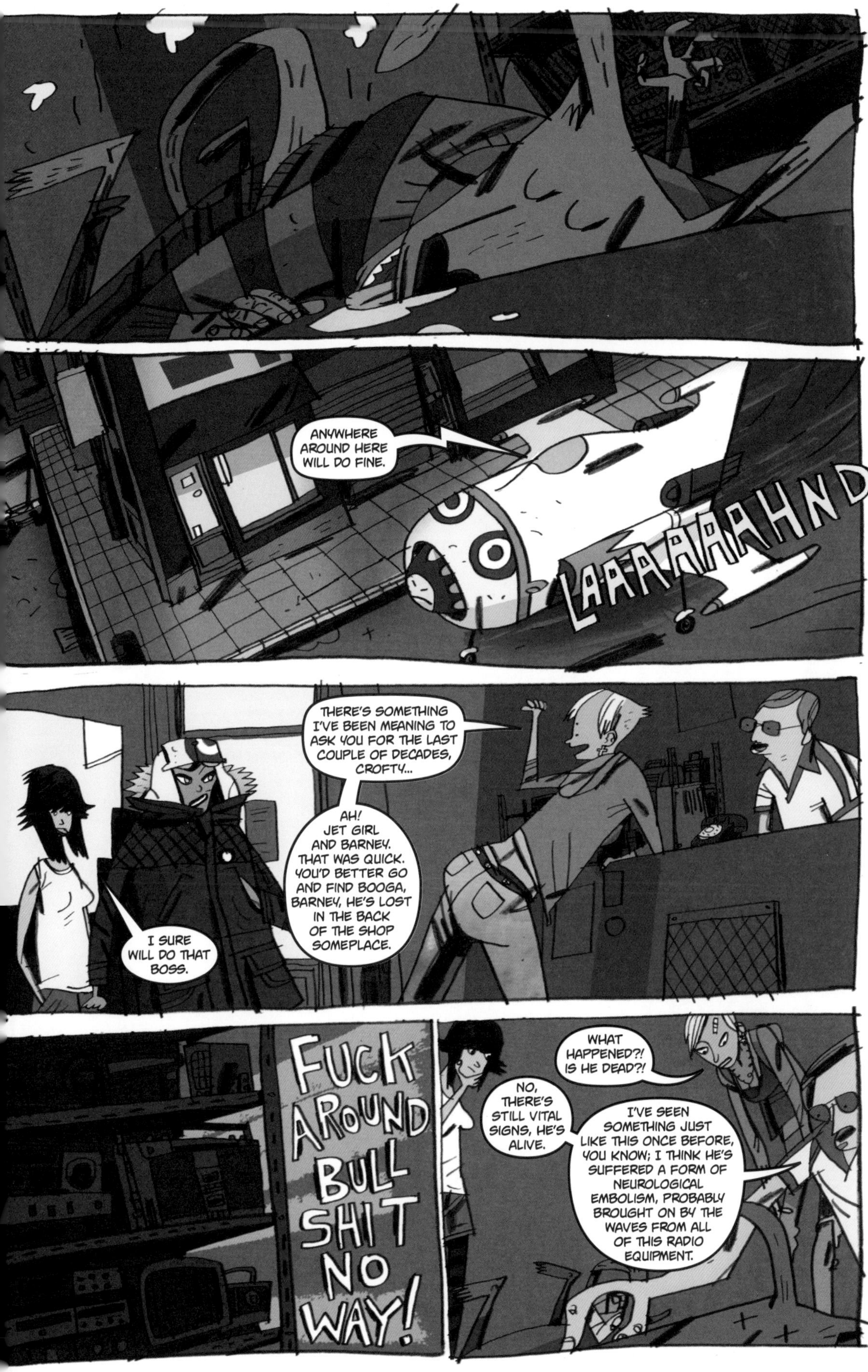
ANYWHERE AROUND HERE WILL DO FINE.
LAAAAAAAHND
THERE'S SOMETHING I'VE BEEN MEANING TO ASK YOU FOR THE LAST COUPLE OF DECADES, CROFTY...
AH! JET GIRL AND BARNEY. THAT WAS QUICK. YOU'D BETTER GO AND FIND BOOGA, BARNEY, HE'S LOST IN THE BACK OF THE SHOP SOMEPLACE.
I SURE WILL DO THAT BOSS.
FUCK AROUND BULL SHIT NO WAY!
WHAT HAPPENED?! IS HE DEAD?!
NO, THERE'S STILL VITAL SIGNS, HE'S ALIVE.
I'VE SEEN SOMETHING JUST LIKE THIS ONCE BEFORE, YOU KNOW; I THINK HE'S SUFFERED A FORM OF NEUROLOGICAL EMBOLISM, PROBABLY BROUGHT ON BY THE WAVES FROM ALL OF THIS RADIO EQUIPMENT.

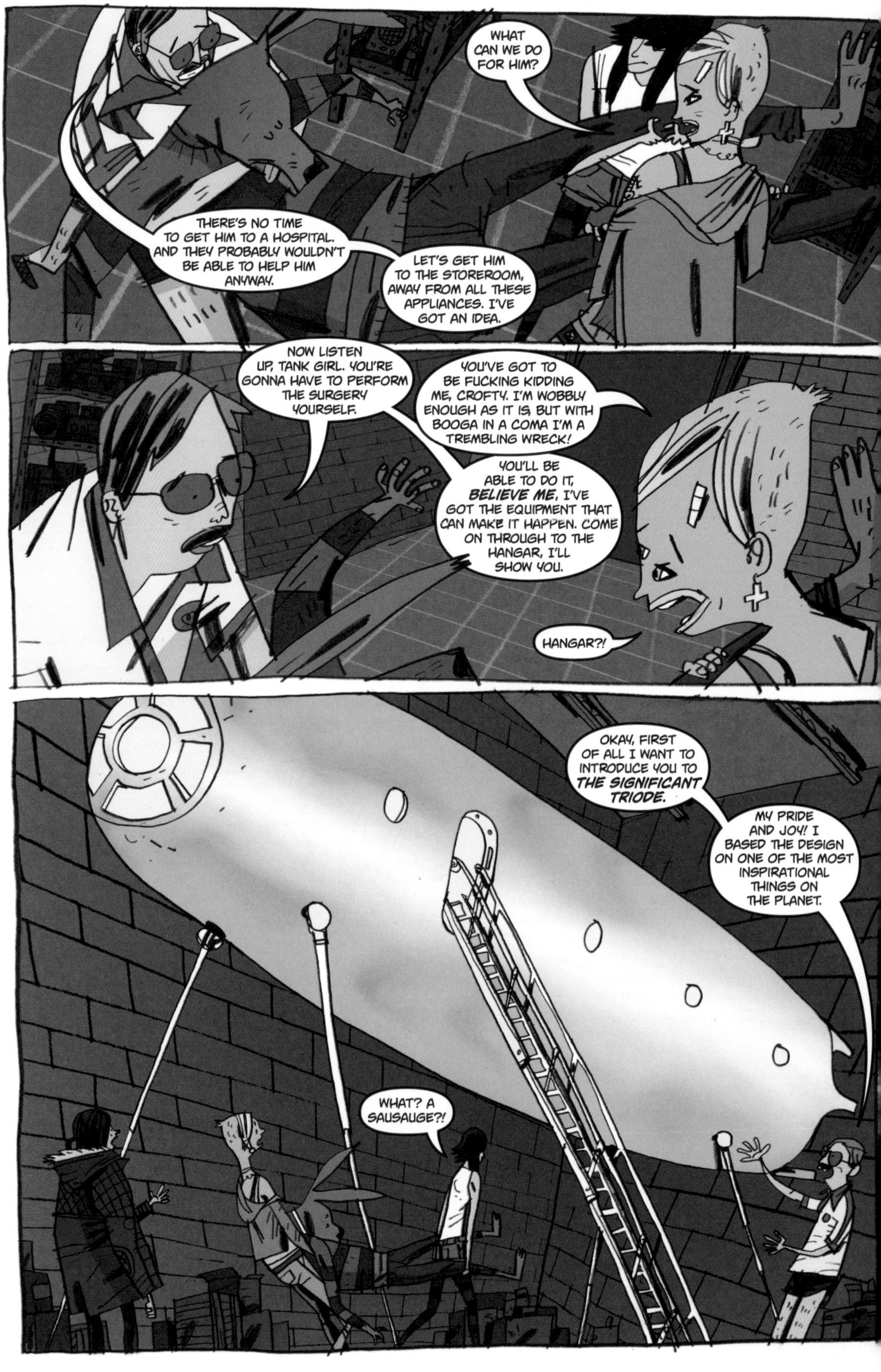
WHAT CAN WE DO FOR HIM?
THERE'S NO TIME TO GET HIM TO A HOSPITAL. AND THEY PROBABLY WOULDN'T BE ABLE TO HELP HIM ANYWAY.
LET'S GET HIM TO THE STOREROOM, AWAY FROM ALL THESE APPLIANCES. I'VE GOT AN IDEA.
NOW LISTEN UP, TANK GIRL. YOU'RE GONNA HAVE TO PERFORM THE SURGERY YOURSELF.
YOU'VE GOT TO BE FUCKING KIDDING ME, CROFTY. I'M WOBBLY ENOUGH AS IT IS, BUT WITH BOOGA IN A COMA I'M A TREMBLING WRECK!
YOU'LL BE ABLE TO DO IT, BELIEVE ME, I'VE GOT THE EQUIPMENT THAT CAN MAKE IT HAPPEN. COME ON THROUGH TO THE HANGAR, I'LL SHOW YOU.
HANGAR?!
OKAY, FIRST OF ALL I WANT TO INTRODUCE YOU TO THE SIGNIFICANT TRIODE.
MY PRIDE AND JOY! I BASED THE DESIGN ON ONE OF THE MOST INSPIRATIONAL THINGS ON THE PLANET.
WHAT? A SAUSAUGE?!

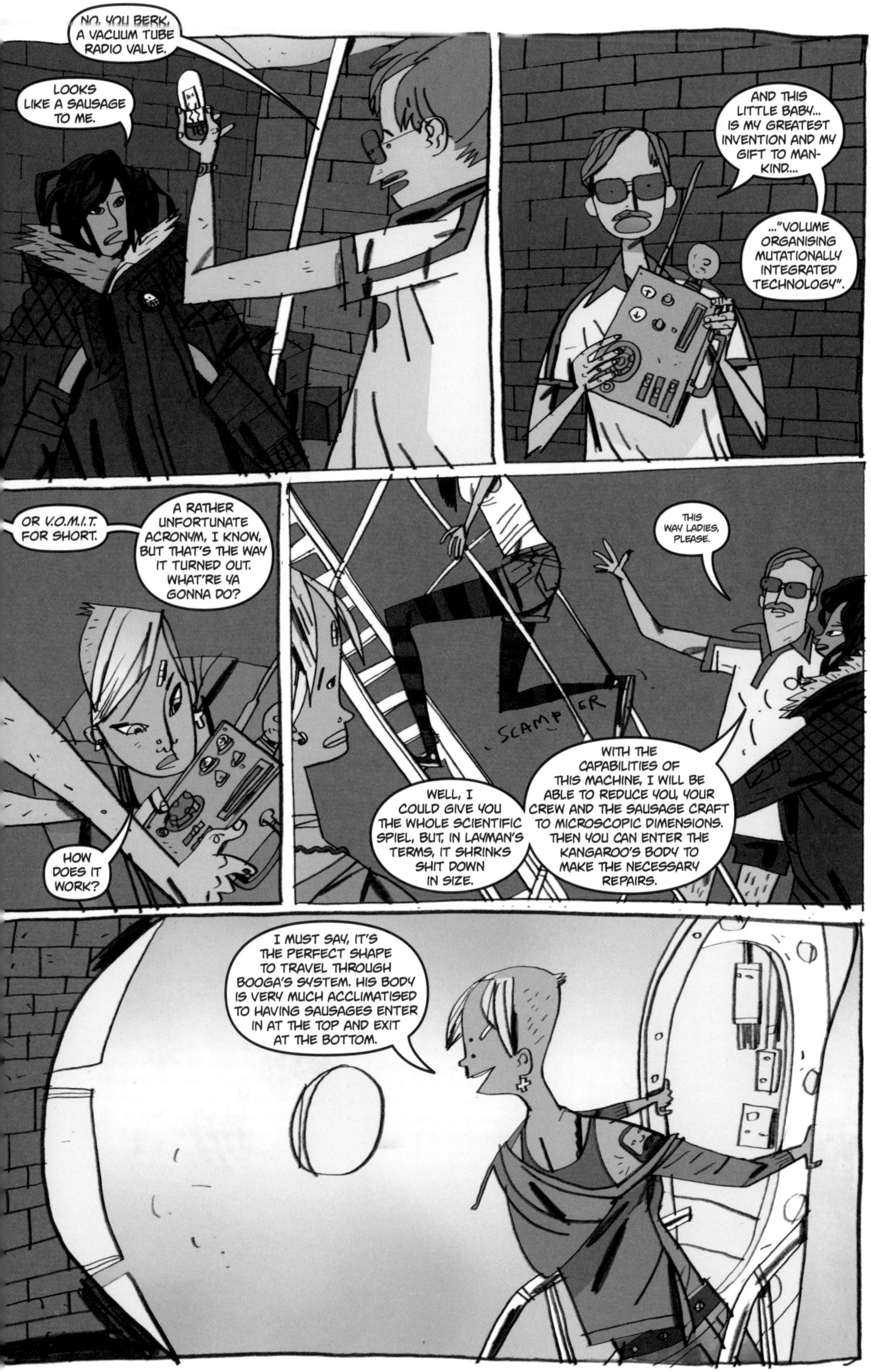
NO, YOU BERK, A VACUUM TUBE RADIO VALVE.
LOOKS LIKE A SAUSAGE TO ME.
AND THIS LITTLE BABY... IS MY GREATEST INVENTION AND MY GIFT TO MAN-KIND...
..."VOLUME ORGANISING MUTATIONALLY INTEGRATED TECHNOLOGY".
OR V.O.M.I.T. FOR SHORT.
A RATHER UNFORTUNATE ACRONYM, I KNOW, BUT THAT'S THE WAY IT TURNED OUT. WHAT'RE YA GONNA DO?
HOW DOES IT WORK?
SCAMPER
THIS WAY LADIES, PLEASE.
WELL, I COULD GIVE YOU THE WHOLE SCIENTIFIC SPIEL, BUT, IN LAYMAN'S TERMS, IT SHRINKS SHIT DOWN IN SIZE.
WITH THE CAPABILITIES OF THIS MACHINE, I WILL BE ABLE TO REDUCE YOU, YOUR CREW AND THE SAUSAGE CRAFT TO MICROSCOPIC DIMENSIONS. THEN YOU CAN ENTER THE KANGAROO'S BODY TO MAKE THE NECESSARY REPAIRS.
I MUST SAY, IT'S THE PERFECT SHAPE TO TRAVEL THROUGH BOOGA'S SYSTEM. HIS BODY IS VERY MUCH ACCLIMATISED TO HAVING SAUSAGES ENTER IN AT THE TOP AND EXIT AT THE BOTTOM.

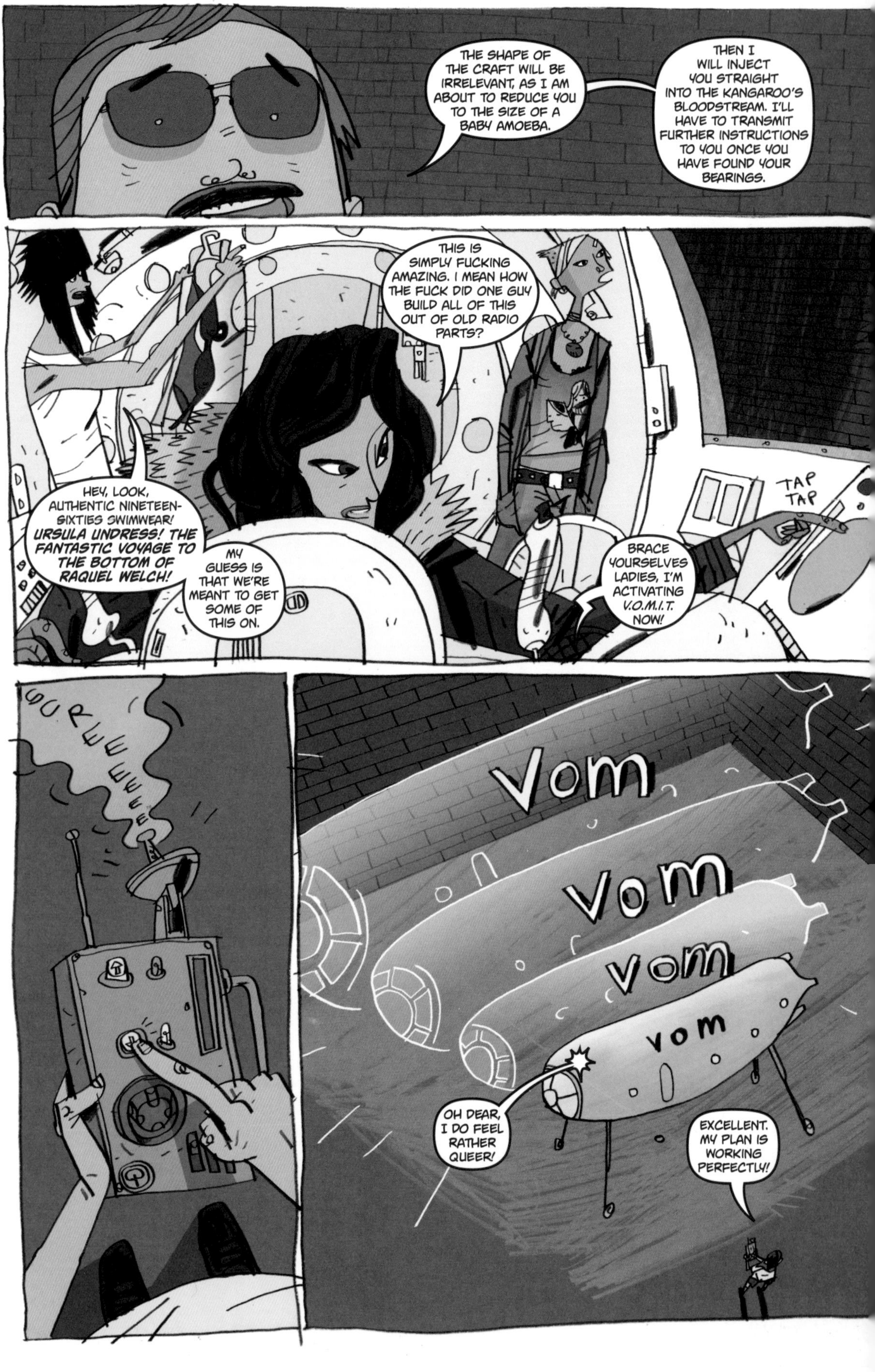
THE SHAPE OF THE CRAFT WILL BE IRRELEVANT, AS I AM ABOUT TO REDUCE YOU TO THE SIZE OF A BABY AMOEBA.
THEN I WILL INJECT YOU STRAIGHT INTO THE KANGAROO'S BLOODSTREAM. I'LL HAVE TO TRANSMIT FURTHER INSTRUCTIONS TO YOU ONCE YOU HAVE FOUND YOUR BEARINGS.
THIS IS SIMPLY FUCKING AMAZING. I MEAN HOW THE FUCK DID ONE GUY BUILD ALL OF THIS OUT OF OLD RADIO PARTS?
HEY, LOOK, AUTHENTIC NINETEEN-SIXTIES SWIMWEAR! URSULA UNDRESS! THE FANTASTIC VOYAGE TO THE BOTTOM OF RAQUEL WELCH!
MY GUESS IS THAT WE'RE MEANT TO GET SOME OF THIS ON.
TAP TAP
BRACE YOURSELVES LADIES, I'M ACTIVATING V.O.M.I.T. NOW!
SQUREEEEEEE
Vom
Vom
vom
vom
OH DEAR, I DO FEEL RATHER QUEER!
EXCELLENT. MY PLAN IS WORKING PERFECTLY!

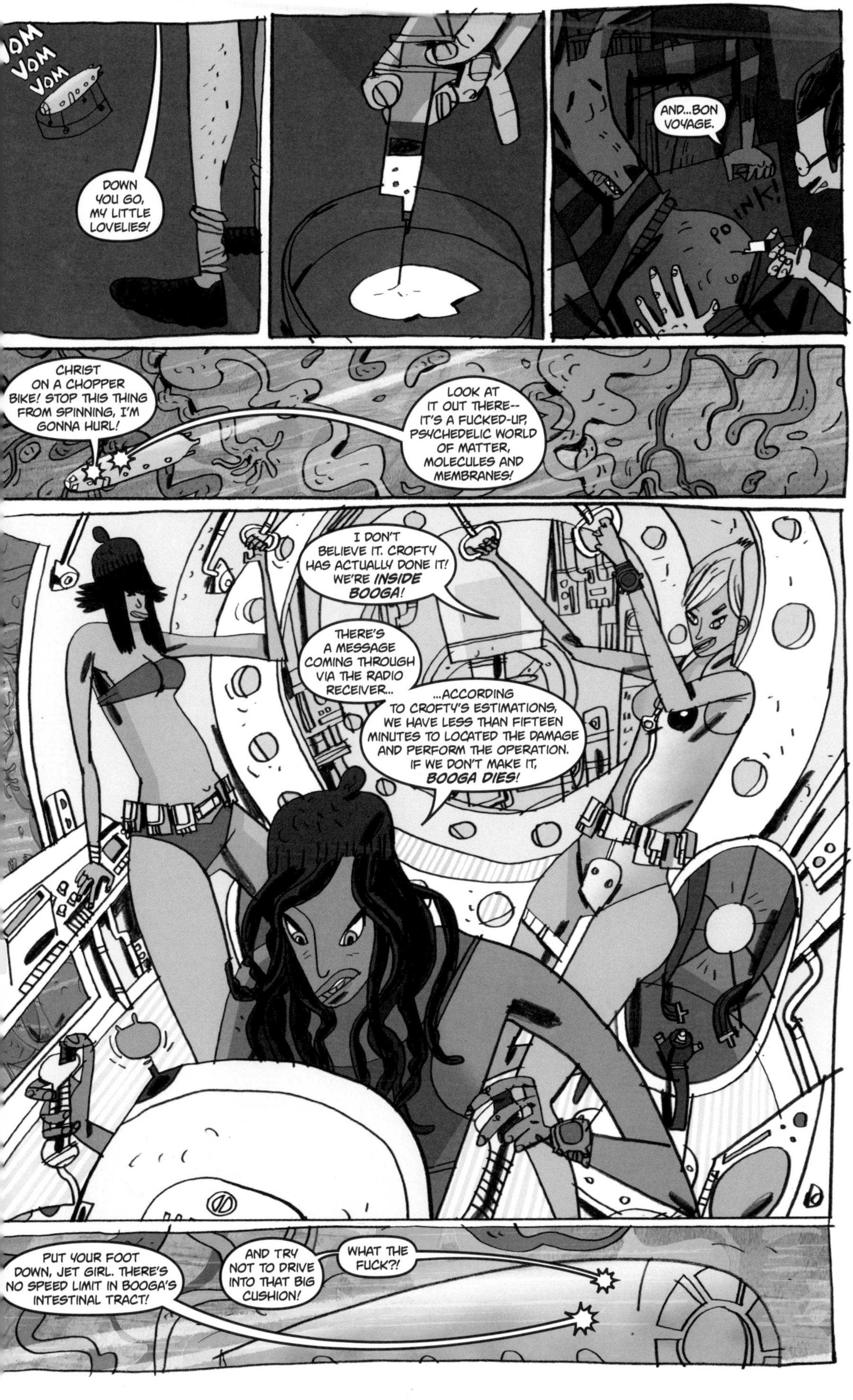
VOM VOM VOM
DOWN YOU GO, MY LITTLE LOVELIES!
AND...BON VOYAGE.
POINK!
CHRIST ON A CHOPPER BIKE! STOP THIS THING FROM SPINNING, I'M GONNA HURL!
LOOK AT IT OUT THERE-- IT'S A FUCKED-UP, PSYCHEDELIC WORLD OF MATTER, MOLECULES AND MEMBRANES!
I DON'T BELIEVE IT. CROFTY HAS ACTUALLY DONE IT! WE'RE *INSIDE BOOGA*!
THERE'S A MESSAGE COMING THROUGH VIA THE RADIO RECEIVER...
...ACCORDING TO CROFTY'S ESTIMATIONS, WE HAVE LESS THAN FIFTEEN MINUTES TO LOCATED THE DAMAGE AND PERFORM THE OPERATION. IF WE DON'T MAKE IT, *BOOGA DIES*!
PUT YOUR FOOT DOWN, JET GIRL. THERE'S NO SPEED LIMIT IN BOOGA'S INTESTINAL TRACT!
AND TRY NOT TO DRIVE INTO THAT BIG CUSHION!
WHAT THE FUCK?!

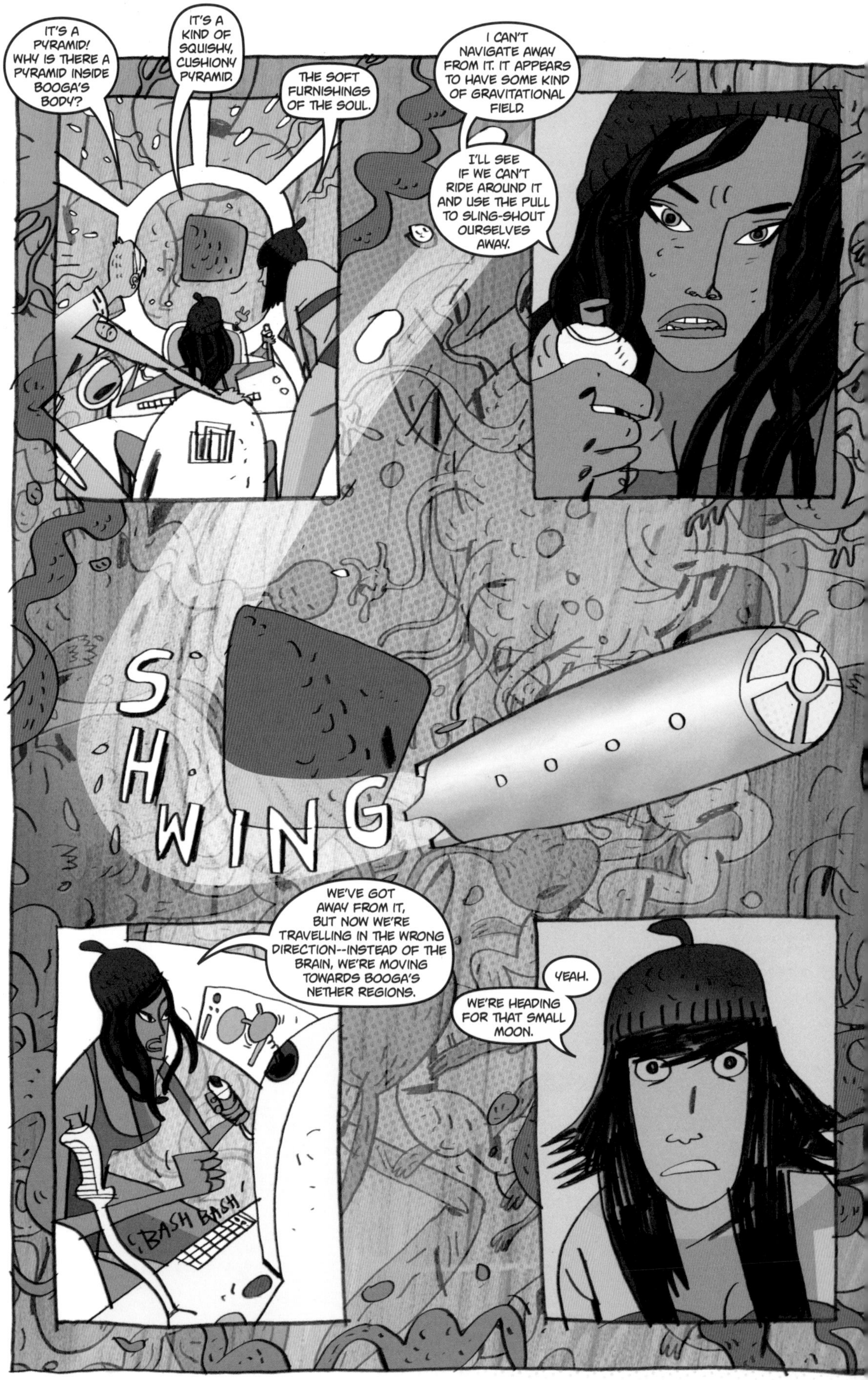
IT'S A PYRAMID! WHY IS THERE A PYRAMID INSIDE BOOGA'S BODY?
IT'S A KIND OF SQUISHY, CUSHIONY PYRAMID.
THE SOFT FURNISHINGS OF THE SOUL.
I CAN'T NAVIGATE AWAY FROM IT. IT APPEARS TO HAVE SOME KIND OF GRAVITATIONAL FIELD.
I'LL SEE IF WE CAN'T RIDE AROUND IT AND USE THE PULL TO SLING-SHOUT OURSELVES AWAY.
SHWING
WE'VE GOT AWAY FROM IT, BUT NOW WE'RE TRAVELLING IN THE WRONG DIRECTION--INSTEAD OF THE BRAIN, WE'RE MOVING TOWARDS BOOGA'S NETHER REGIONS.
BASH BASH
YEAH.
WE'RE HEADING FOR THAT SMALL MOON.

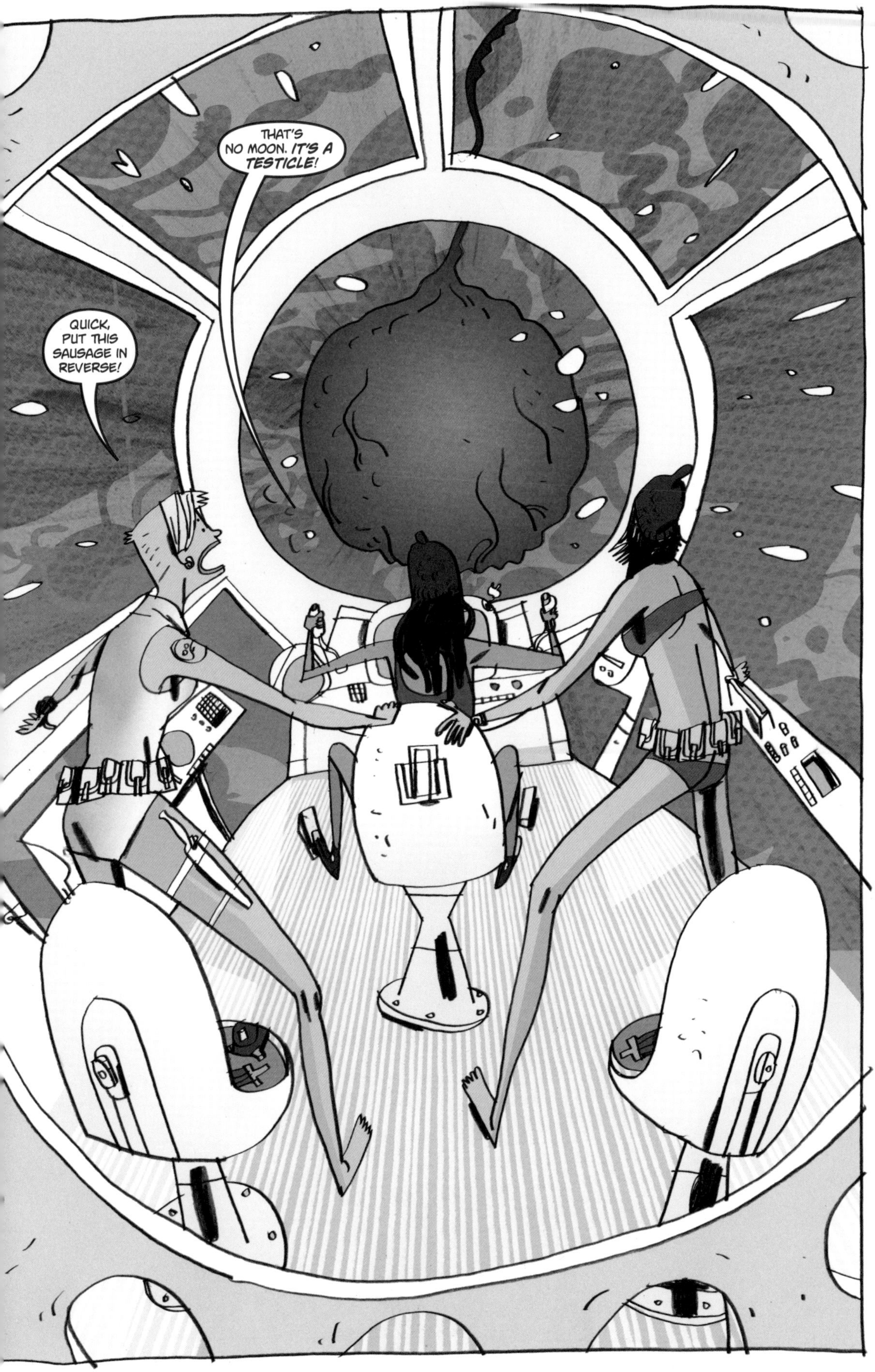
THAT'S NO MOON. IT'S A TESTICLE!
QUICK, PUT THIS SAUSAGE IN REVERSE!

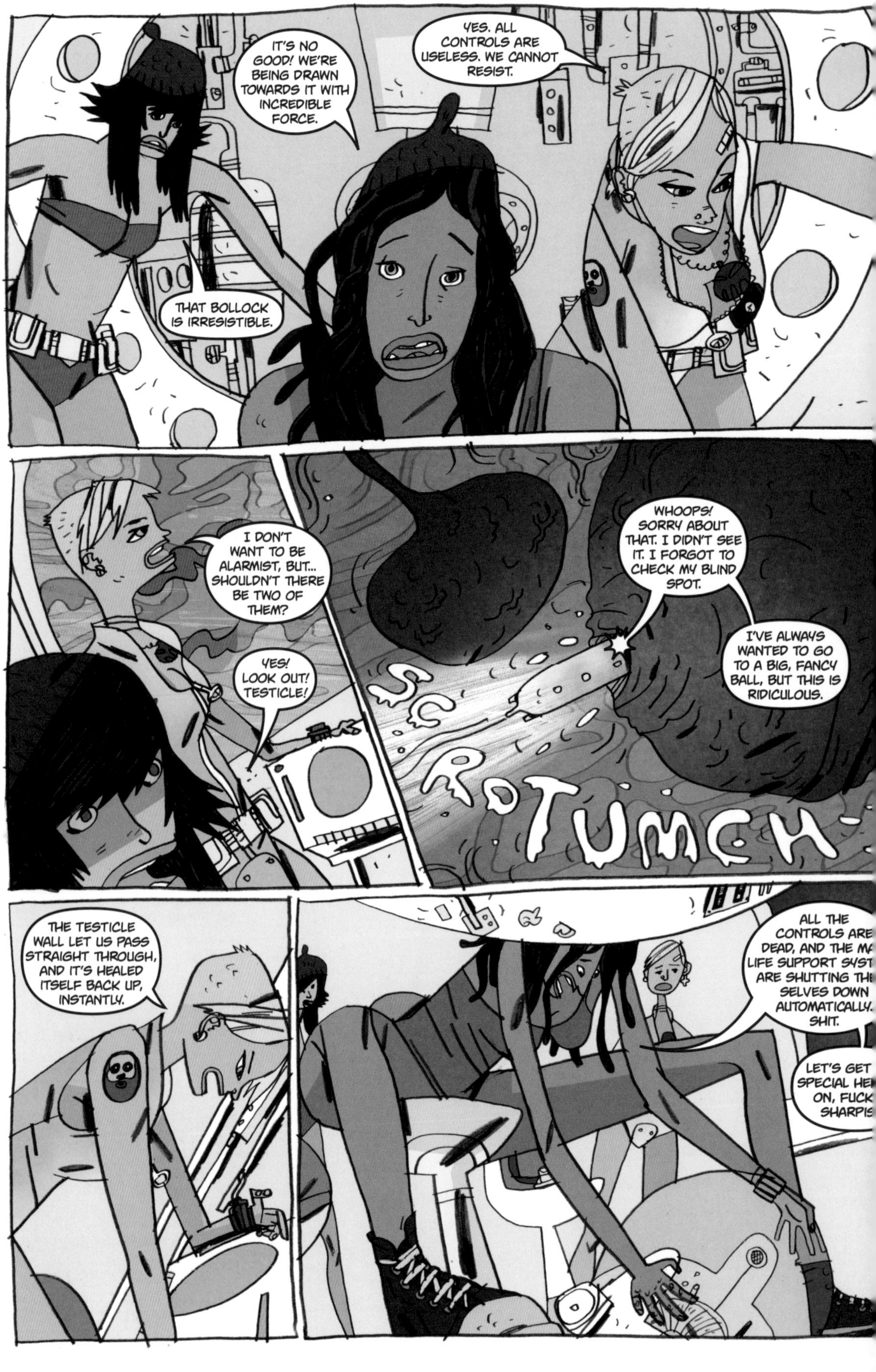
IT'S NO GOOD! WE'RE BEING DRAWN TOWARDS IT WITH INCREDIBLE FORCE.
YES. ALL CONTROLS ARE USELESS. WE CANNOT RESIST.
THAT BOLLOCK IS IRRESISTIBLE.
I DON'T WANT TO BE ALARMIST, BUT... SHOULDN'T THERE BE TWO OF THEM?
YES! LOOK OUT! TESTICLE!
WHOOPS! SORRY ABOUT THAT. I DIDN'T SEE IT. I FORGOT TO CHECK MY BLIND SPOT.
I'VE ALWAYS WANTED TO GO TO A BIG, FANCY BALL, BUT THIS IS RIDICULOUS.
SCROTUMCH
THE TESTICLE WALL LET US PASS STRAIGHT THROUGH, AND IT'S HEALED ITSELF BACK UP, INSTANTLY.
ALL THE CONTROLS ARE DEAD, AND THE MA LIFE SUPPORT SYST ARE SHUTTING THE SELVES DOWN AUTOMATICALLY. SHIT.
LET'S GET SPECIAL HE ON, FUCK SHARPIS

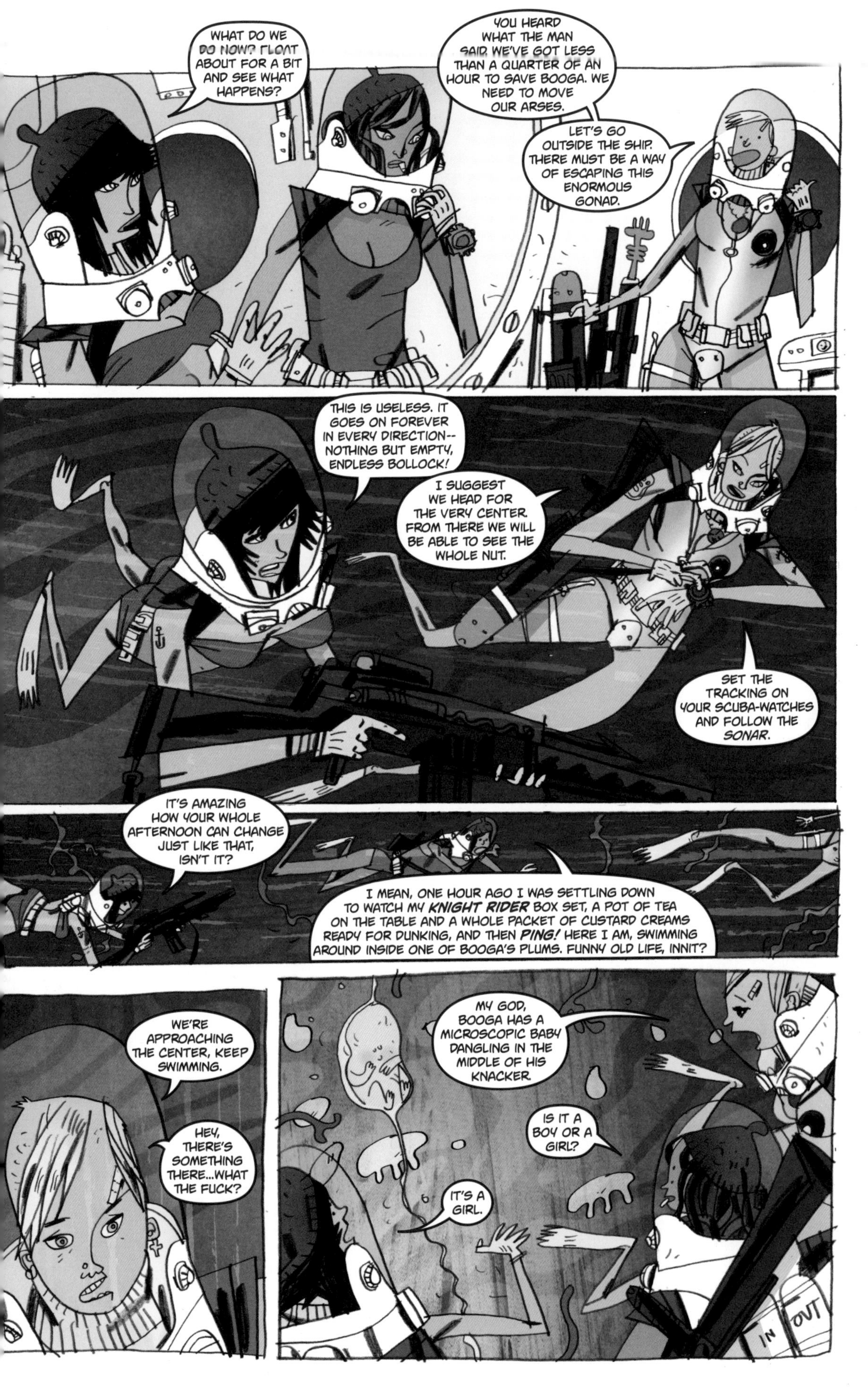
WHAT DO WE DO NOW? FLOAT ABOUT FOR A BIT AND SEE WHAT HAPPENS?
YOU HEARD WHAT THE MAN SAID. WE'VE GOT LESS THAN A QUARTER OF AN HOUR TO SAVE BOOGA. WE NEED TO MOVE OUR ARSES.
LET'S GO OUTSIDE THE SHIP. THERE MUST BE A WAY OF ESCAPING THIS ENORMOUS GONAD.
THIS IS USELESS. IT GOES ON FOREVER IN EVERY DIRECTION-- NOTHING BUT EMPTY, ENDLESS BOLLOCK!
I SUGGEST WE HEAD FOR THE VERY CENTER. FROM THERE WE WILL BE ABLE TO SEE THE WHOLE NUT.
SET THE TRACKING ON YOUR SCUBA-WATCHES AND FOLLOW THE *SONAR*.
IT'S AMAZING HOW YOUR WHOLE AFTERNOON CAN CHANGE JUST LIKE THAT, ISN'T IT?
I MEAN, ONE HOUR AGO I WAS SETTLING DOWN TO WATCH MY ***KNIGHT RIDER*** BOX SET, A POT OF TEA ON THE TABLE AND A WHOLE PACKET OF CUSTARD CREAMS READY FOR DUNKING, AND THEN ***PING!*** HERE I AM, SWIMMING AROUND INSIDE ONE OF BOOGA'S PLUMS. FUNNY OLD LIFE, INNIT?
WE'RE APPROACHING THE CENTER, KEEP SWIMMING.
HEY, THERE'S SOMETHING THERE...WHAT THE FUCK?
MY GOD, BOOGA HAS A MICROSCOPIC BABY DANGLING IN THE MIDDLE OF HIS KNACKER.
IS IT A BOY OR A GIRL?
IT'S A GIRL.
IN
OUT

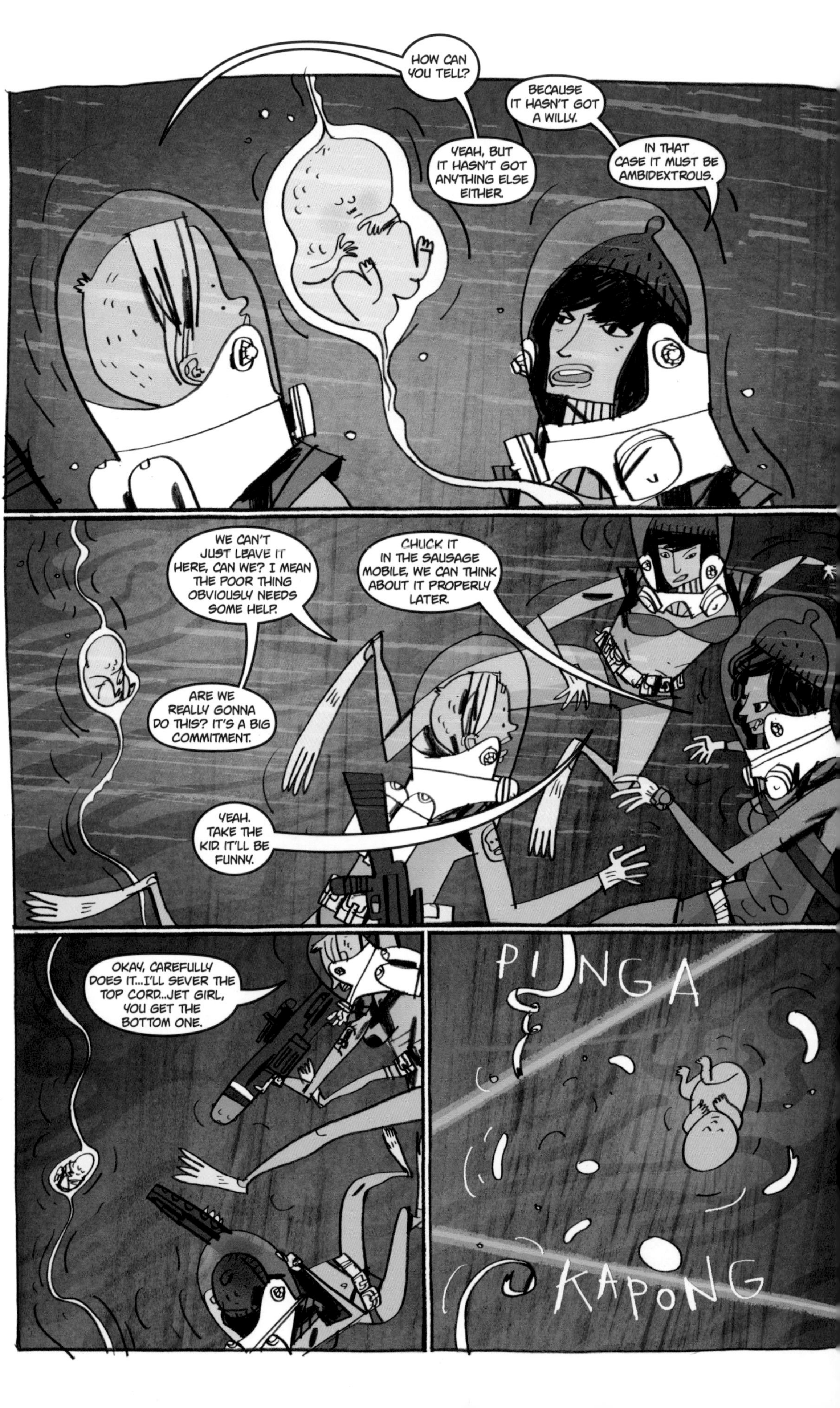
HOW CAN YOU TELL?
BECAUSE IT HASN'T GOT A WILLY.
YEAH, BUT IT HASN'T GOT ANYTHING ELSE EITHER.
IN THAT CASE IT MUST BE AMBIDEXTROUS.
WE CAN'T JUST LEAVE IT HERE, CAN WE? I MEAN THE POOR THING OBVIOUSLY NEEDS SOME HELP.
CHUCK IT IN THE SAUSAGE MOBILE, WE CAN THINK ABOUT IT PROPERLY LATER.
ARE WE REALLY GONNA DO THIS? IT'S A BIG COMMITMENT.
YEAH. TAKE THE KID. IT'LL BE FUNNY.
OKAY, CAREFULLY DOES IT...I'LL SEVER THE TOP CORD...JET GIRL, YOU GET THE BOTTOM ONE.
PINGA
KAPONG

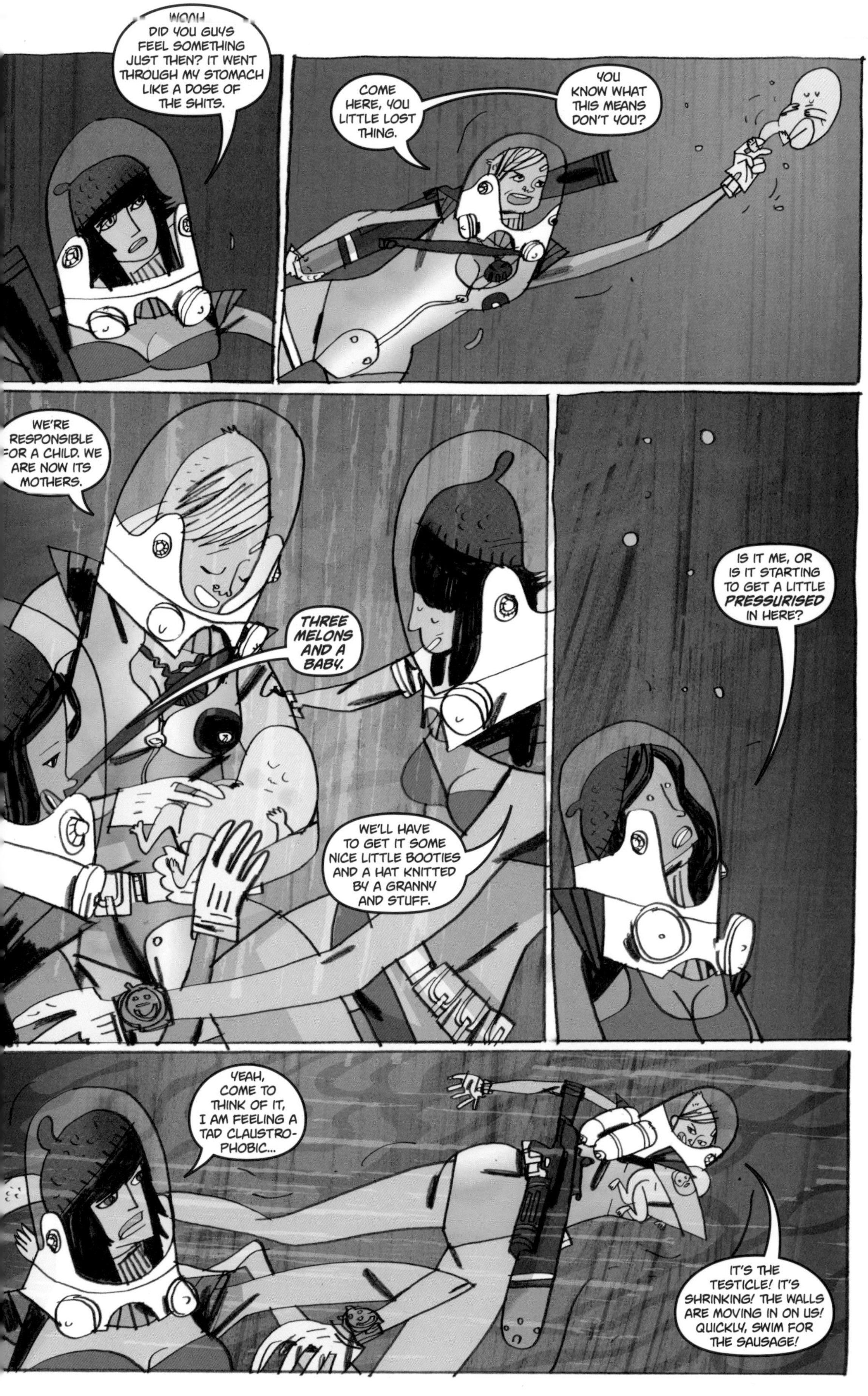
WOAH
DID YOU GUYS FEEL SOMETHING JUST THEN? IT WENT THROUGH MY STOMACH LIKE A DOSE OF THE SHITS.
COME HERE, YOU LITTLE LOST THING.
YOU KNOW WHAT THIS MEANS DON'T YOU?
WE'RE RESPONSIBLE FOR A CHILD. WE ARE NOW ITS MOTHERS.
THREE MELONS AND A BABY.
WE'LL HAVE TO GET IT SOME NICE LITTLE BOOTIES AND A HAT KNITTED BY A GRANNY AND STUFF.
IS IT ME, OR IS IT STARTING TO GET A LITTLE PRESSURISED IN HERE?
YEAH, COME TO THINK OF IT, I AM FEELING A TAD CLAUSTRO-PHOBIC...
IT'S THE TESTICLE! IT'S SHRINKING! THE WALLS ARE MOVING IN ON US! QUICKLY, SWIM FOR THE SAUSAGE!

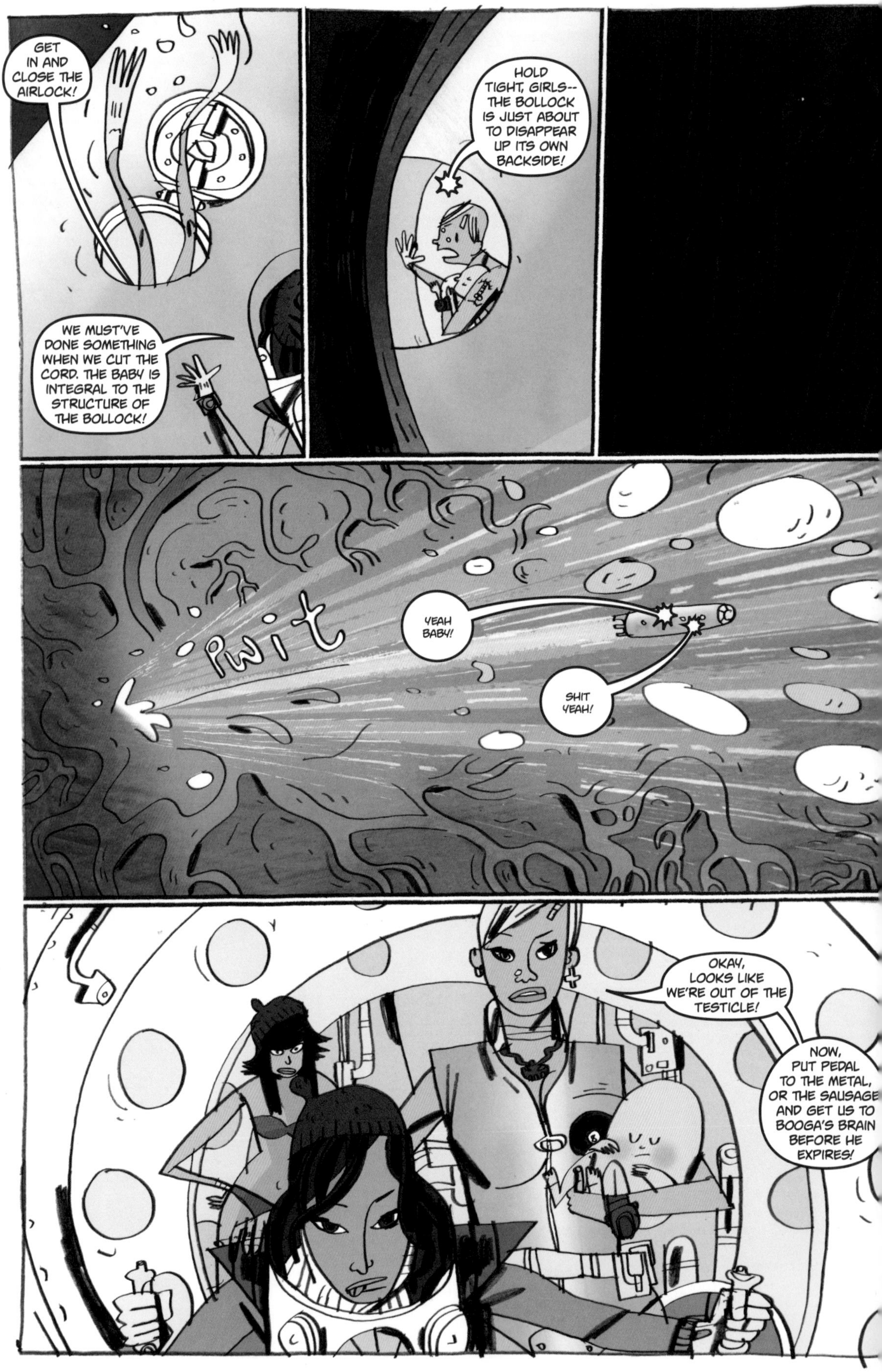
GET IN AND CLOSE THE AIRLOCK!
WE MUST'VE DONE SOMETHING WHEN WE CUT THE CORD. THE BABY IS INTEGRAL TO THE STRUCTURE OF THE BOLLOCK!
HOLD TIGHT, GIRLS-- THE BOLLOCK IS JUST ABOUT TO DISAPPEAR UP ITS OWN BACKSIDE!
PWIT
YEAH BABY!
SHIT YEAH!
OKAY, LOOKS LIKE WE'RE OUT OF THE TESTICLE!
NOW, PUT PEDAL TO THE METAL, OR THE SAUSAGE AND GET US TO BOOGA'S BRAIN BEFORE HE EXPIRES!

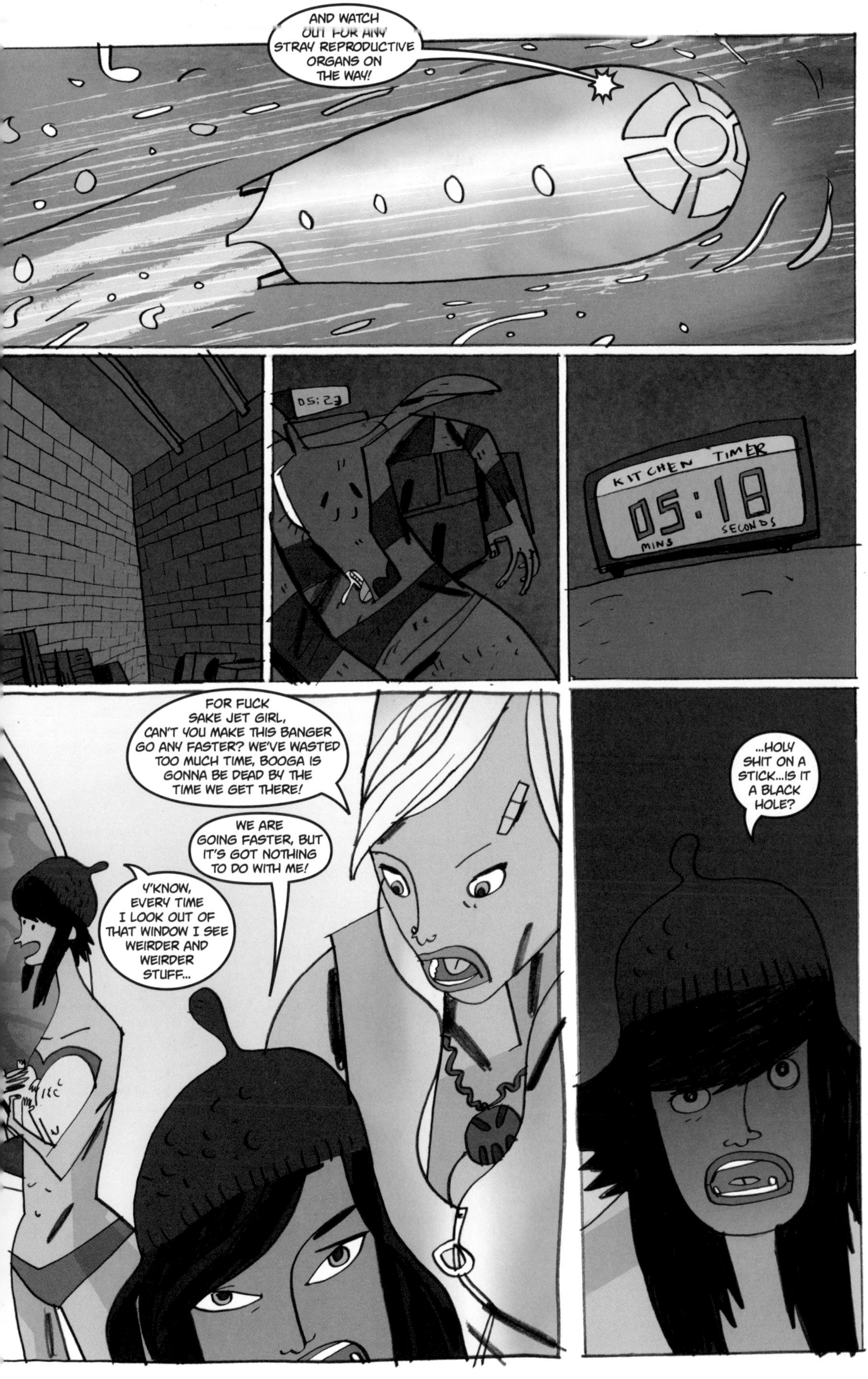
AND WATCH OUT FOR ANY STRAY REPRODUCTIVE ORGANS ON THE WAY!
05:23
KITCHEN TIMER
05:18
MINS
SECONDS
FOR FUCK SAKE JET GIRL, CAN'T YOU MAKE THIS BANGER GO ANY FASTER? WE'VE WASTED TOO MUCH TIME, BOOGA IS GONNA BE DEAD BY THE TIME WE GET THERE!
WE ARE GOING FASTER, BUT IT'S GOT NOTHING TO DO WITH ME!
Y'KNOW, EVERY TIME I LOOK OUT OF THAT WINDOW I SEE WEIRDER AND WEIRDER STUFF...
...HOLY SHIT ON A STICK...IS IT A BLACK HOLE?

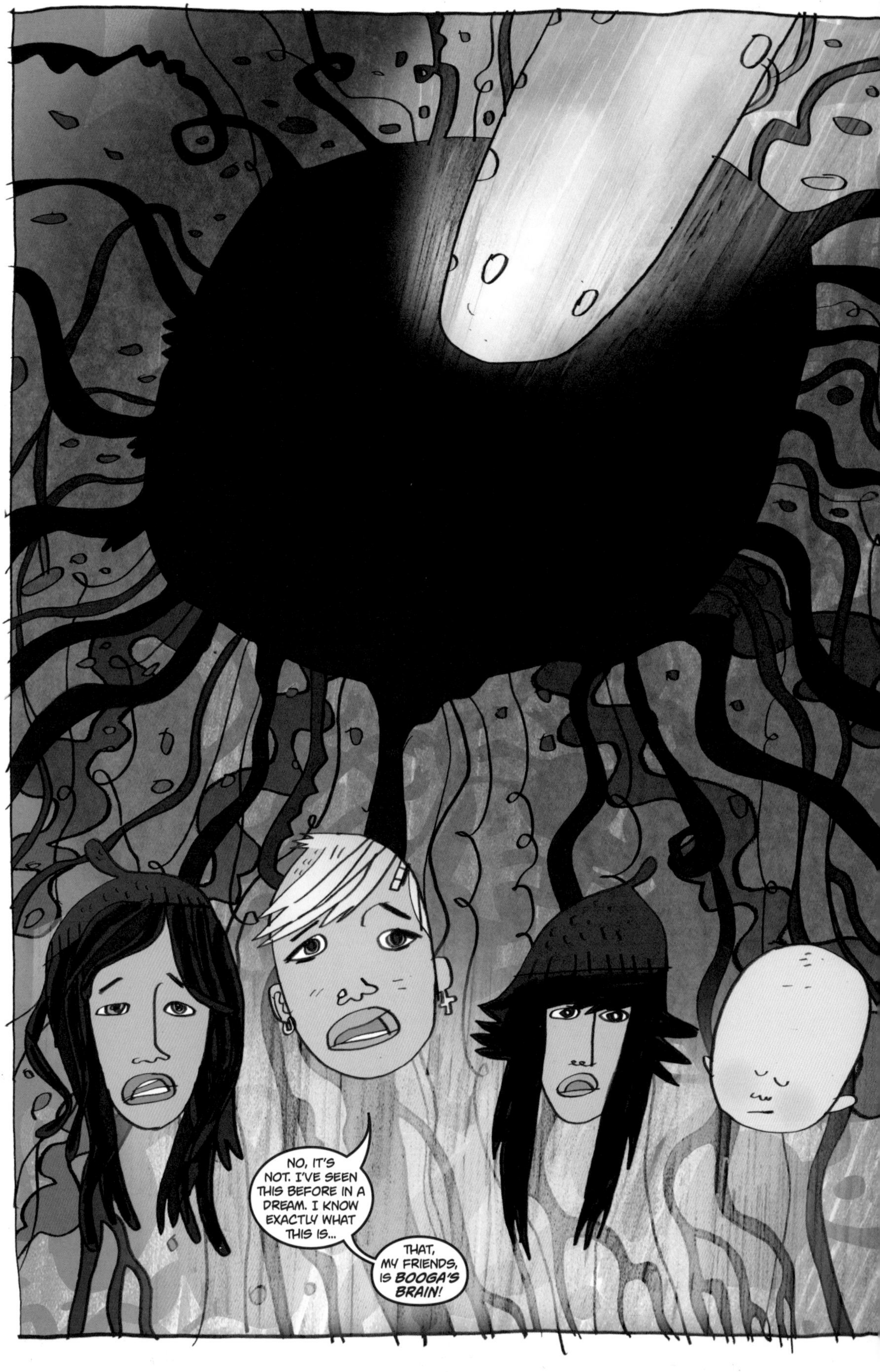
NO, IT'S NOT. I'VE SEEN THIS BEFORE IN A DREAM. I KNOW EXACTLY WHAT THIS IS...
THAT, MY FRIENDS, IS *BOOGA'S BRAIN!*

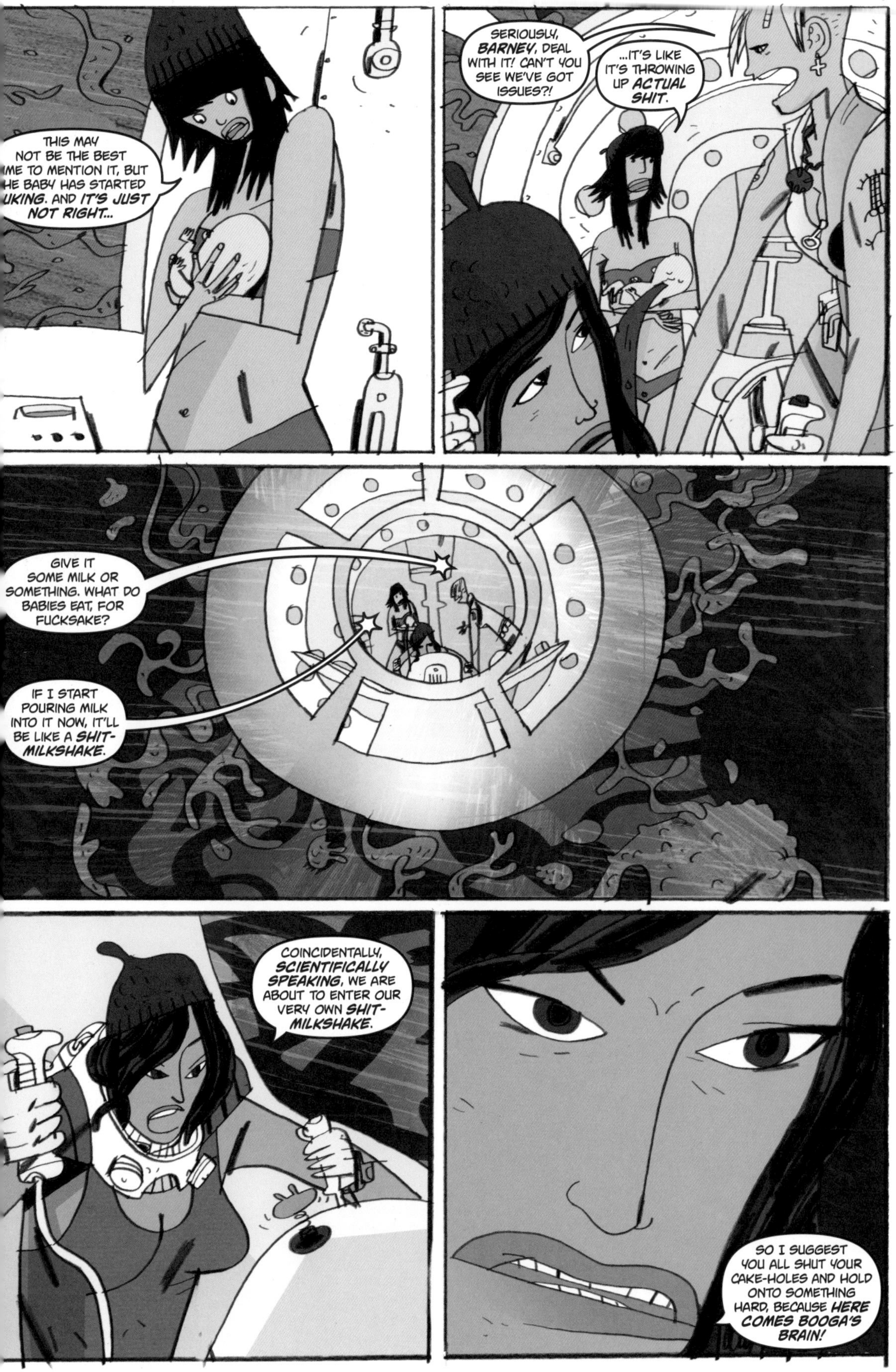

THIS MAY NOT BE THE BEST ME TO MENTION IT, BUT HE BABY HAS STARTED UKING. AND IT'S JUST NOT RIGHT...
SERIOUSLY, BARNEY, DEAL WITH IT! CAN'T YOU SEE WE'VE GOT ISSUES?!
...IT'S LIKE IT'S THROWING UP ACTUAL SHIT.
GIVE IT SOME MILK OR SOMETHING. WHAT DO BABIES EAT, FOR FUCKSAKE?
IF I START POURING MILK INTO IT NOW, IT'LL BE LIKE A SHIT-MILKSHAKE.
COINCIDENTALLY, SCIENTIFICALLY SPEAKING, WE ARE ABOUT TO ENTER OUR VERY OWN SHIT-MILKSHAKE.
SO I SUGGEST YOU ALL SHUT YOUR CAKE-HOLES AND HOLD ONTO SOMETHING HARD, BECAUSE HERE COMES BOOGA'S BRAIN!

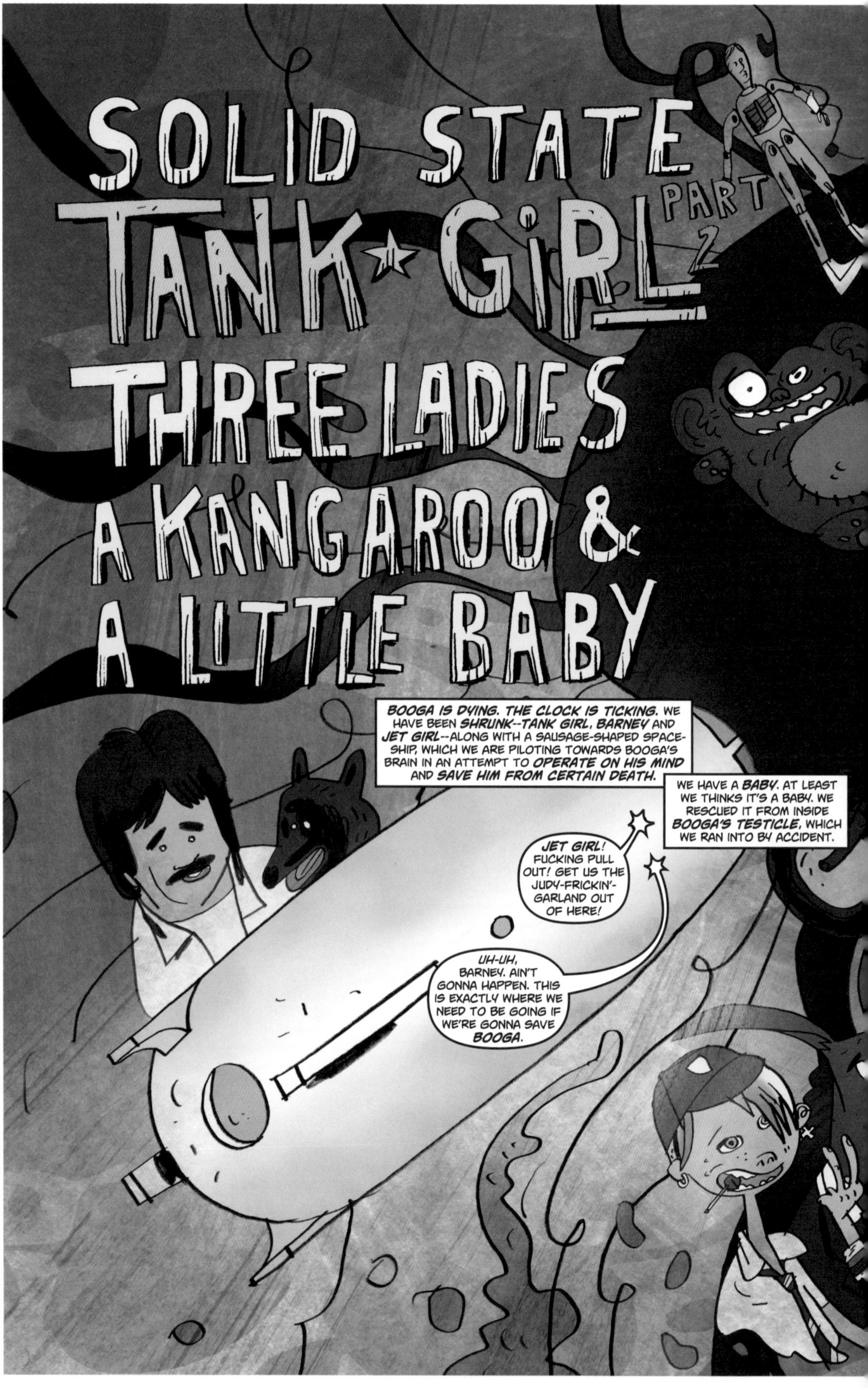
SOLID STATE TANK GIRL PART 2
THREE LADIES A KANGAROO & A LITTLE BABY
BOOGA IS DYING. THE CLOCK IS TICKING. WE HAVE BEEN SHRUNK--TANK GIRL, BARNEY AND JET GIRL--ALONG WITH A SAUSAGE-SHAPED SPACE-SHIP, WHICH WE ARE PILOTING TOWARDS BOOGA'S BRAIN IN AN ATTEMPT TO OPERATE ON HIS MIND AND SAVE HIM FROM CERTAIN DEATH.
WE HAVE A BABY. AT LEAST WE THINKS IT'S A BABY. WE RESCUED IT FROM INSIDE BOOGA'S TESTICLE, WHICH WE RAN INTO BY ACCIDENT.
JET GIRL! FUCKING PULL OUT! GET US THE JUDY-FRICKIN'-GARLAND OUT OF HERE!
UH-UH, BARNEY. AIN'T GONNA HAPPEN. THIS IS EXACTLY WHERE WE NEED TO BE GOING IF WE'RE GONNA SAVE BOOGA.

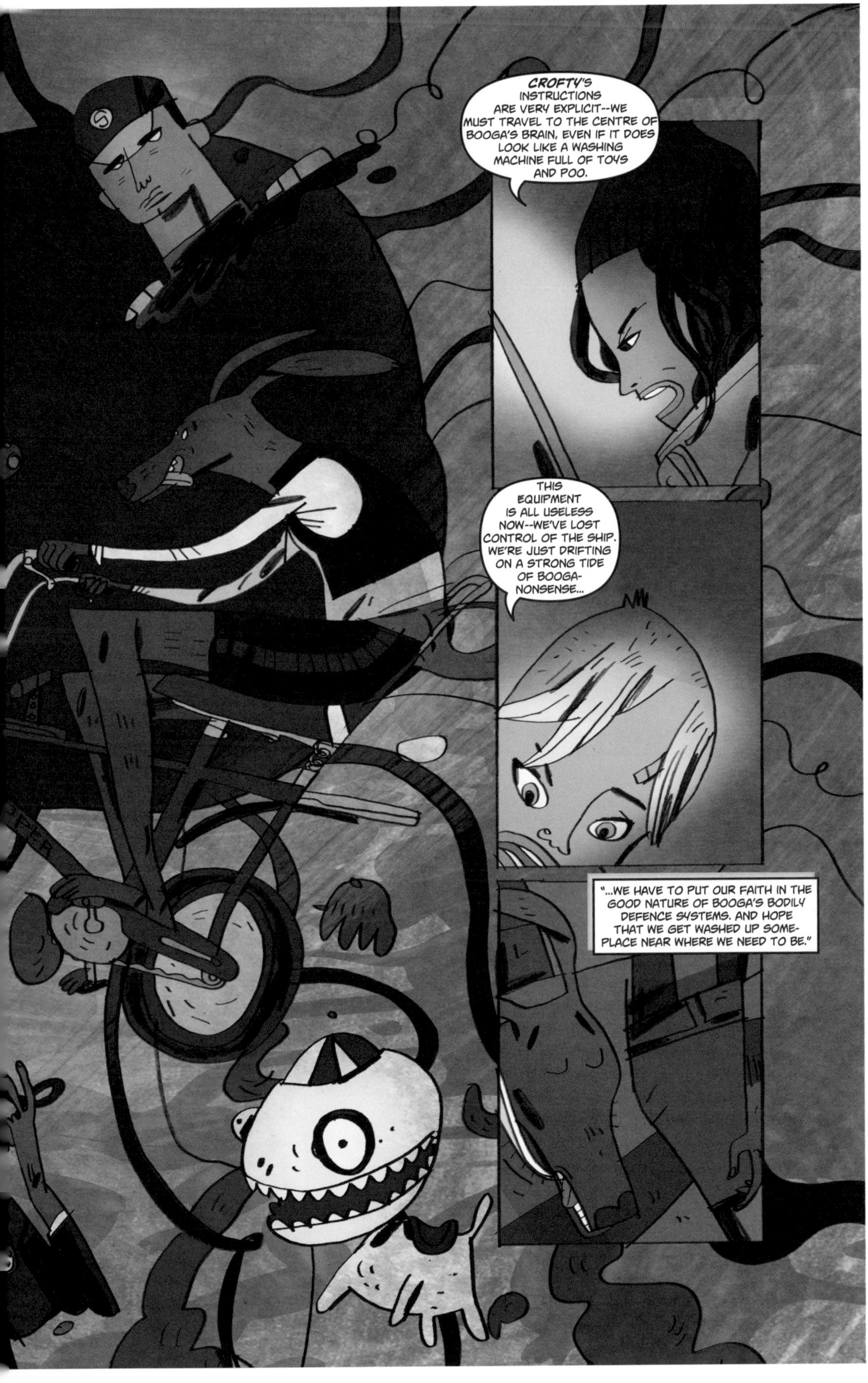
CROFTY'S INSTRUCTIONS ARE VERY EXPLICIT--WE MUST TRAVEL TO THE CENTRE OF BOOGA'S BRAIN, EVEN IF IT DOES LOOK LIKE A WASHING MACHINE FULL OF TOYS AND POO.
THIS EQUIPMENT IS ALL USELESS NOW--WE'VE LOST CONTROL OF THE SHIP. WE'RE JUST DRIFTING ON A STRONG TIDE OF BOOGA-NONSENSE...
"...WE HAVE TO PUT OUR FAITH IN THE GOOD NATURE OF BOOGA'S BODILY DEFENCE SYSTEMS. AND HOPE THAT WE GET WASHED UP SOME-PLACE NEAR WHERE WE NEED TO BE."

THAT'S NOT OUR ONLY PROBLEM--IF BOOGA EXPIRES, HIS BLOOD WILL CLOT AND HIS BODY WILL SEIZE UP. WE'LL BE STUCK LIKE SHIT IN YOUR GRIPS.

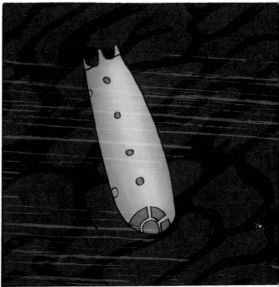

YEAH, WELL, BOOGA AIN'T GONNA DIE. *I WON'T LET HIM.*

CAN WE TELL IF THIS THING IS STILL MOVING?

ACCORDING TO THE MOTION DETECTORS, WE'VE STOPPED DEAD.

RIGHT. TIME TO SORT THIS SHIT OUT ONCE AND FOR ALL. I'M GOING OUT.

ALONE.

CLICK

I MAY BE SOME TIME.

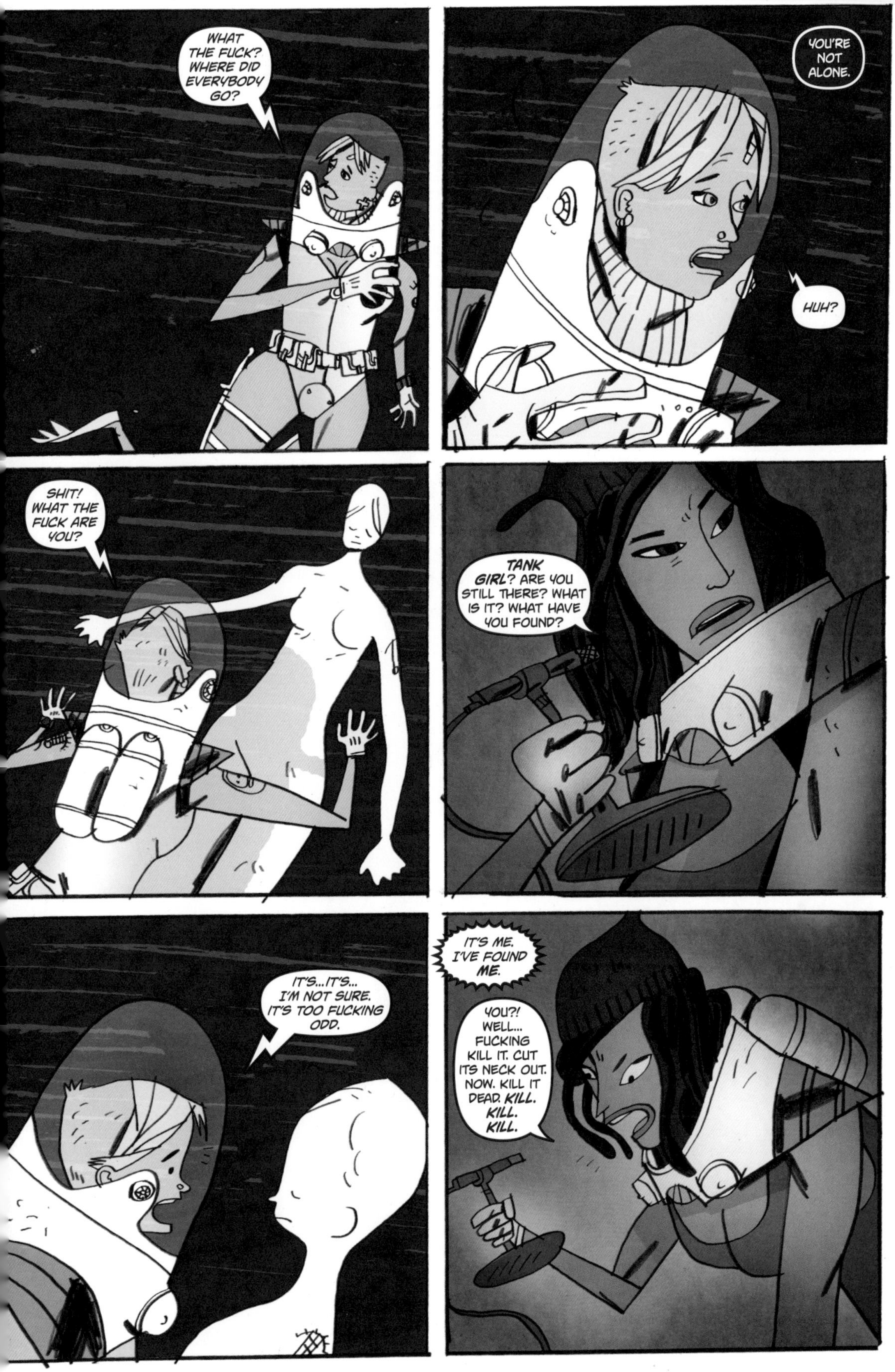
WHAT THE FUCK? WHERE DID EVERYBODY GO?
YOU'RE NOT ALONE.
HUH?
SHIT! WHAT THE FUCK ARE YOU?
TANK GIRL? ARE YOU STILL THERE? WHAT IS IT? WHAT HAVE YOU FOUND?
IT'S...IT'S... I'M NOT SURE. IT'S TOO FUCKING ODD.
IT'S ME. I'VE FOUND ME.
YOU?! WELL... FUCKING KILL IT. CUT ITS NECK OUT. NOW. KILL IT DEAD. KILL. KILL. KILL.

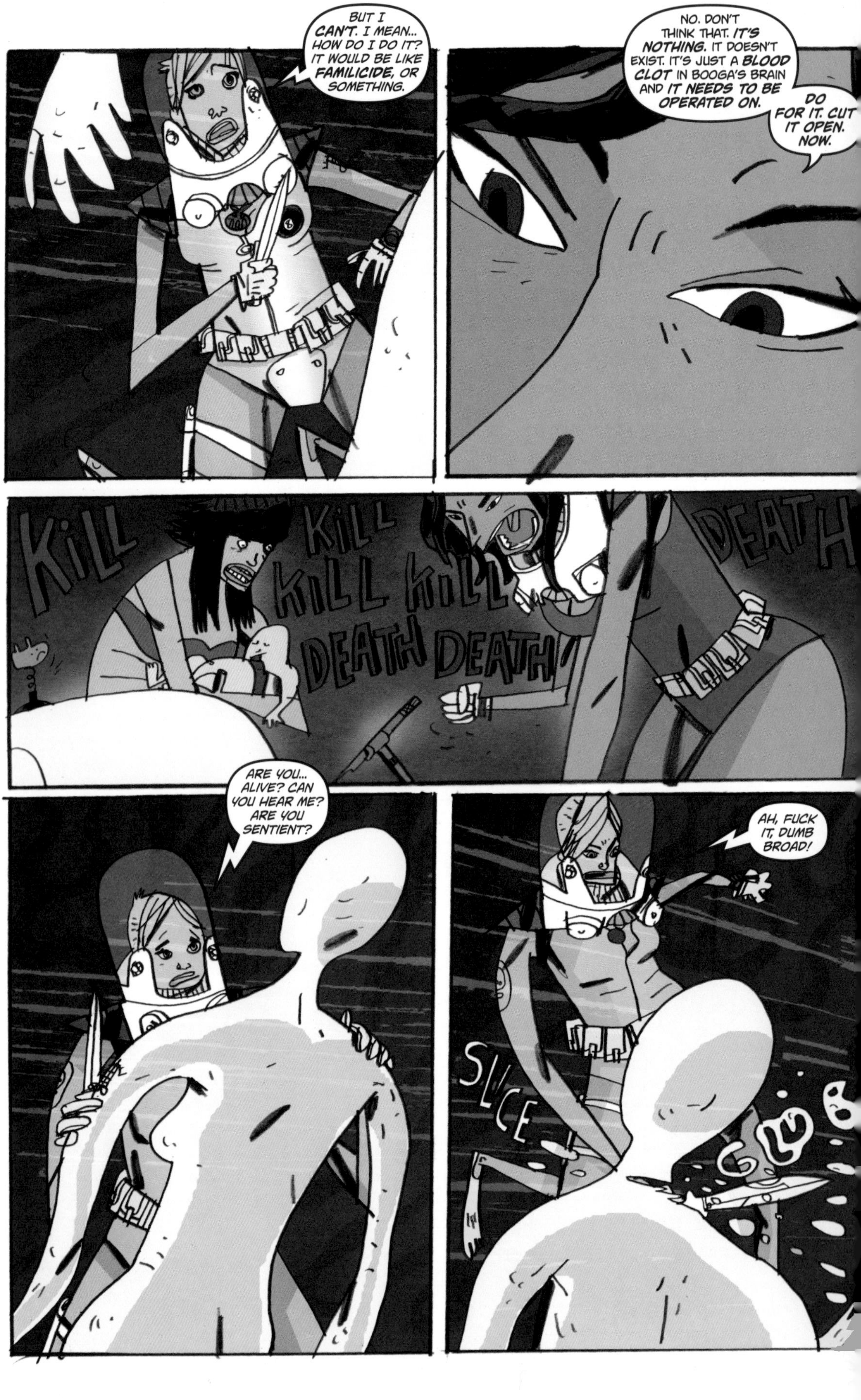
BUT I CAN'T. I MEAN... HOW DO I DO IT? IT WOULD BE LIKE FAMILICIDE, OR SOMETHING.
NO. DON'T THINK THAT. IT'S NOTHING. IT DOESN'T EXIST. IT'S JUST A BLOOD CLOT IN BOOGA'S BRAIN AND IT NEEDS TO BE OPERATED ON.
DO FOR IT. CUT IT OPEN. NOW.
KILL KILL KILL KILL
DEATH DEATH DEATH
ARE YOU... ALIVE? CAN YOU HEAR ME? ARE YOU SENTIENT?
AH, FUCK IT, DUMB BROAD!
SLICE
GLUG

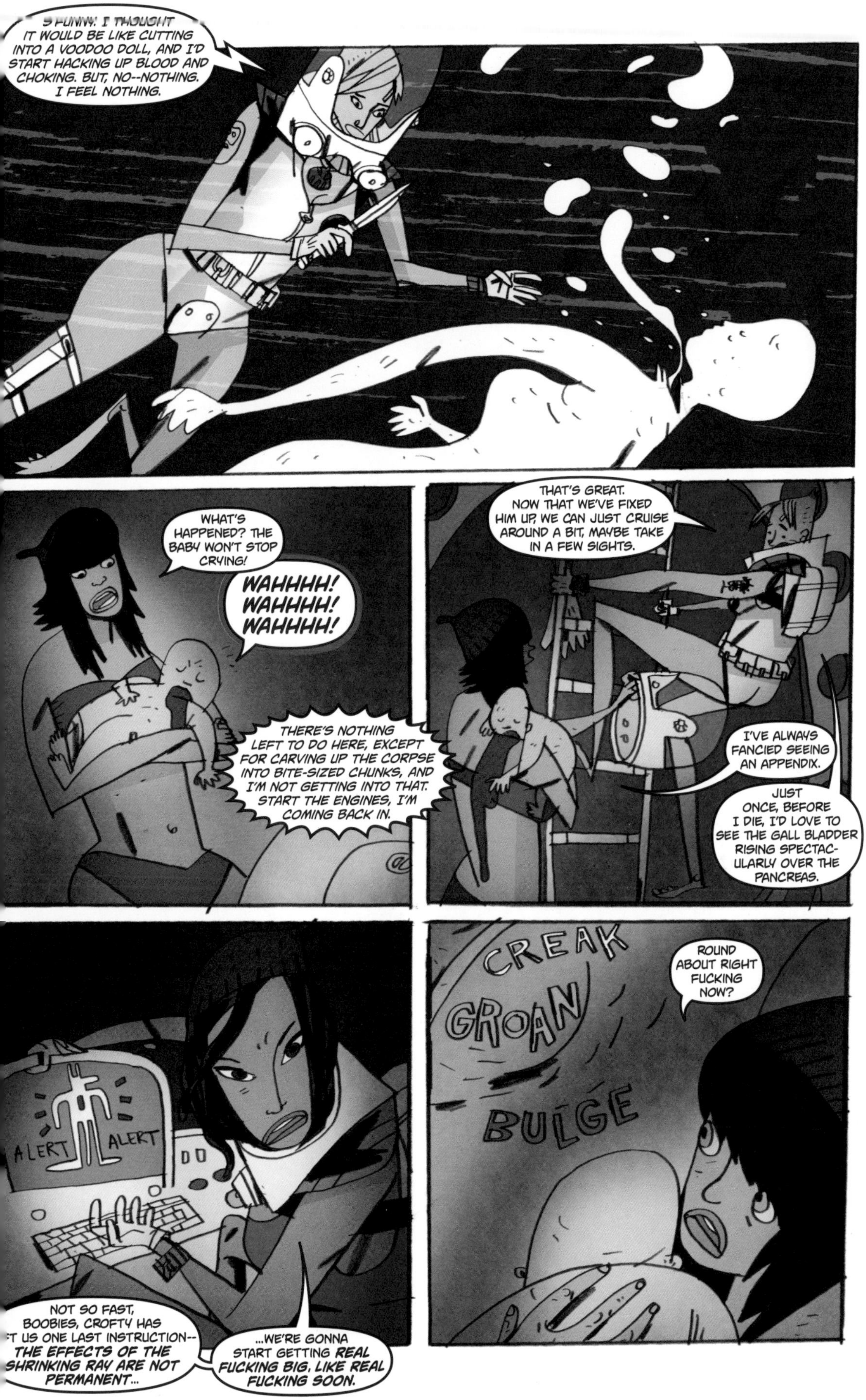
'S FUNNY. I THOUGHT IT WOULD BE LIKE CUTTING INTO A VOODOO DOLL, AND I'D START HACKING UP BLOOD AND CHOKING. BUT, NO--NOTHING. I FEEL NOTHING.
WHAT'S HAPPENED? THE BABY WON'T STOP CRYING!
WAHHHH! WAHHHH! WAHHHH!
THERE'S NOTHING LEFT TO DO HERE, EXCEPT FOR CARVING UP THE CORPSE INTO BITE-SIZED CHUNKS, AND I'M NOT GETTING INTO THAT. START THE ENGINES, I'M COMING BACK IN.
THAT'S GREAT. NOW THAT WE'VE FIXED HIM UP, WE CAN JUST CRUISE AROUND A BIT, MAYBE TAKE IN A FEW SIGHTS.
I'VE ALWAYS FANCIED SEEING AN APPENDIX.
JUST ONCE, BEFORE I DIE, I'D LOVE TO SEE THE GALL BLADDER RISING SPECTAC-ULARLY OVER THE PANCREAS.
ALERT
ALERT
NOT SO FAST, BOOBIES, CROFTY HAS 'T US ONE LAST INSTRUCTION-- THE EFFECTS OF THE SHRINKING RAY ARE NOT PERMANENT...
...WE'RE GONNA START GETTING REAL FUCKING BIG, LIKE REAL FUCKING SOON.
CREAK
GROAN
BULGE
ROUND ABOUT RIGHT FUCKING NOW?

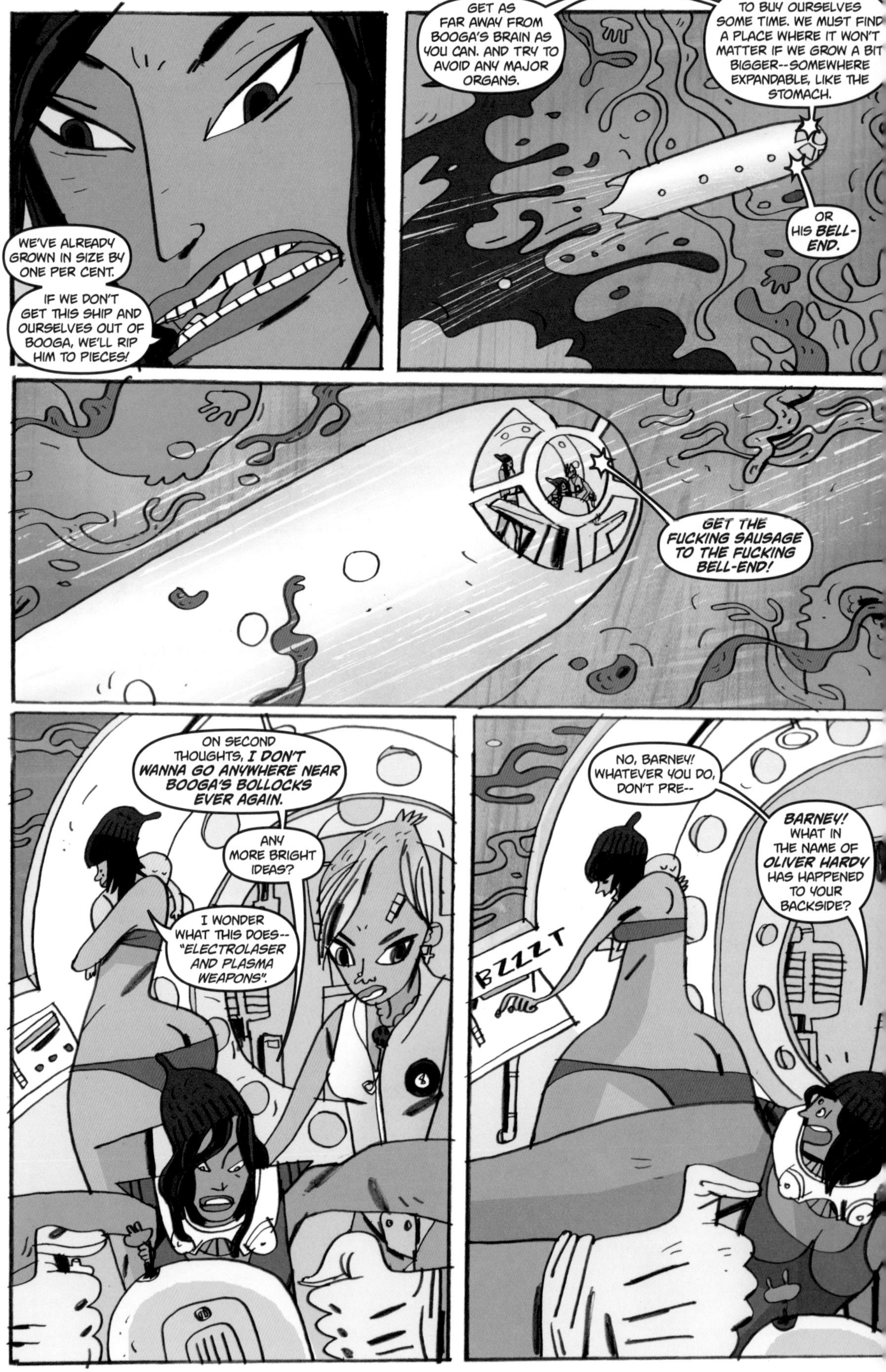
WE'VE ALREADY GROWN IN SIZE BY ONE PER CENT.
IF WE DON'T GET THIS SHIP AND OURSELVES OUT OF BOOGA, WE'LL RIP HIM TO PIECES!
GET AS FAR AWAY FROM BOOGA'S BRAIN AS YOU CAN. AND TRY TO AVOID ANY MAJOR ORGANS.
WE'VE GOT TO BUY OURSELVES SOME TIME. WE MUST FIND A PLACE WHERE IT WON'T MATTER IF WE GROW A BIT BIGGER--SOMEWHERE EXPANDABLE, LIKE THE STOMACH.
OR HIS BELL-END.
GET THE FUCKING SAUSAGE TO THE FUCKING BELL-END!
ON SECOND THOUGHTS, I DON'T WANNA GO ANYWHERE NEAR BOOGA'S BOLLOCKS EVER AGAIN.
ANY MORE BRIGHT IDEAS?
I WONDER WHAT THIS DOES--"ELECTROLASER AND PLASMA WEAPONS".
NO, BARNEY! WHATEVER YOU DO, DON'T PRE--
BZZZT
BARNEY! WHAT IN THE NAME OF OLIVER HARDY HAS HAPPENED TO YOUR BACKSIDE?

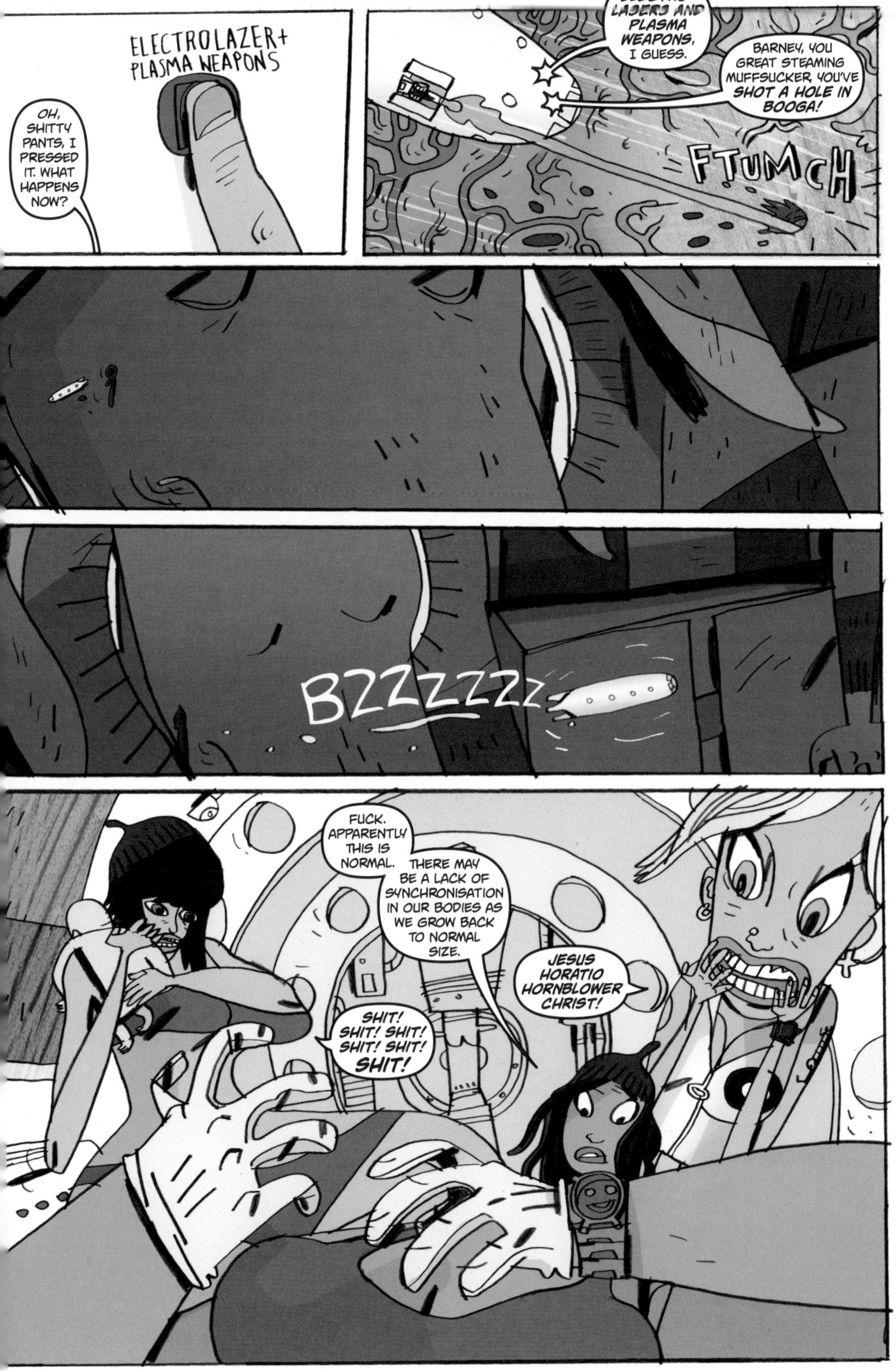
OH, SHITTY PANTS, I PRESSED IT. WHAT HAPPENS NOW?
ELECTROLAZER+ PLASMA WEAPONS
ELECTRO-LAZERS AND PLASMA WEAPONS, I GUESS.
BARNEY, YOU GREAT STEAMING MUFFSUCKER, YOU'VE SHOT A HOLE IN BOOGA!
FTUMCH
BZZZZZZz
FUCK. APPARENTLY THIS IS NORMAL.
THERE MAY BE A LACK OF SYNCHRONISATION IN OUR BODIES AS WE GROW BACK TO NORMAL SIZE.
JESUS HORATIO HORNBLOWER CHRIST!
SHIT! SHIT! SHIT! SHIT! SHIT! SHIT!

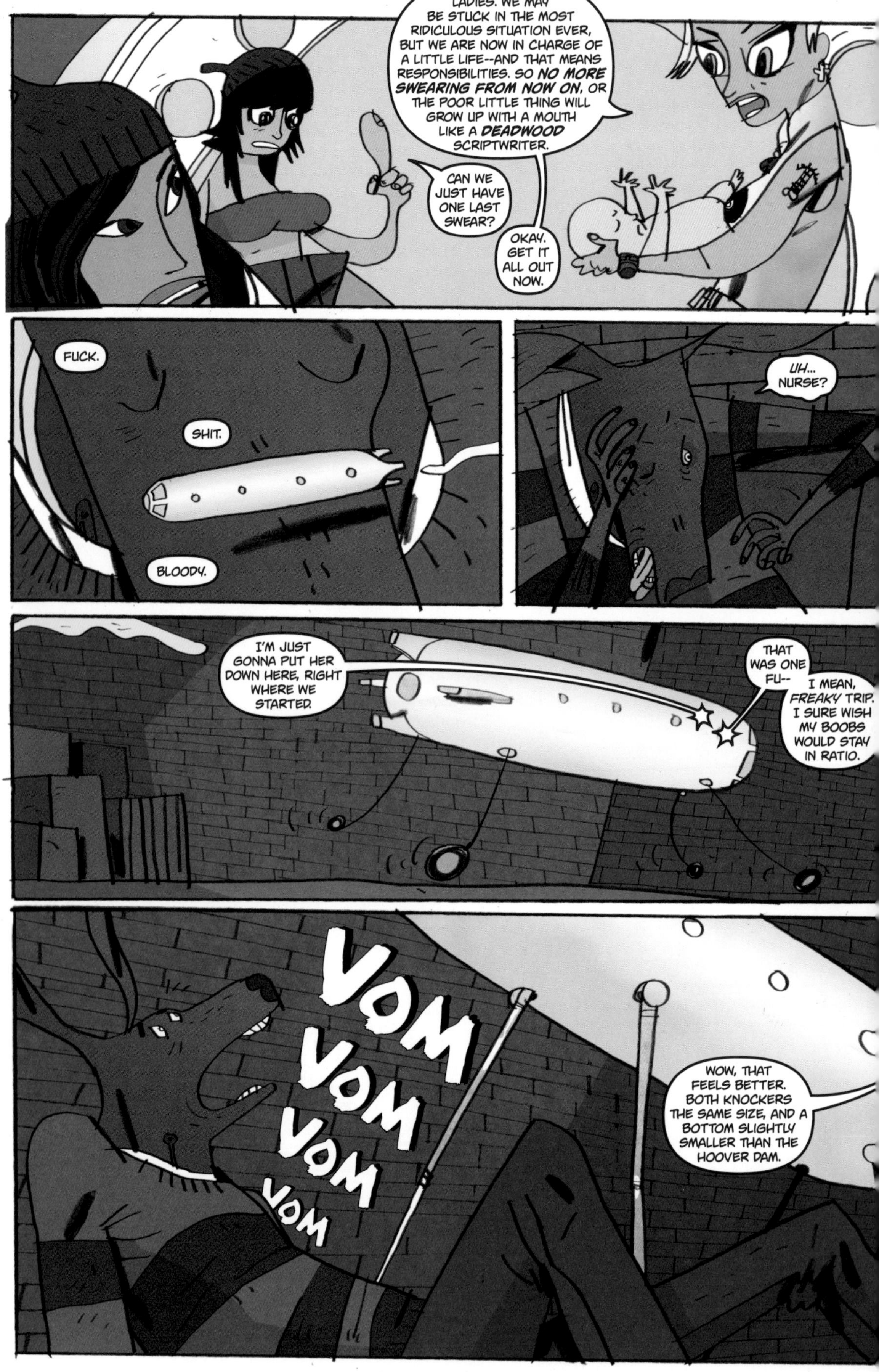

LISTEN UP, LADIES. WE MAY BE STUCK IN THE MOST RIDICULOUS SITUATION EVER, BUT WE ARE NOW IN CHARGE OF A LITTLE LIFE--AND THAT MEANS RESPONSIBILITIES. SO **NO MORE SWEARING FROM NOW ON**, OR THE POOR LITTLE THING WILL GROW UP WITH A MOUTH LIKE A **DEADWOOD** SCRIPTWRITER.
CAN WE JUST HAVE ONE LAST SWEAR?
OKAY. GET IT ALL OUT NOW.
FUCK.
SHIT.
BLOODY.
UH... NURSE?
I'M JUST GONNA PUT HER DOWN HERE, RIGHT WHERE WE STARTED.
THAT WAS ONE FU--
I MEAN, *FREAKY* TRIP. I SURE WISH MY BOOBS WOULD STAY IN RATIO.
VOM
VOM
VOM
VOM
VOM
WOW, THAT FEELS BETTER. BOTH KNOCKERS THE SAME SIZE, AND A BOTTOM SLIGHTLY SMALLER THAN THE HOOVER DAM.

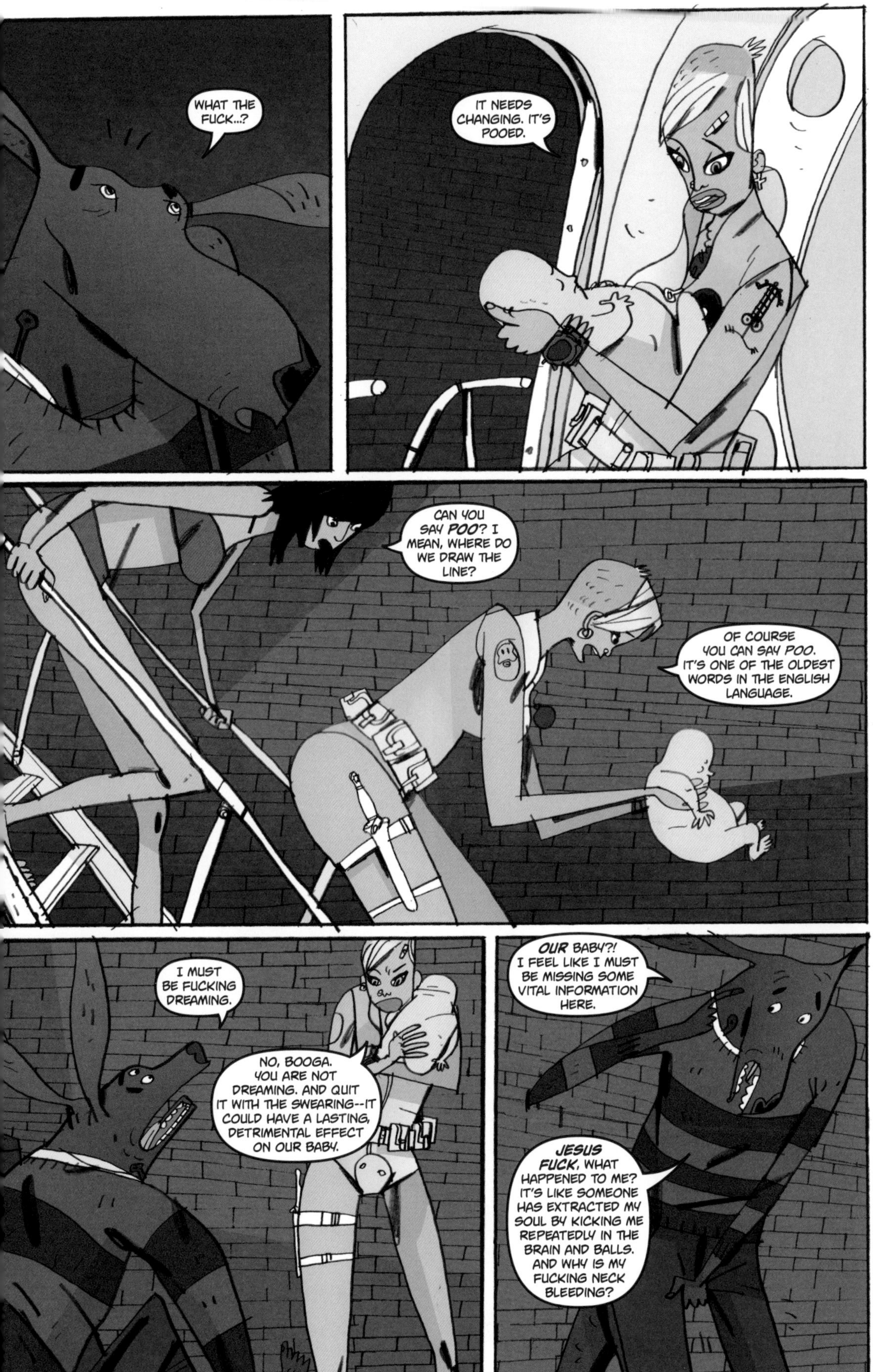
WHAT THE FUCK...?
IT NEEDS CHANGING. IT'S POOED.
CAN YOU SAY *POO*? I MEAN, WHERE DO WE DRAW THE LINE?
OF COURSE YOU CAN SAY *POO*. IT'S ONE OF THE OLDEST WORDS IN THE ENGLISH LANGUAGE.
I MUST BE FUCKING DREAMING.
NO, BOOGA. YOU ARE NOT DREAMING. AND QUIT IT WITH THE SWEARING--IT COULD HAVE A LASTING, DETRIMENTAL EFFECT ON OUR BABY.
OUR BABY?! I FEEL LIKE I MUST BE MISSING SOME VITAL INFORMATION HERE.
JESUS FUCK, WHAT HAPPENED TO ME? IT'S LIKE SOMEONE HAS EXTRACTED MY SOUL BY KICKING ME REPEATEDLY IN THE BRAIN AND BALLS. AND WHY IS MY FUCKING NECK BLEEDING?

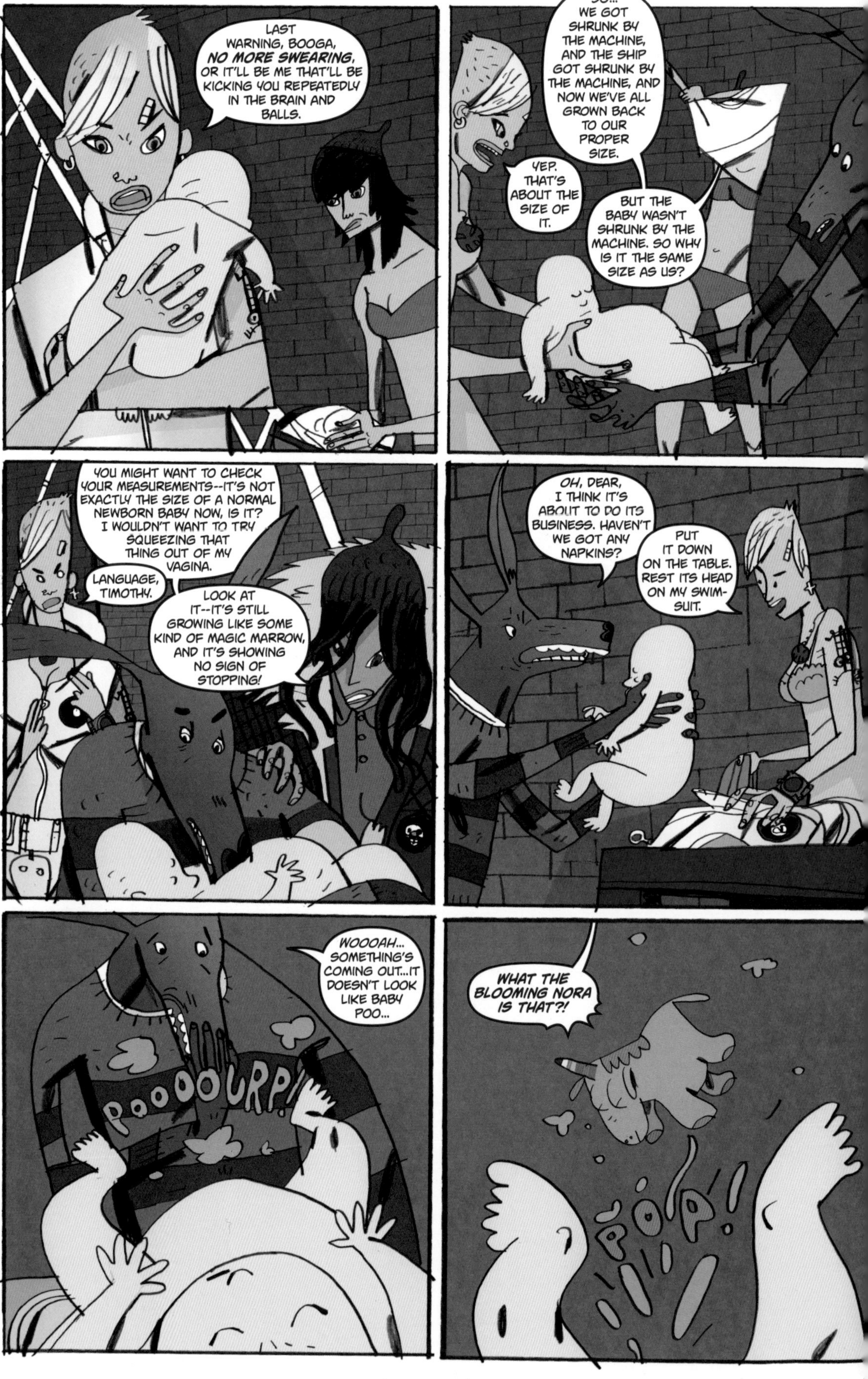

LAST WARNING, BOOGA, NO MORE SWEARING, OR IT'LL BE ME THAT'LL BE KICKING YOU REPEATEDLY IN THE BRAIN AND BALLS.
SO... WE GOT SHRUNK BY THE MACHINE, AND THE SHIP GOT SHRUNK BY THE MACHINE, AND NOW WE'VE ALL GROWN BACK TO OUR PROPER SIZE.
YEP. THAT'S ABOUT THE SIZE OF IT.
BUT THE BABY WASN'T SHRUNK BY THE MACHINE. SO WHY IS IT THE SAME SIZE AS US?
YOU MIGHT WANT TO CHECK YOUR MEASUREMENTS--IT'S NOT EXACTLY THE SIZE OF A NORMAL NEWBORN BABY NOW, IS IT? I WOULDN'T WANT TO TRY SQUEEZING THAT THING OUT OF MY VAGINA.
LANGUAGE, TIMOTHY.
LOOK AT IT--IT'S STILL GROWING LIKE SOME KIND OF MAGIC MARROW, AND IT'S SHOWING NO SIGN OF STOPPING!
OH, DEAR, I THINK IT'S ABOUT TO DO ITS BUSINESS. HAVEN'T WE GOT ANY NAPKINS?
PUT IT DOWN ON THE TABLE. REST ITS HEAD ON MY SWIM-SUIT.
WOOOAH... SOMETHING'S COMING OUT...IT DOESN'T LOOK LIKE BABY POO...
POOOOURP!
WHAT THE BLOOMING NORA IS THAT?!
POP!!

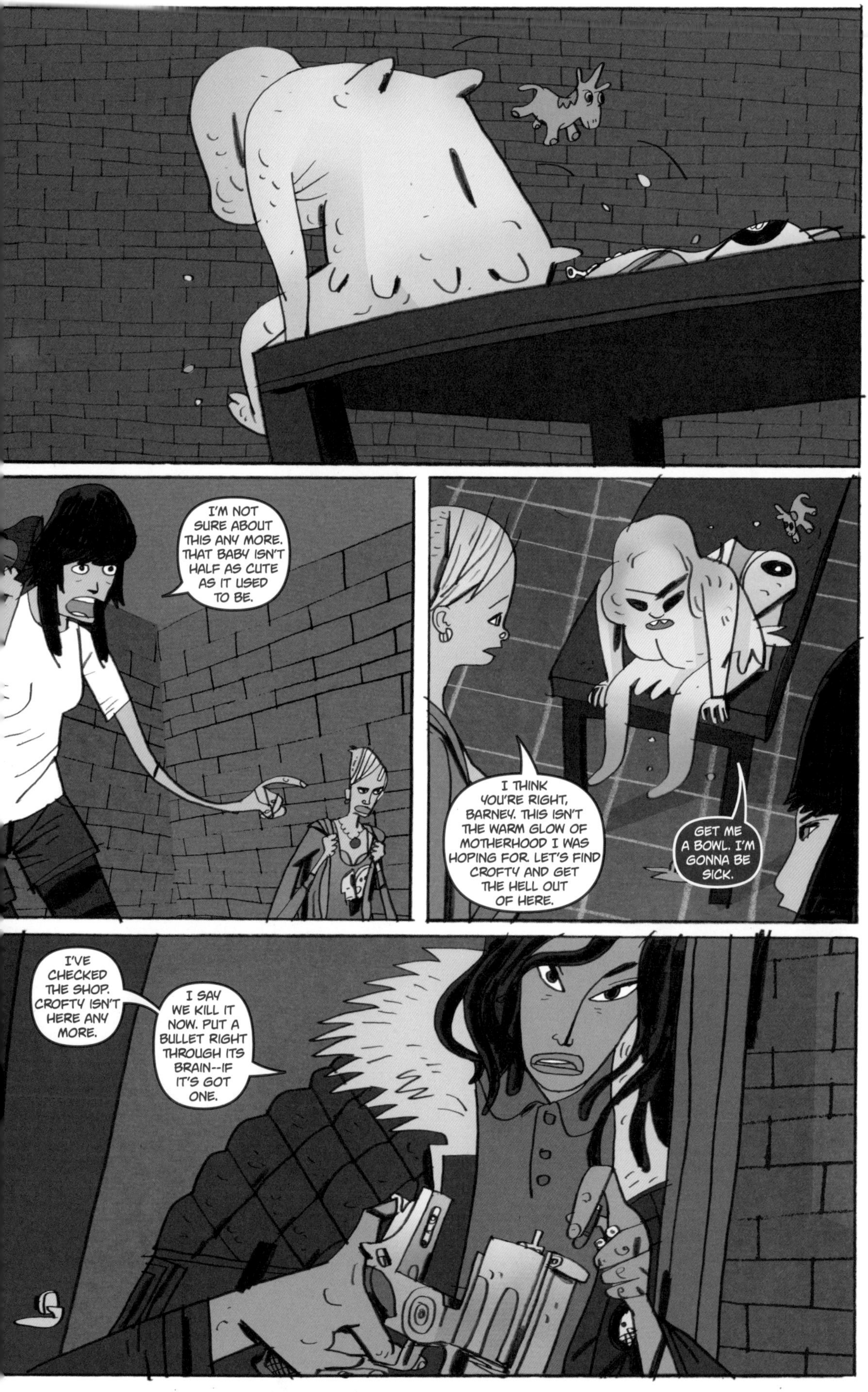
I'M NOT SURE ABOUT THIS ANY MORE. THAT BABY ISN'T HALF AS CUTE AS IT USED TO BE.
I THINK YOU'RE RIGHT, BARNEY. THIS ISN'T THE WARM GLOW OF MOTHERHOOD I WAS HOPING FOR. LET'S FIND CROFTY AND GET THE HELL OUT OF HERE.
GET ME A BOWL. I'M GONNA BE SICK.
I'VE CHECKED THE SHOP. CROFTY ISN'T HERE ANY MORE.
I SAY WE KILL IT NOW. PUT A BULLET RIGHT THROUGH ITS BRAIN--IF IT'S GOT ONE.

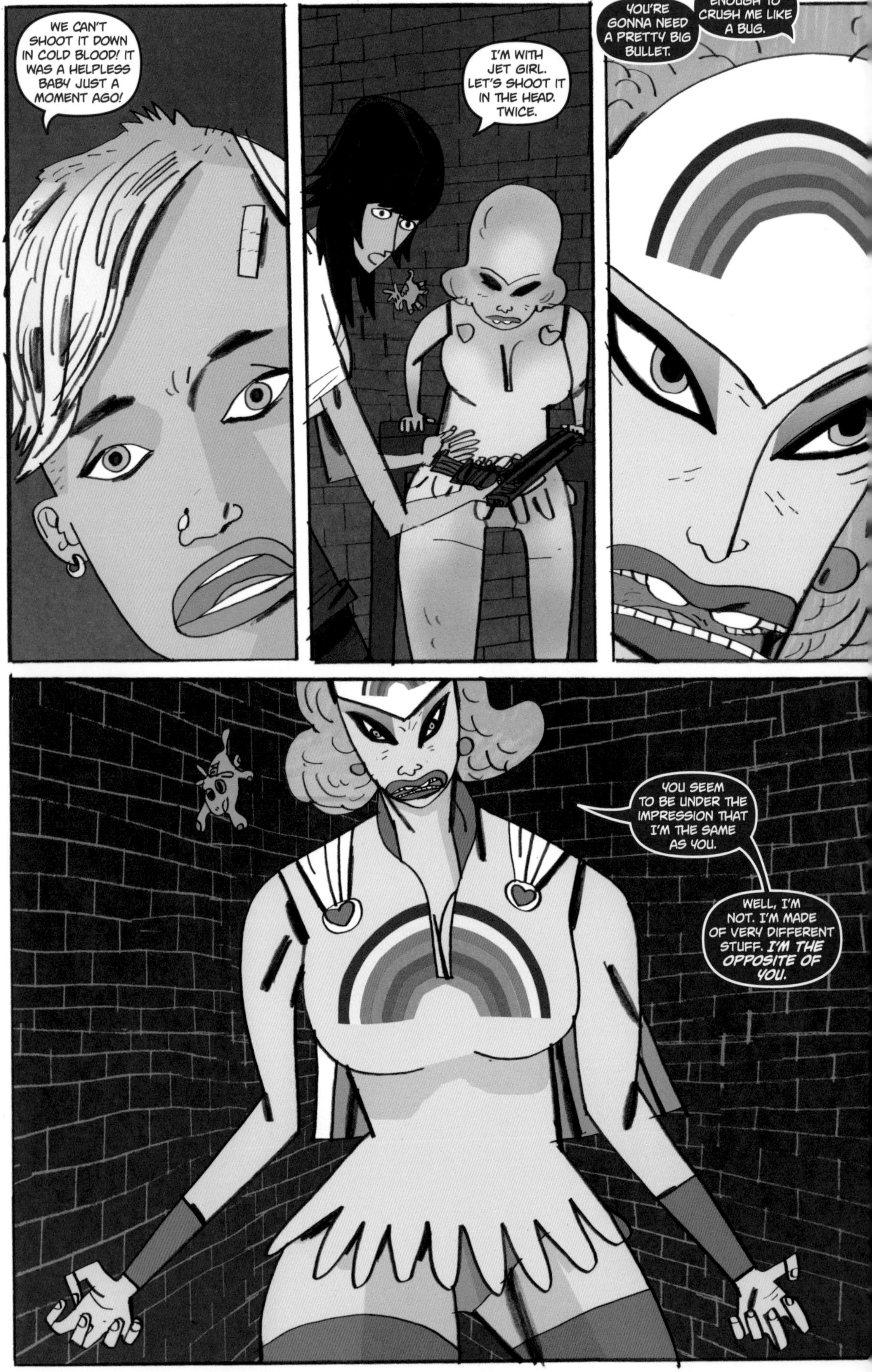
WE CAN'T SHOOT IT DOWN IN COLD BLOOD! IT WAS A HELPLESS BABY JUST A MOMENT AGO!
I'M WITH JET GIRL. LET'S SHOOT IT IN THE HEAD. TWICE.
YOU'RE GONNA NEED A PRETTY BIG BULLET.
ONE BIG ENOUGH TO CRUSH ME LIKE A BUG.
YOU SEEM TO BE UNDER THE IMPRESSION THAT I'M THE SAME AS YOU.
WELL, I'M NOT. I'M MADE OF VERY DIFFERENT STUFF. *I'M THE OPPOSITE OF YOU.*

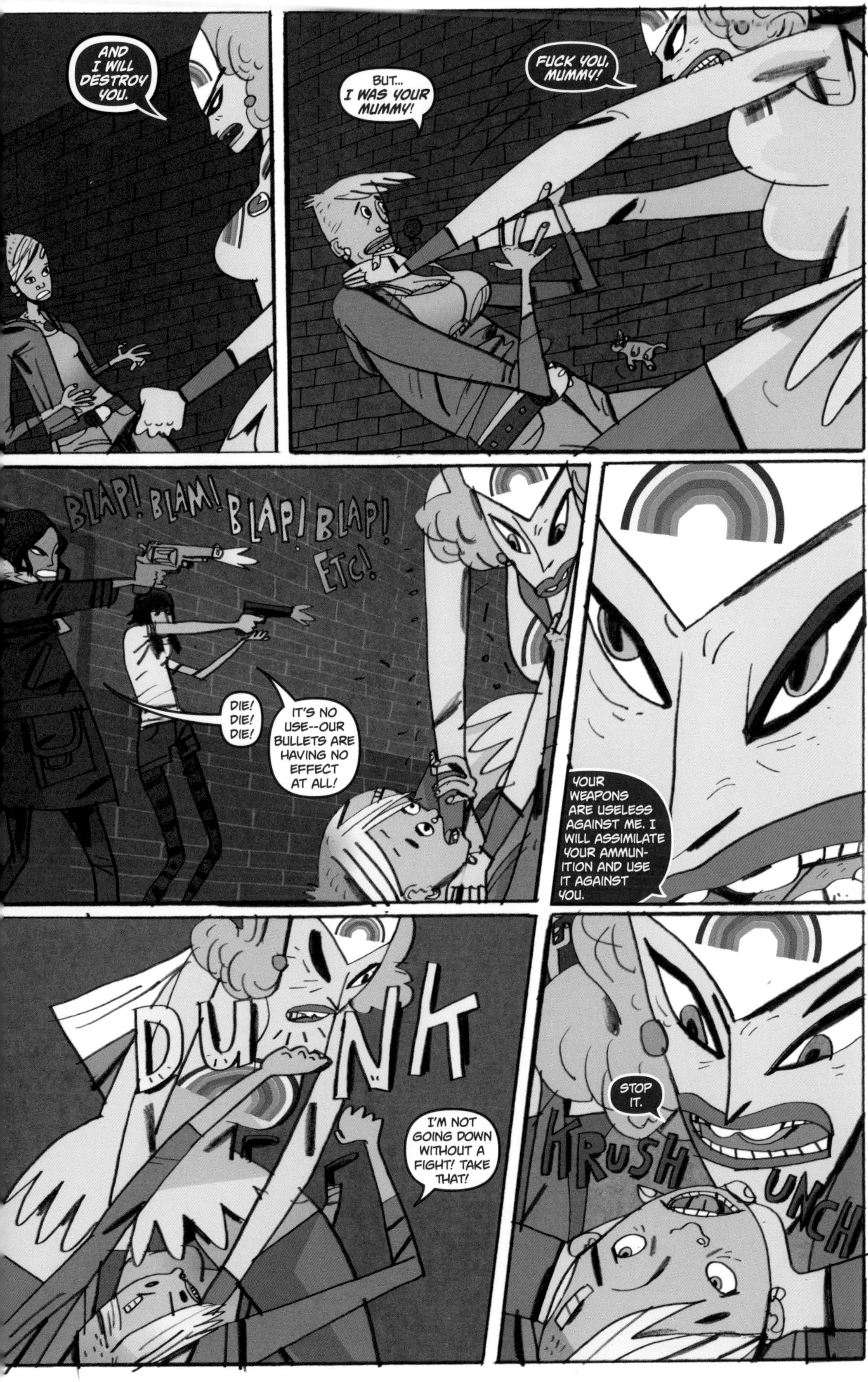
AND I WILL DESTROY YOU.
BUT... I WAS YOUR MUMMY!
FUCK YOU, MUMMY!
BLAP! BLAM! BLAP! BLAP! ETC!
DIE! DIE! DIE!
IT'S NO USE--OUR BULLETS ARE HAVING NO EFFECT AT ALL!
YOUR WEAPONS ARE USELESS AGAINST ME. I WILL ASSIMILATE YOUR AMMUNITION AND USE IT AGAINST YOU.
DUNK
I'M NOT GOING DOWN WITHOUT A FIGHT! TAKE THAT!
STOP IT.
KRUSH
UNCH

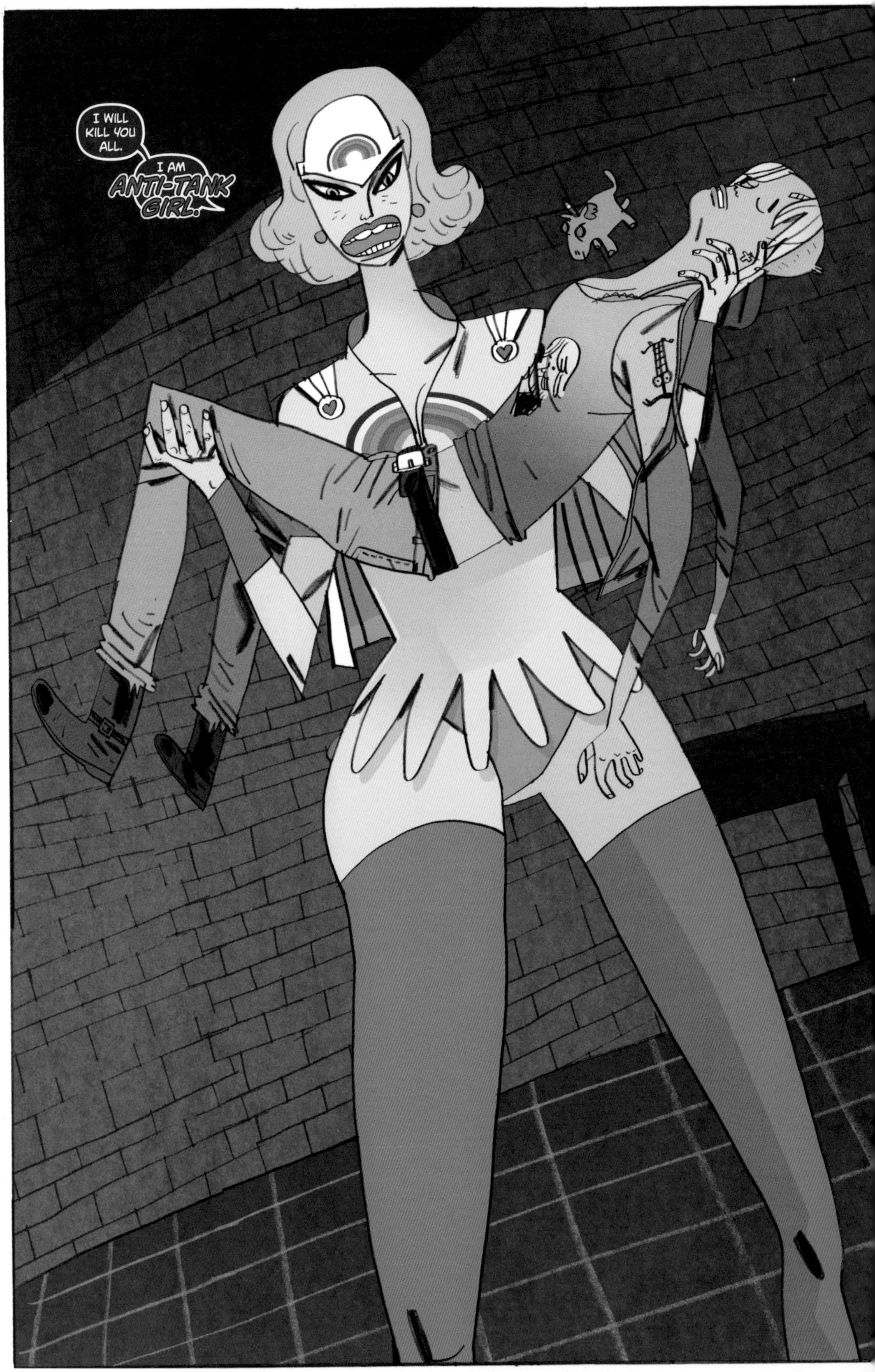
I WILL KILL YOU ALL.
I AM ANTI-TANK GIRL.

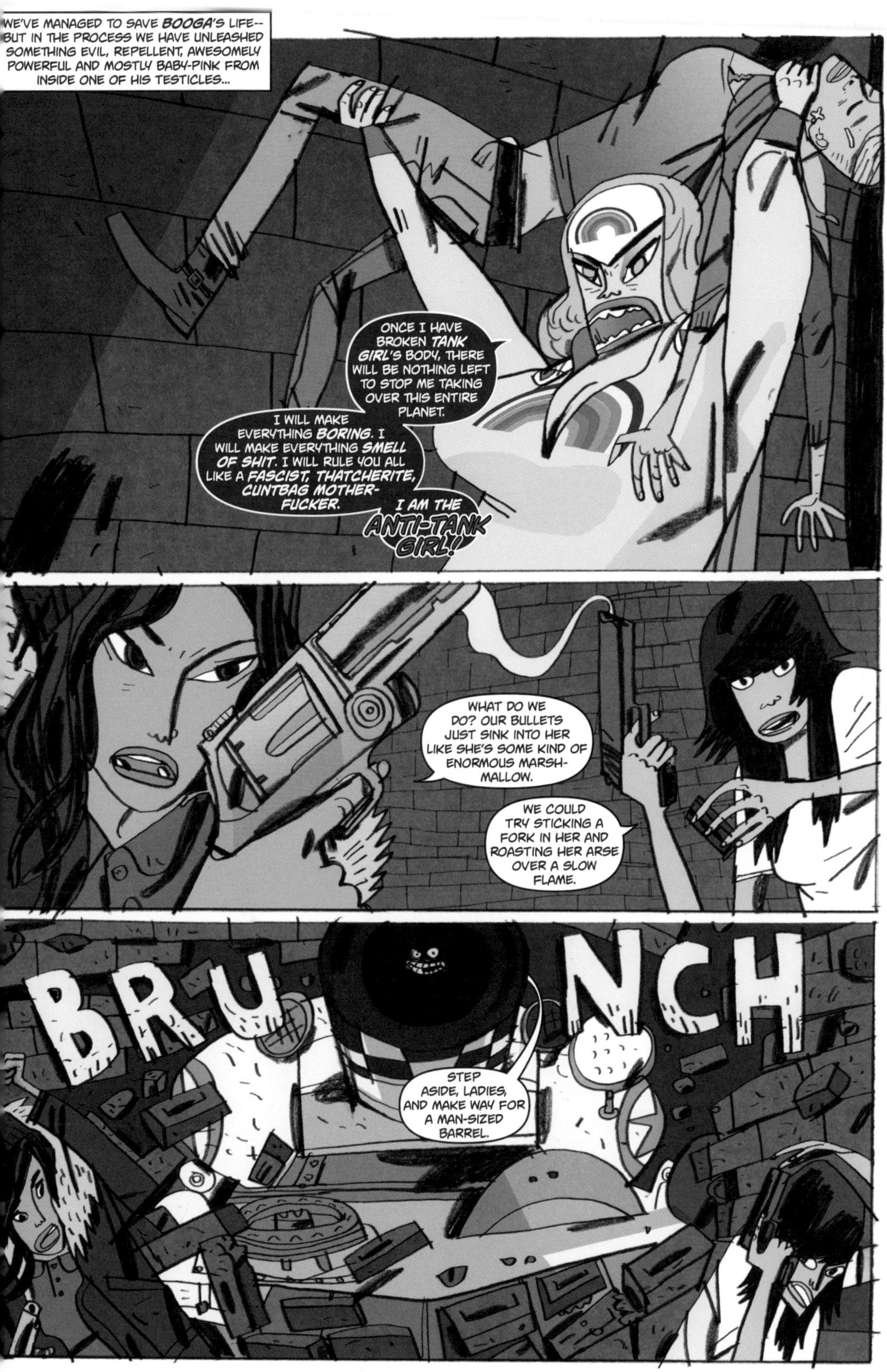
WE'VE MANAGED TO SAVE BOOGA'S LIFE-- BUT IN THE PROCESS WE HAVE UNLEASHED SOMETHING EVIL, REPELLENT, AWESOMELY POWERFUL AND MOSTLY BABY-PINK FROM INSIDE ONE OF HIS TESTICLES...
ONCE I HAVE BROKEN TANK GIRL'S BODY, THERE WILL BE NOTHING LEFT TO STOP ME TAKING OVER THIS ENTIRE PLANET.
I WILL MAKE EVERYTHING BORING. I WILL MAKE EVERYTHING SMELL OF SHIT. I WILL RULE YOU ALL LIKE A FASCIST, THATCHERITE, CUNTBAG MOTHER-FUCKER.
I AM THE ANTI-TANK GIRL!
WHAT DO WE DO? OUR BULLETS JUST SINK INTO HER LIKE SHE'S SOME KIND OF ENORMOUS MARSH-MALLOW.
WE COULD TRY STICKING A FORK IN HER AND ROASTING HER ARSE OVER A SLOW FLAME.
BRUNCH
STEP ASIDE, LADIES, AND MAKE WAY FOR A MAN-SIZED BARREL.

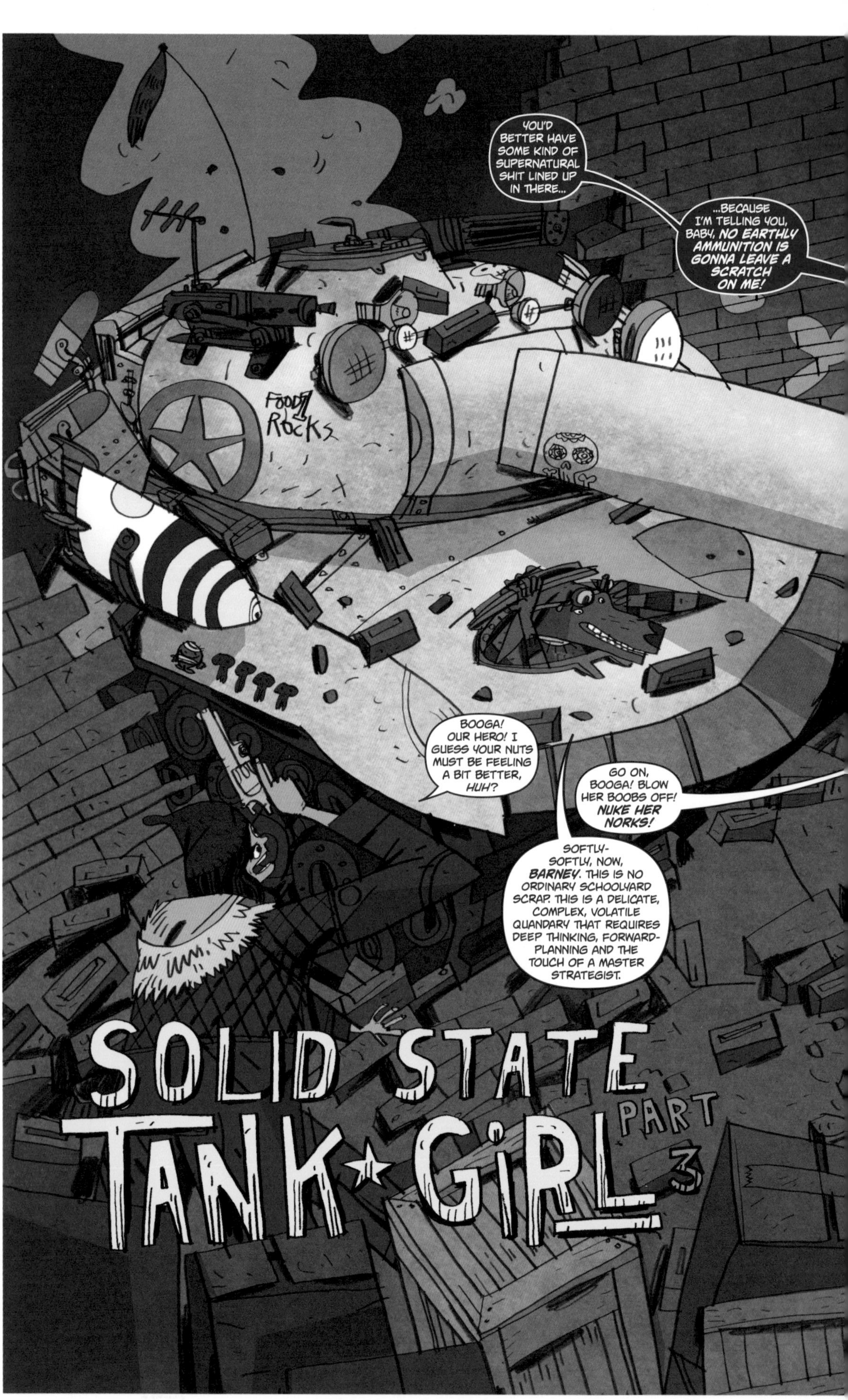
YOU'D BETTER HAVE SOME KIND OF SUPERNATURAL SHIT LINED UP IN THERE...
...BECAUSE I'M TELLING YOU, BABY, NO EARTHLY AMMUNITION IS GONNA LEAVE A SCRATCH ON ME!
FOOD 1 ROCKS
BOOGA! OUR HERO! I GUESS YOUR NUTS MUST BE FEELING A BIT BETTER, HUH?
GO ON, BOOGA! BLOW HER BOOBS OFF! NUKE HER NORKS!
SOFTLY-SOFTLY, NOW, BARNEY. THIS IS NO ORDINARY SCHOOLYARD SCRAP. THIS IS A DELICATE, COMPLEX, VOLATILE QUANDARY THAT REQUIRES DEEP THINKING, FORWARD-PLANNING AND THE TOUCH OF A MASTER STRATEGIST.
SOLID STATE TANK GIRL PART 3

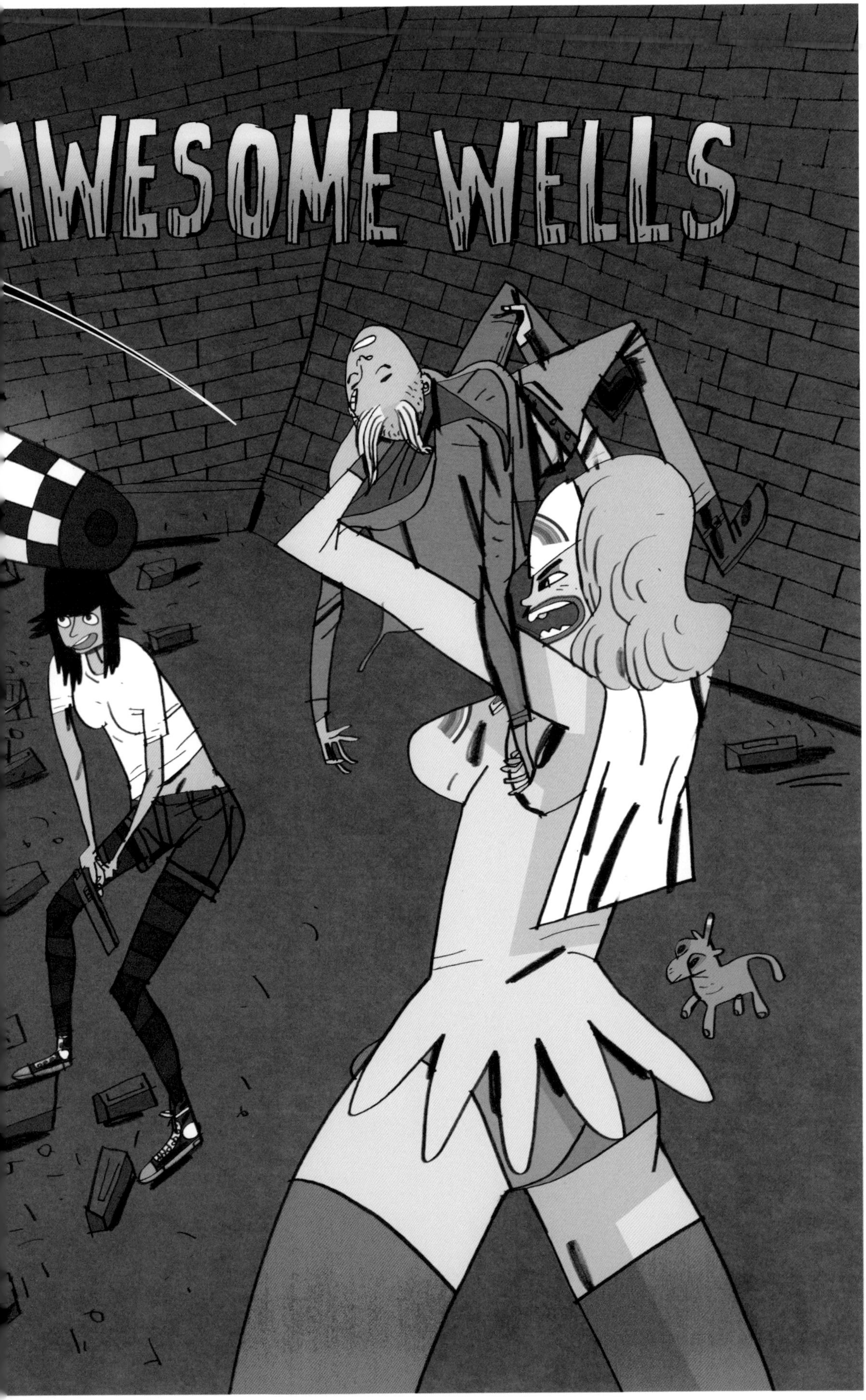
AWESOME WELLS

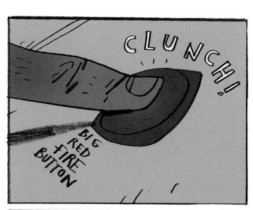

CLUNCH!

BIG RED FIRE BUTTON

LUNCH

SLUNCH!

¿AHK!¿ I CAN'T SEE! WHAT THE FUCK IS THIS STUFF?

YOU MEAN TO SAY THAT YOU STUCK YOUR FILTHY KNOB IN THIS STUFF AND THEN SPRAYED IT ALL OVER ME? I'LL TEAR OUT YOUR SOUL AND SHOVE IT UP YOUR JACKSY!

IT'S ORGANIC LIVE YOGHURT. I'VE BEEN USING IT TO TREAT A RATHER NASTY CASE OF THRUSH, SO WE'VE GOT A GOOD SUPPLY IN THE FRIDGE.

JET GIRL, BARNEY--QUICK, TICKLE HER ARMPITS!

TICKLE-LICKLE-LICKLE!

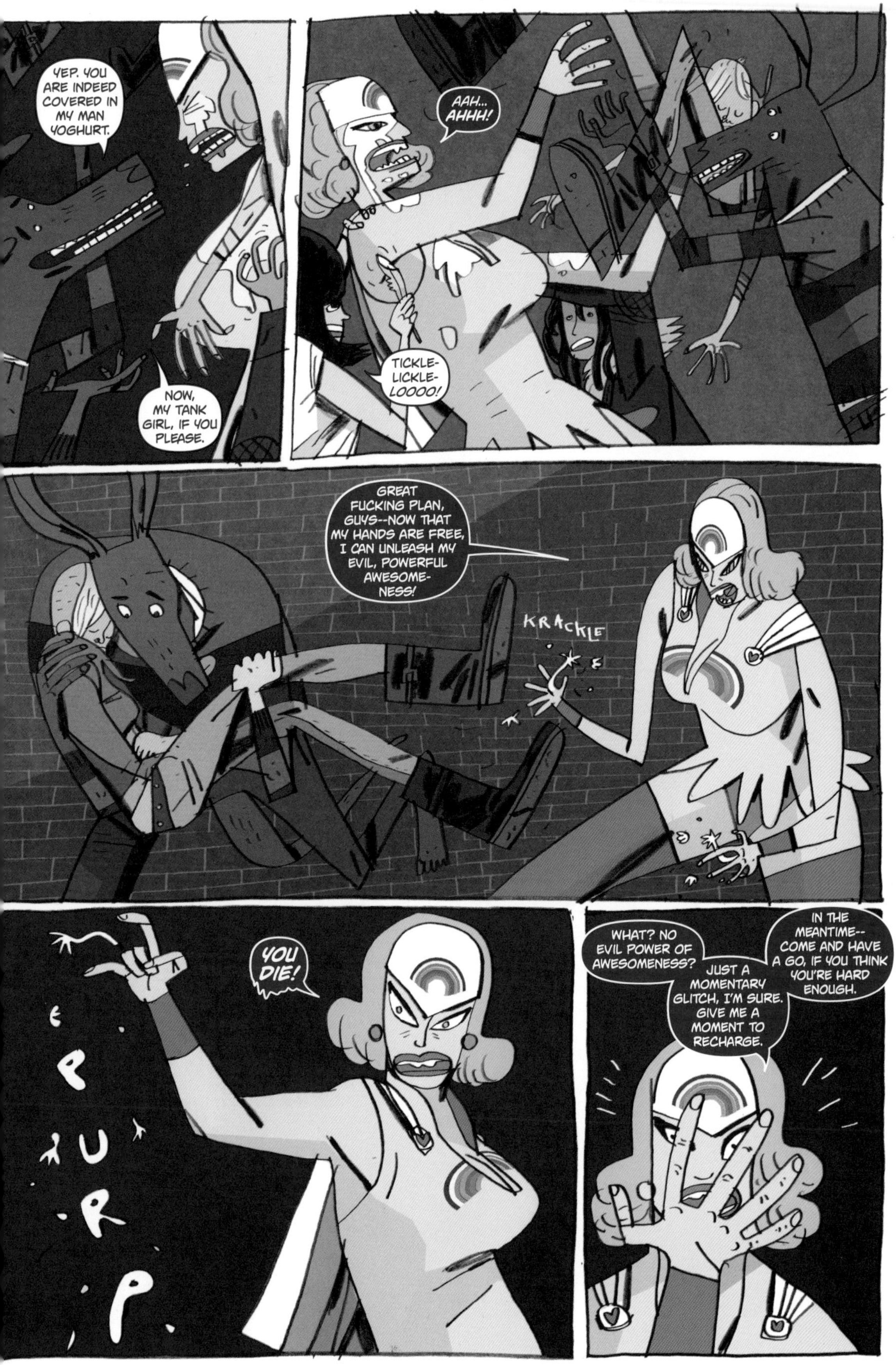
YEP. YOU ARE INDEED COVERED IN MY MAN YOGHURT.
NOW, MY TANK GIRL, IF YOU PLEASE.
AAH... AHHH!
TICKLE-LICKLE-LOOOO!
GREAT FUCKING PLAN, GUYS--NOW THAT MY HANDS ARE FREE, I CAN UNLEASH MY EVIL, POWERFUL AWESOME-NESS!
KRACKLE
PURP
YOU DIE!
WHAT? NO EVIL POWER OF AWESOMENESS?
JUST A MOMENTARY GLITCH, I'M SURE. GIVE ME A MOMENT TO RECHARGE.
IN THE MEANTIME--COME AND HAVE A GO, IF YOU THINK YOU'RE HARD ENOUGH.

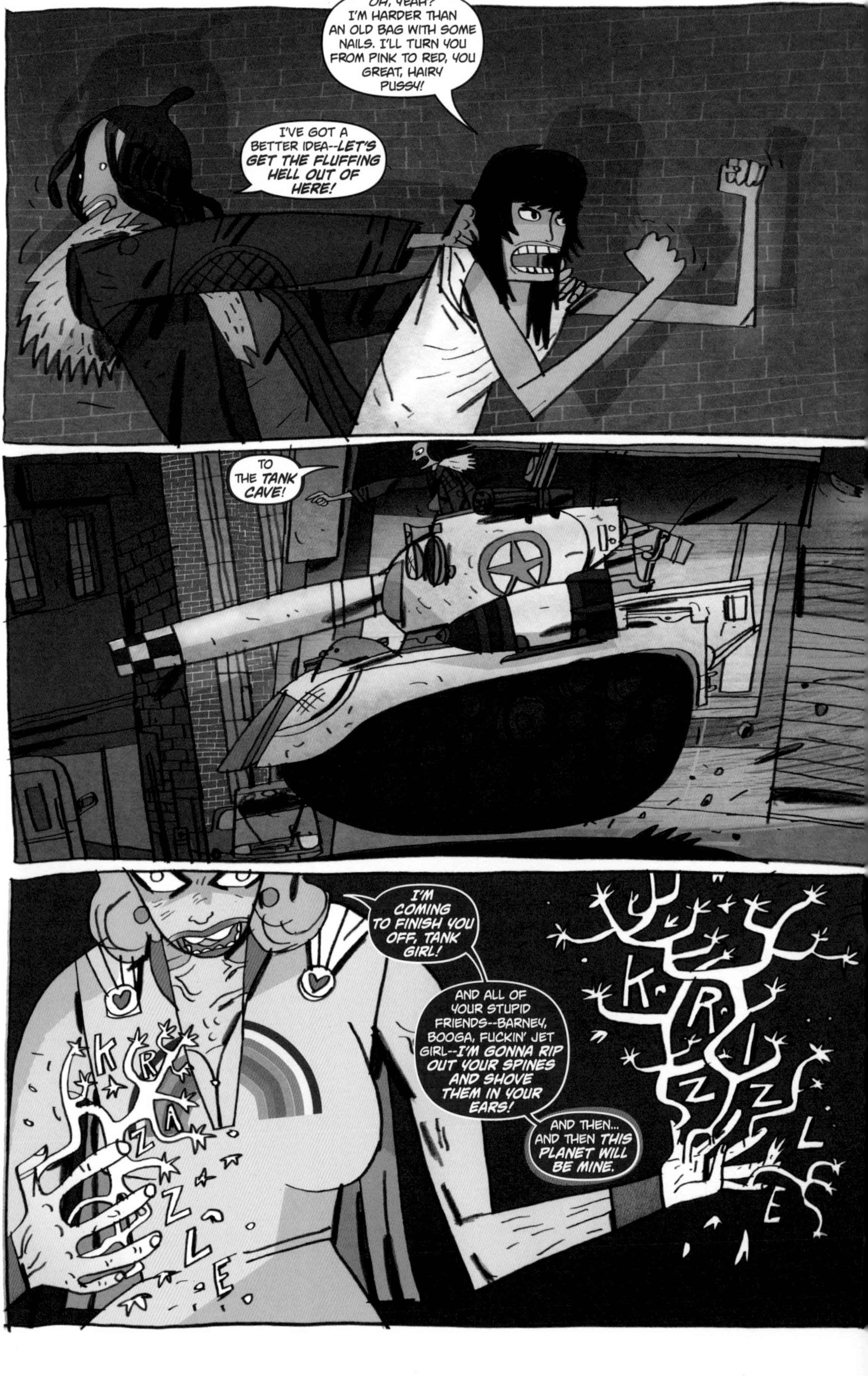
OH, YEAH? I'M HARDER THAN AN OLD BAG WITH SOME NAILS. I'LL TURN YOU FROM PINK TO RED, YOU GREAT, HAIRY PUSSY!
I'VE GOT A BETTER IDEA--LET'S GET THE FLUFFING HELL OUT OF HERE!
TO THE TANK CAVE!
I'M COMING TO FINISH YOU OFF, TANK GIRL!
AND ALL OF YOUR STUPID FRIENDS--BARNEY, BOOGA, FUCKIN' JET GIRL--I'M GONNA RIP OUT YOUR SPINES AND SHOVE THEM IN YOUR EARS!
AND THEN... AND THEN THIS PLANET WILL BE MINE.
KRIZZLE
KRIZZLE

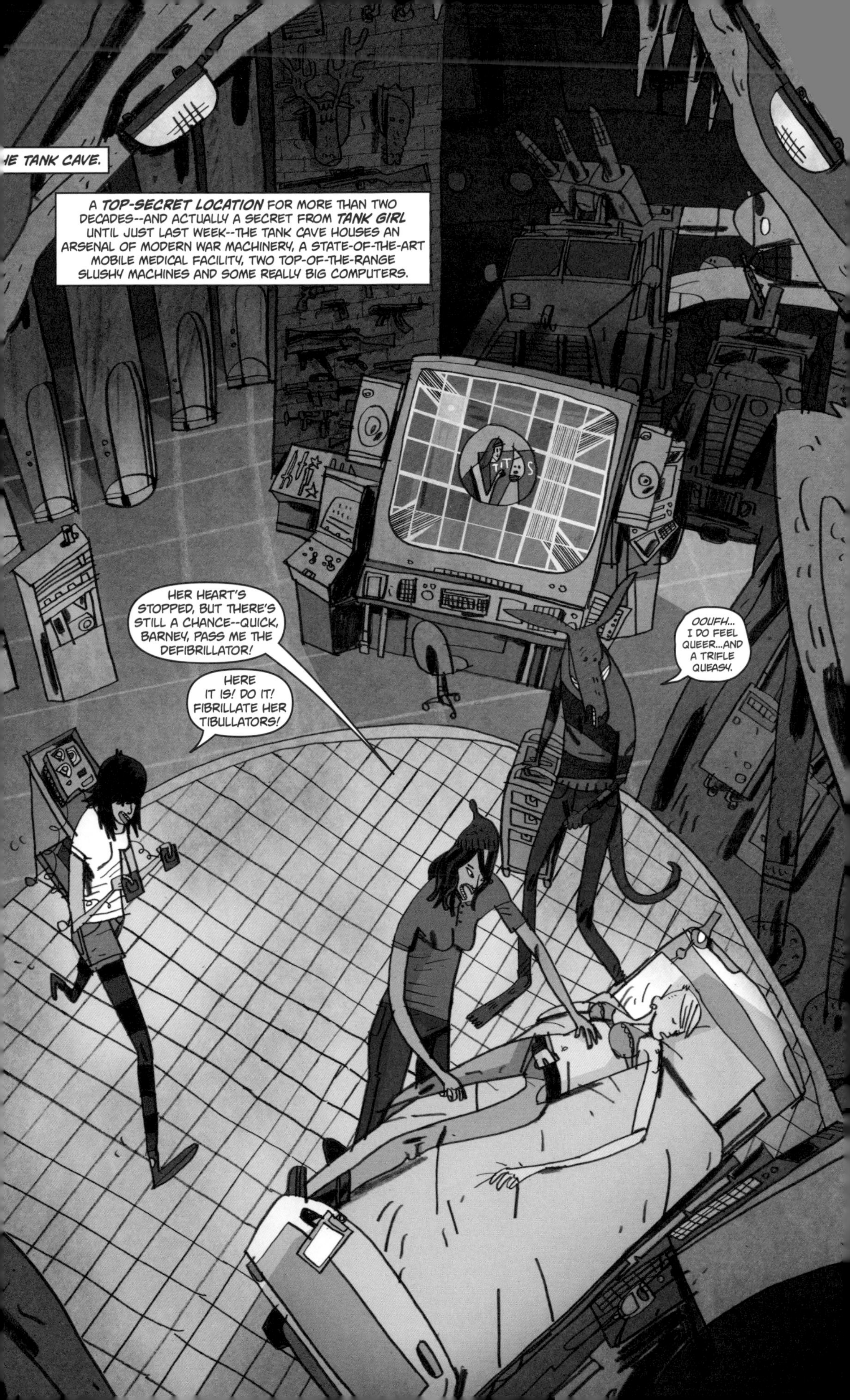

HE TANK CAVE.
A TOP-SECRET LOCATION FOR MORE THAN TWO DECADES--AND ACTUALLY A SECRET FROM TANK GIRL UNTIL JUST LAST WEEK--THE TANK CAVE HOUSES AN ARSENAL OF MODERN WAR MACHINERY, A STATE-OF-THE-ART MOBILE MEDICAL FACILITY, TWO TOP-OF-THE-RANGE SLUSHY MACHINES AND SOME REALLY BIG COMPUTERS.
HER HEART'S STOPPED, BUT THERE'S STILL A CHANCE--QUICK, BARNEY, PASS ME THE DEFIBRILLATOR!
HERE IT IS! DO IT! FIBRILLATE HER TIBULLATORS!
OOUFH... I DO FEEL QUEER...AND A TRIFLE QUEASY.

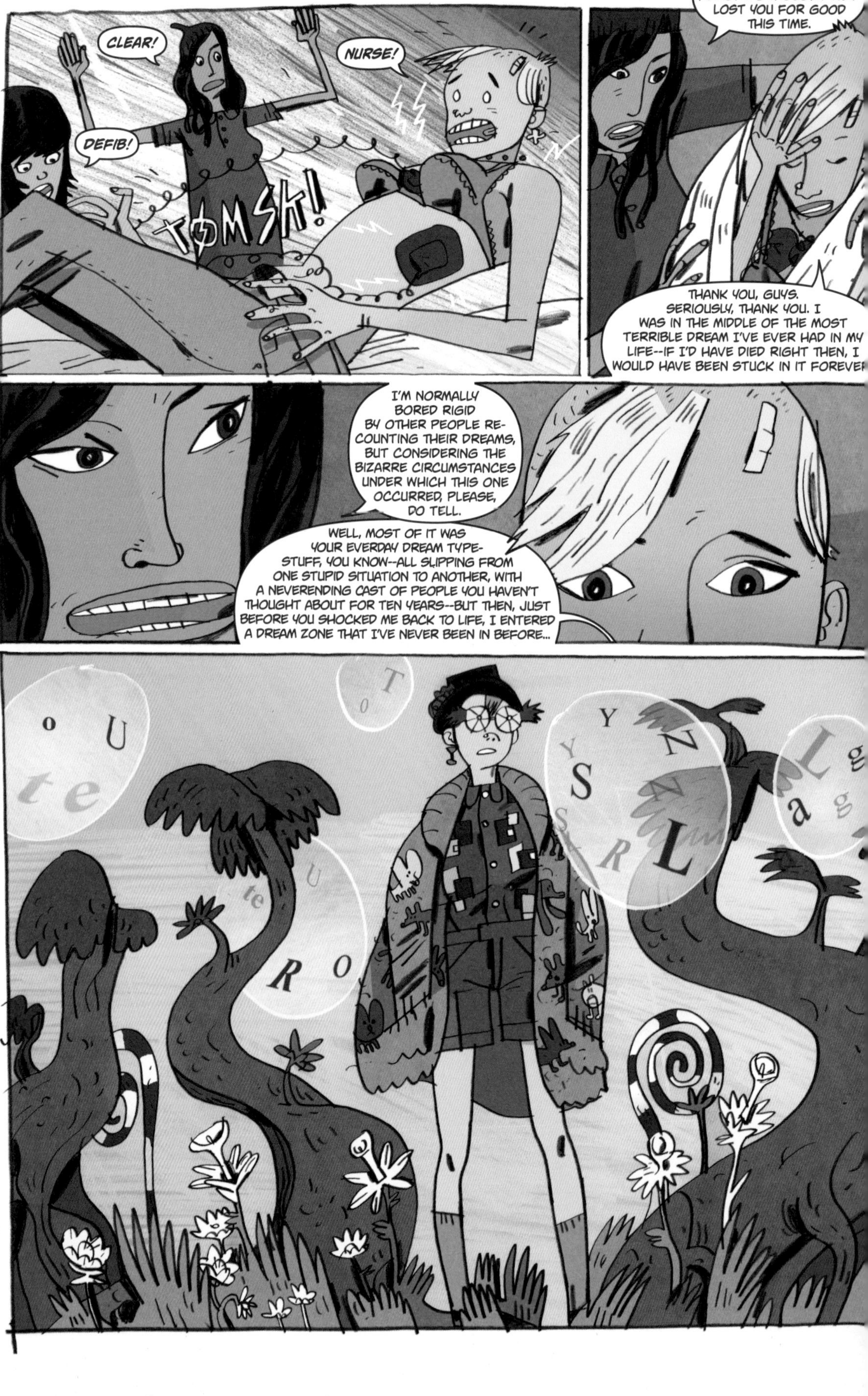
CLEAR!
DEFIB!
NURSE!
TØMSK!
TANK GIRL! THANK GOD YOU'RE ALRIGHT. I THOUGHT WE'D LOST YOU FOR GOOD THIS TIME.
THANK YOU, GUYS. SERIOUSLY, THANK YOU. I WAS IN THE MIDDLE OF THE MOST TERRIBLE DREAM I'VE EVER HAD IN MY LIFE--IF I'D HAVE DIED RIGHT THEN, I WOULD HAVE BEEN STUCK IN IT FOREVER
I'M NORMALLY BORED RIGID BY OTHER PEOPLE RE-COUNTING THEIR DREAMS, BUT CONSIDERING THE BIZARRE CIRCUMSTANCES UNDER WHICH THIS ONE OCCURRED, PLEASE, DO TELL.
WELL, MOST OF IT WAS YOUR EVERDAY DREAM TYPE-STUFF, YOU KNOW--ALL SLIPPING FROM ONE STUPID SITUATION TO ANOTHER, WITH A NEVERENDING CAST OF PEOPLE YOU HAVEN'T THOUGHT ABOUT FOR TEN YEARS--BUT THEN, JUST BEFORE YOU SHOCKED ME BACK TO LIFE, I ENTERED A DREAM ZONE THAT I'VE NEVER BEEN IN BEFORE...

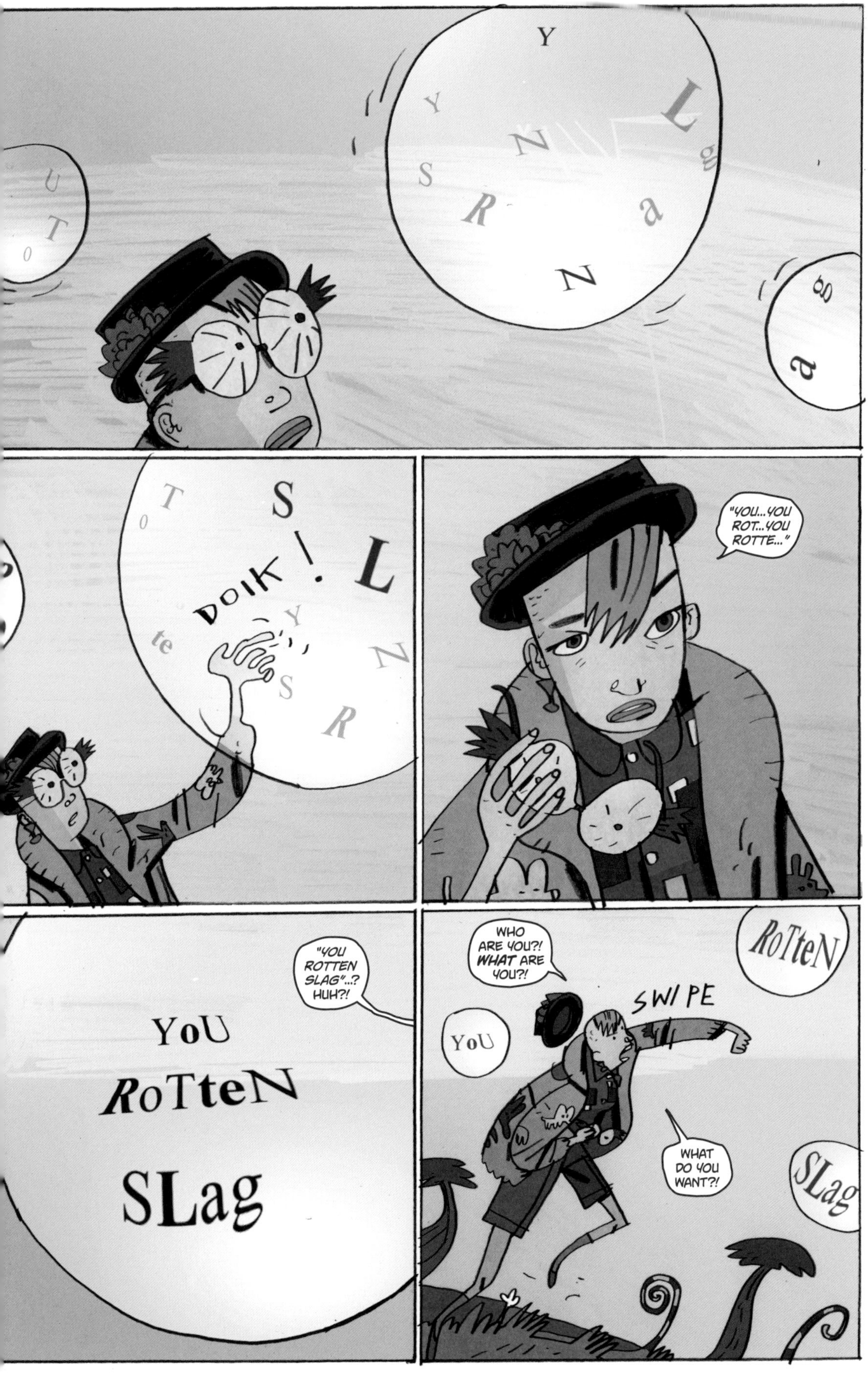
DOIK !
"YOU...YOU ROT...YOU ROTTE..."
YoU RoTteN SLag
"YOU ROTTEN SLAG"...? HUH?!
WHO ARE YOU?! WHAT ARE YOU?!
RoTteN
SWIPE
YoU
WHAT DO YOU WANT?!
SLag

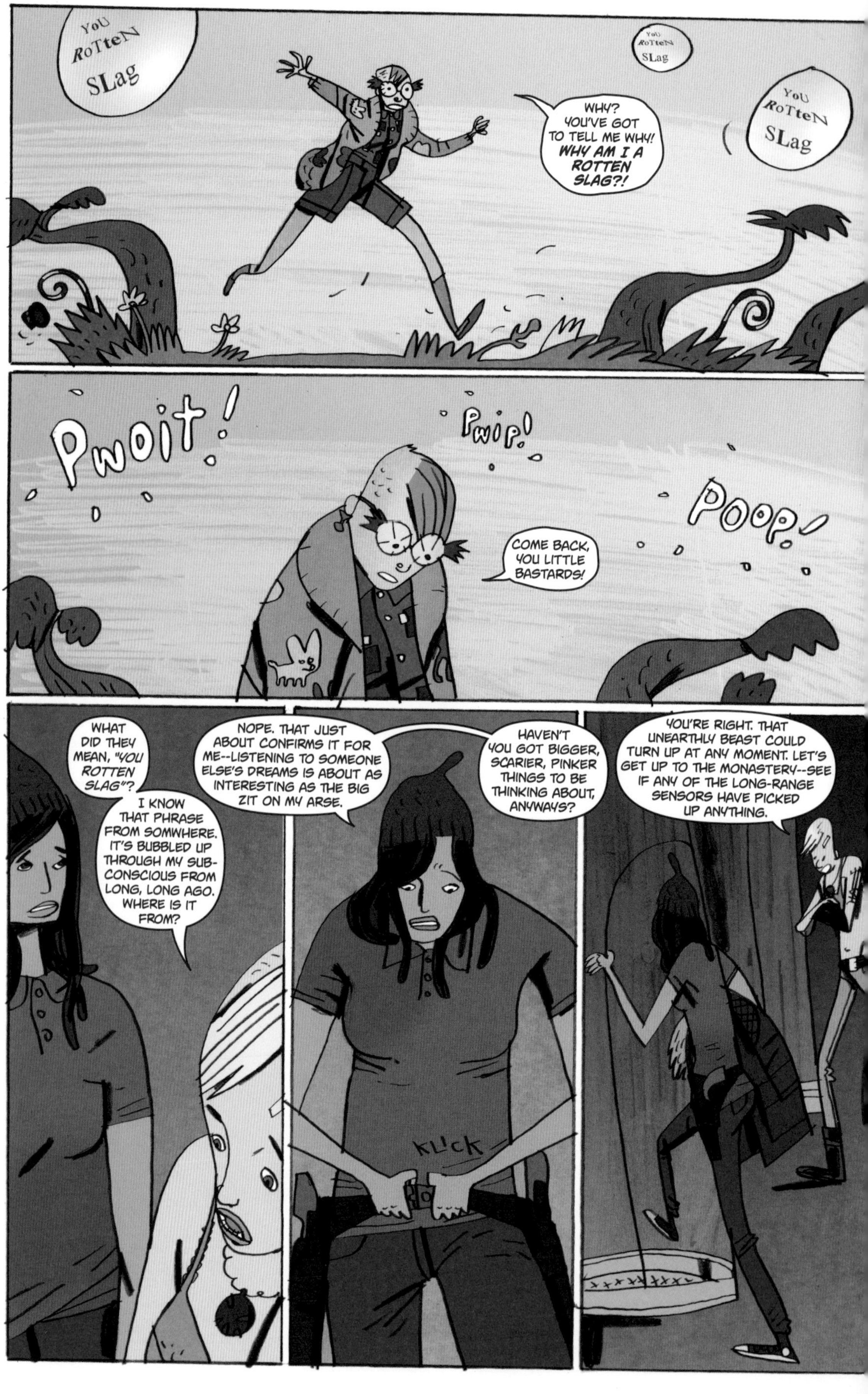
YOU ROTTEN SLAG
YOU ROTTEN SLAG
WHY? YOU'VE GOT TO TELL ME WHY! WHY AM I A ROTTEN SLAG?!
YOU ROTTEN SLAG
PWOIT!
PWIP!
POOP!
COME BACK, YOU LITTLE BASTARDS!
WHAT DID THEY MEAN, "YOU ROTTEN SLAG"?
I KNOW THAT PHRASE FROM SOMWHERE. IT'S BUBBLED UP THROUGH MY SUB-CONSCIOUS FROM LONG, LONG AGO. WHERE IS IT FROM?
NOPE. THAT JUST ABOUT CONFIRMS IT FOR ME--LISTENING TO SOMEONE ELSE'S DREAMS IS ABOUT AS INTERESTING AS THE BIG ZIT ON MY ARSE.
HAVEN'T YOU GOT BIGGER, SCARIER, PINKER THINGS TO BE THINKING ABOUT, ANYWAYS?
KLICK
YOU'RE RIGHT. THAT UNEARTHLY BEAST COULD TURN UP AT ANY MOMENT. LET'S GET UP TO THE MONASTERY--SEE IF ANY OF THE LONG-RANGE SENSORS HAVE PICKED UP ANYTHING.

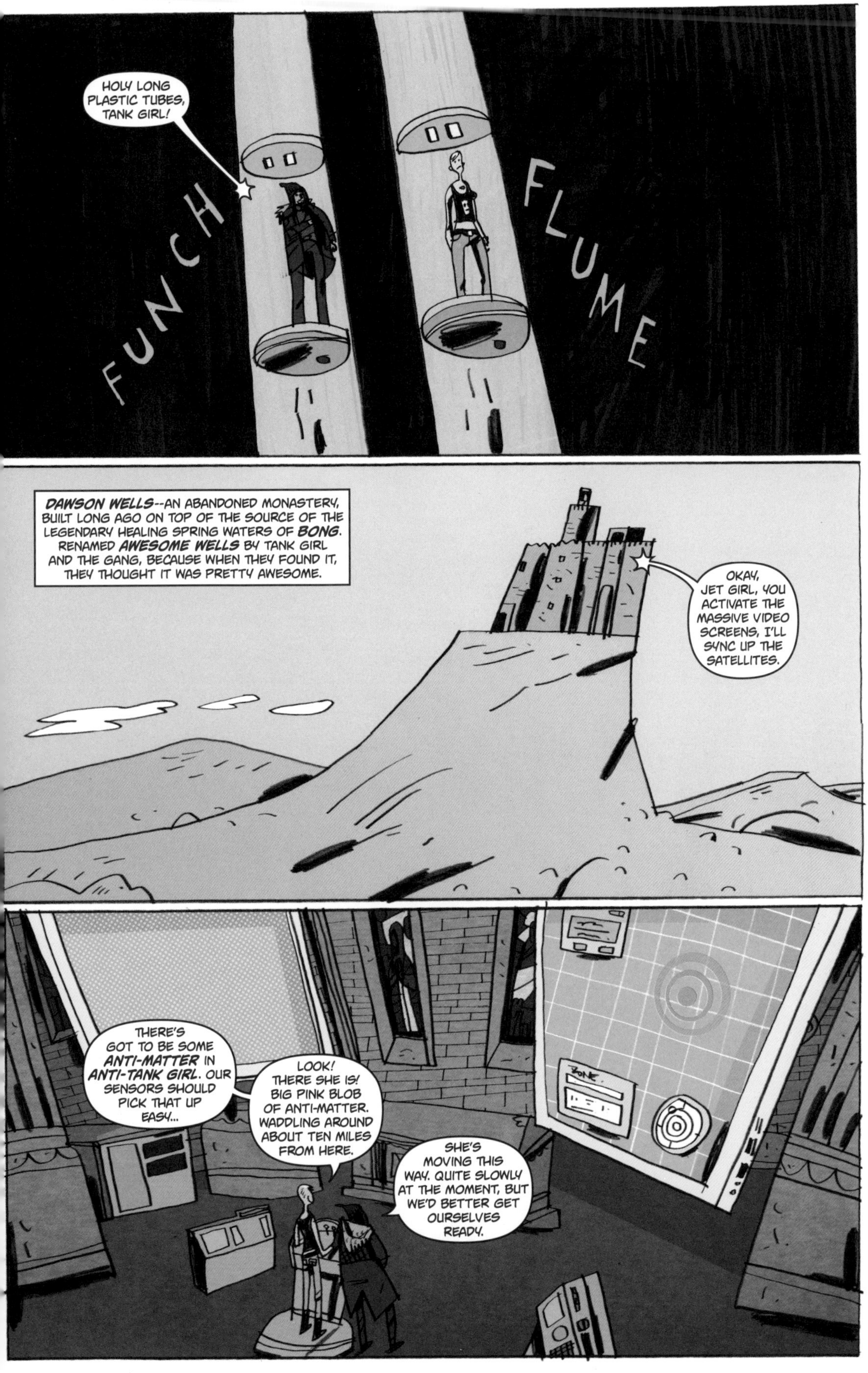
HOLY LONG PLASTIC TUBES, TANK GIRL!
FUNCH
FLUME
DAWSON WELLS--AN ABANDONED MONASTERY, BUILT LONG AGO ON TOP OF THE SOURCE OF THE LEGENDARY HEALING SPRING WATERS OF BONG. RENAMED AWESOME WELLS BY TANK GIRL AND THE GANG, BECAUSE WHEN THEY FOUND IT, THEY THOUGHT IT WAS PRETTY AWESOME.
OKAY, JET GIRL, YOU ACTIVATE THE MASSIVE VIDEO SCREENS, I'LL SYNC UP THE SATELLITES.
THERE'S GOT TO BE SOME ANTI-MATTER IN ANTI-TANK GIRL. OUR SENSORS SHOULD PICK THAT UP EASY...
LOOK! THERE SHE IS! BIG PINK BLOB OF ANTI-MATTER. WADDLING AROUND ABOUT TEN MILES FROM HERE.
SHE'S MOVING THIS WAY. QUITE SLOWLY AT THE MOMENT, BUT WE'D BETTER GET OURSELVES READY.

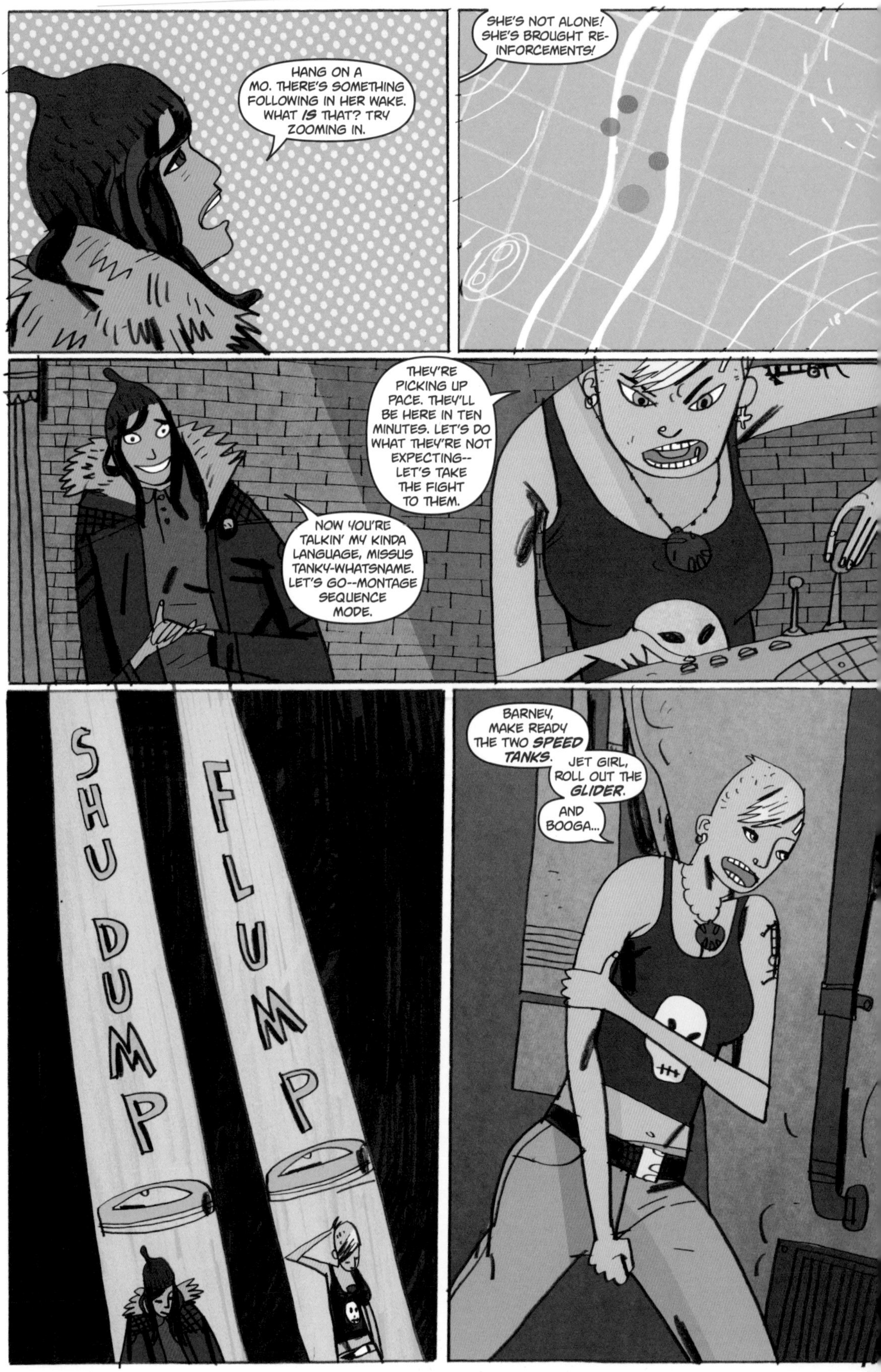
HANG ON A MO. THERE'S SOMETHING FOLLOWING IN HER WAKE. WHAT *IS* THAT? TRY ZOOMING IN.
SHE'S NOT ALONE! SHE'S BROUGHT RE-INFORCEMENTS!
THEY'RE PICKING UP PACE. THEY'LL BE HERE IN TEN MINUTES. LET'S DO WHAT THEY'RE NOT EXPECTING-- LET'S TAKE THE FIGHT TO THEM.
NOW YOU'RE TALKIN' MY KINDA LANGUAGE, MISSUS TANKY-WHATSNAME. LET'S GO--MONTAGE SEQUENCE MODE.
SHU DUMP
FLUMP
BARNEY, MAKE READY THE TWO **SPEED TANKS**.
JET GIRL, ROLL OUT THE **GLIDER**.
AND BOOGA...

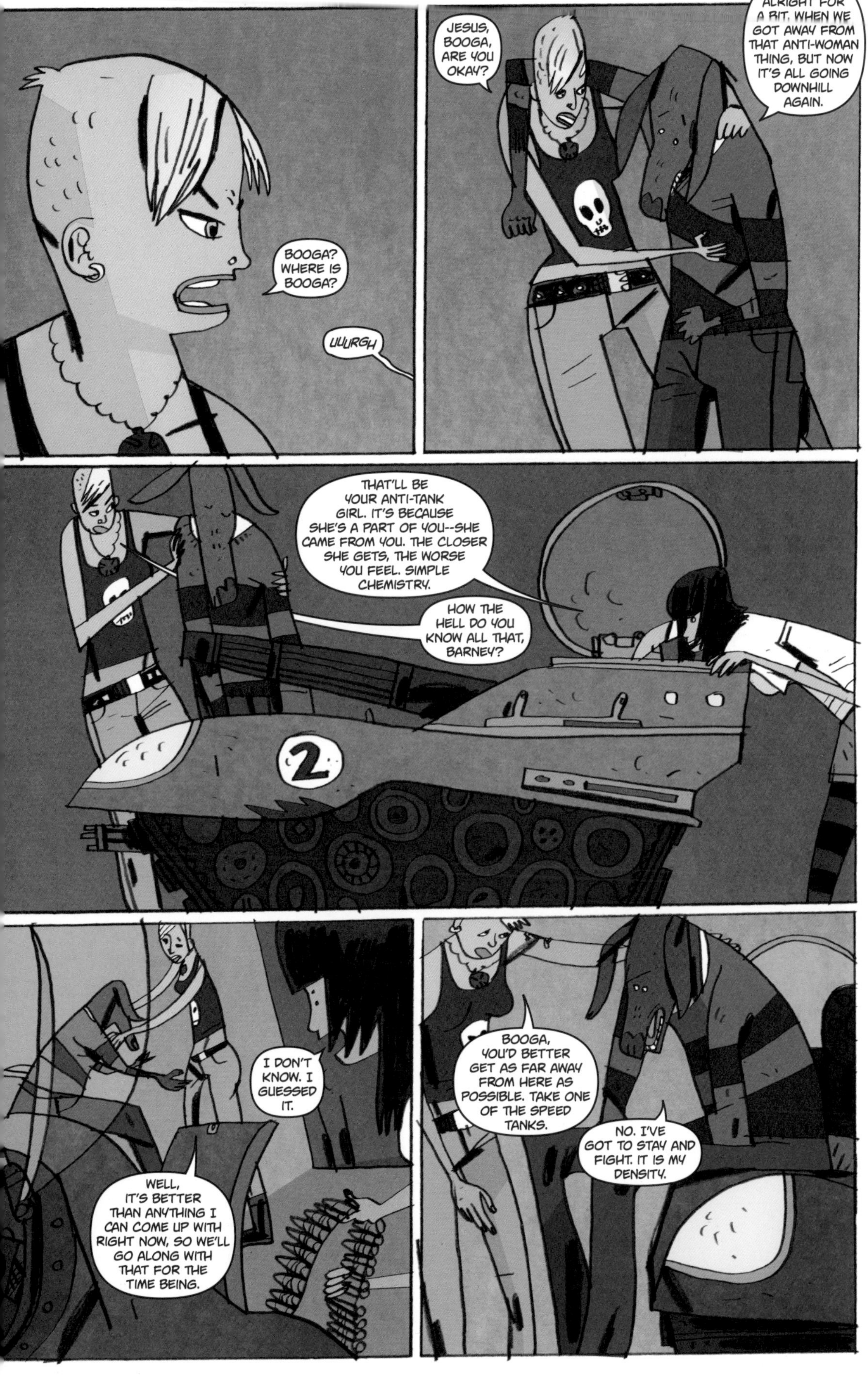
BOOGA? WHERE IS BOOGA?
UUURGH
JESUS, BOOGA, ARE YOU OKAY?
I FELT ALRIGHT FOR A BIT, WHEN WE GOT AWAY FROM THAT ANTI-WOMAN THING, BUT NOW IT'S ALL GOING DOWNHILL AGAIN.
THAT'LL BE YOUR ANTI-TANK GIRL. IT'S BECAUSE SHE'S A PART OF YOU--SHE CAME FROM YOU. THE CLOSER SHE GETS, THE WORSE YOU FEEL. SIMPLE CHEMISTRY.
HOW THE HELL DO YOU KNOW ALL THAT, BARNEY?
I DON'T KNOW. I GUESSED IT.
WELL, IT'S BETTER THAN ANYTHING I CAN COME UP WITH RIGHT NOW, SO WE'LL GO ALONG WITH THAT FOR THE TIME BEING.
BOOGA, YOU'D BETTER GET AS FAR AWAY FROM HERE AS POSSIBLE. TAKE ONE OF THE SPEED TANKS.
NO. I'VE GOT TO STAY AND FIGHT. IT IS MY DENSITY.

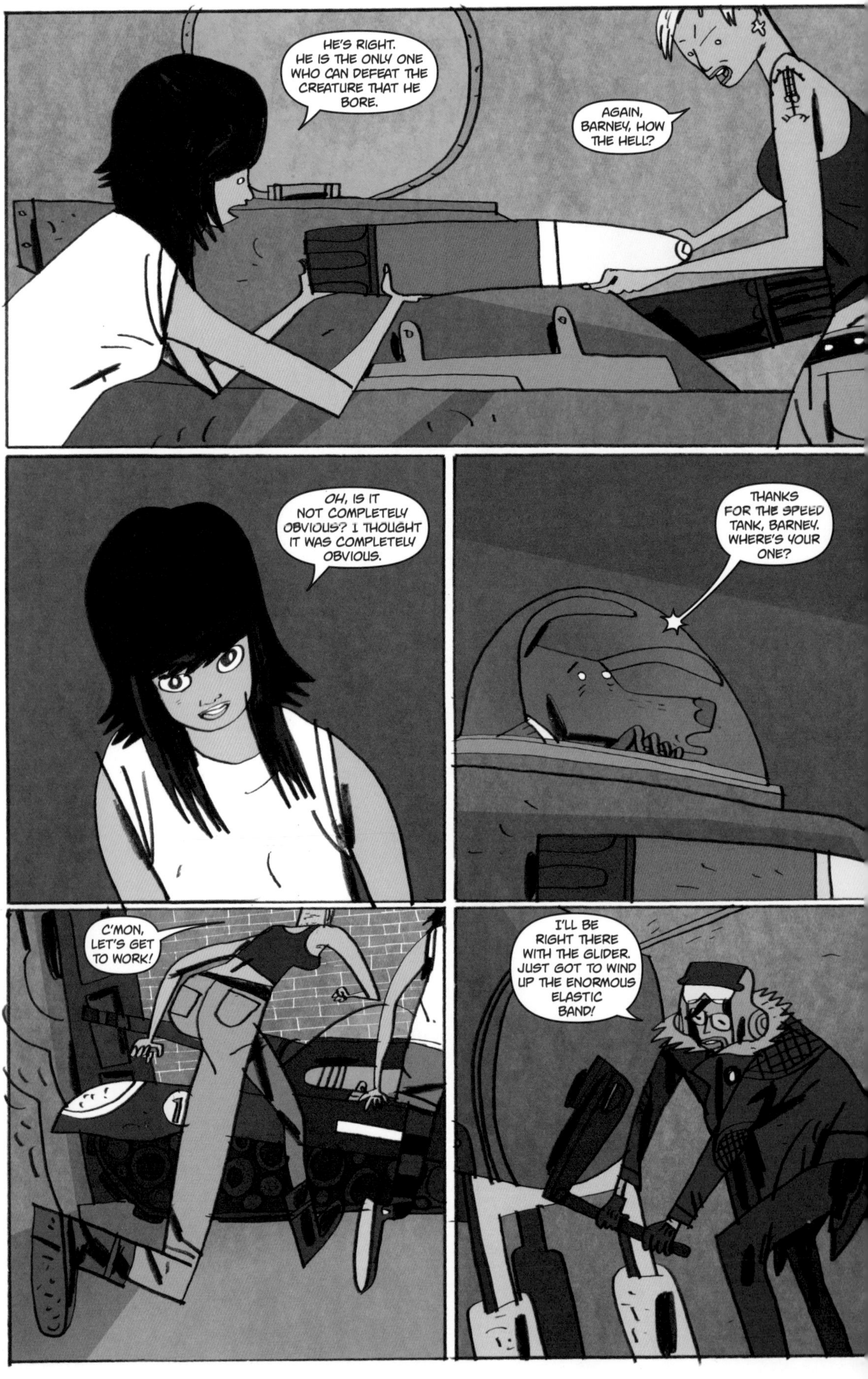
HE'S RIGHT. HE IS THE ONLY ONE WHO CAN DEFEAT THE CREATURE THAT HE BORE.
AGAIN, BARNEY, HOW THE HELL?
OH, IS IT NOT COMPLETELY OBVIOUS? I THOUGHT IT WAS COMPLETELY OBVIOUS.
THANKS FOR THE SPEED TANK, BARNEY. WHERE'S YOUR ONE?
C'MON, LET'S GET TO WORK!
I'LL BE RIGHT THERE WITH THE GLIDER. JUST GOT TO WIND UP THE ENORMOUS ELASTIC BAND!

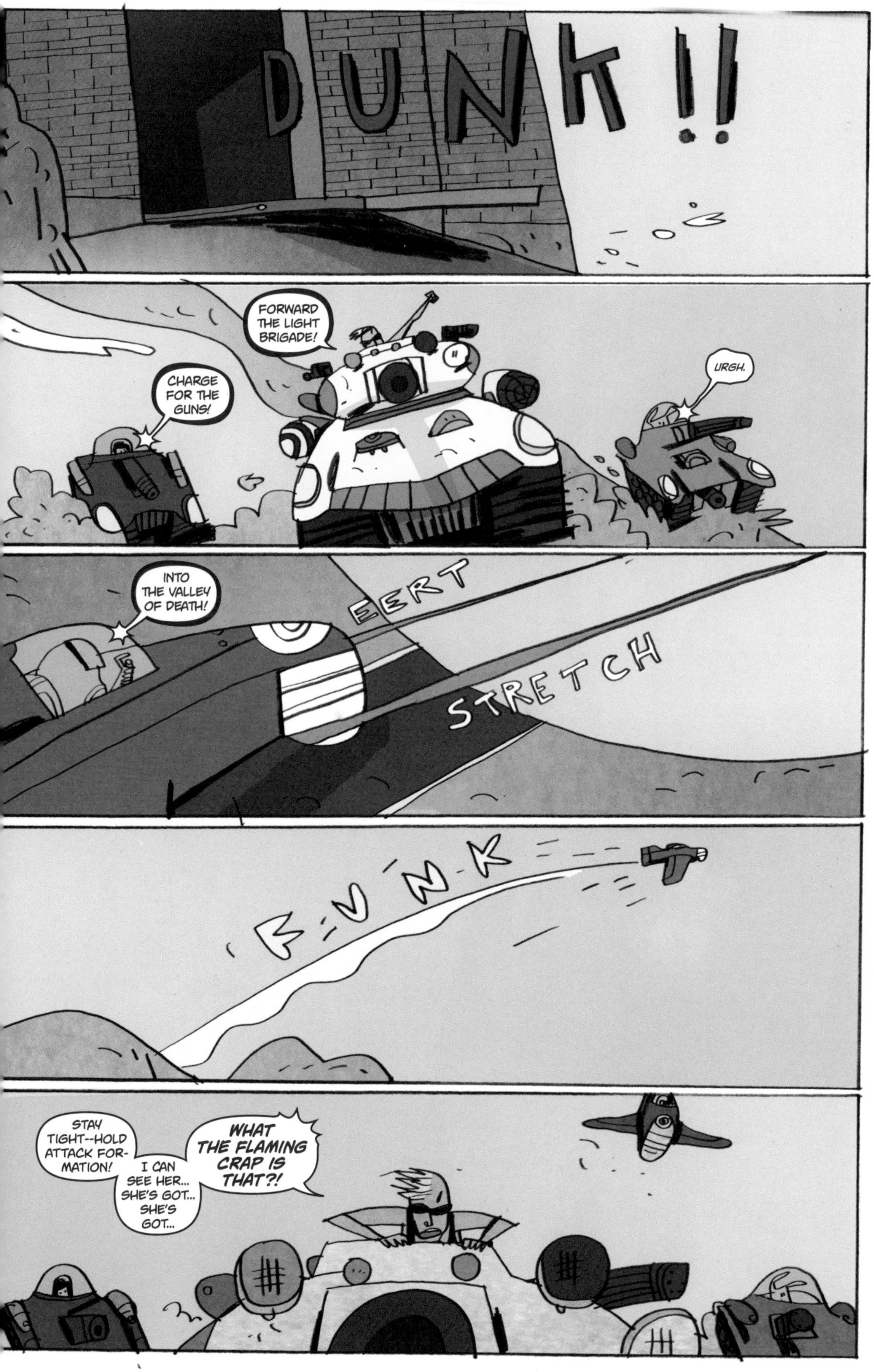
DUNK!!
FORWARD THE LIGHT BRIGADE!
CHARGE FOR THE GUNS!
URGH.
INTO THE VALLEY OF DEATH!
EERT
STRETCH
FUNK
STAY TIGHT--HOLD ATTACK FORMATION!
I CAN SEE HER... SHE'S GOT... SHE'S GOT...
WHAT THE FLAMING CRAP IS THAT?!

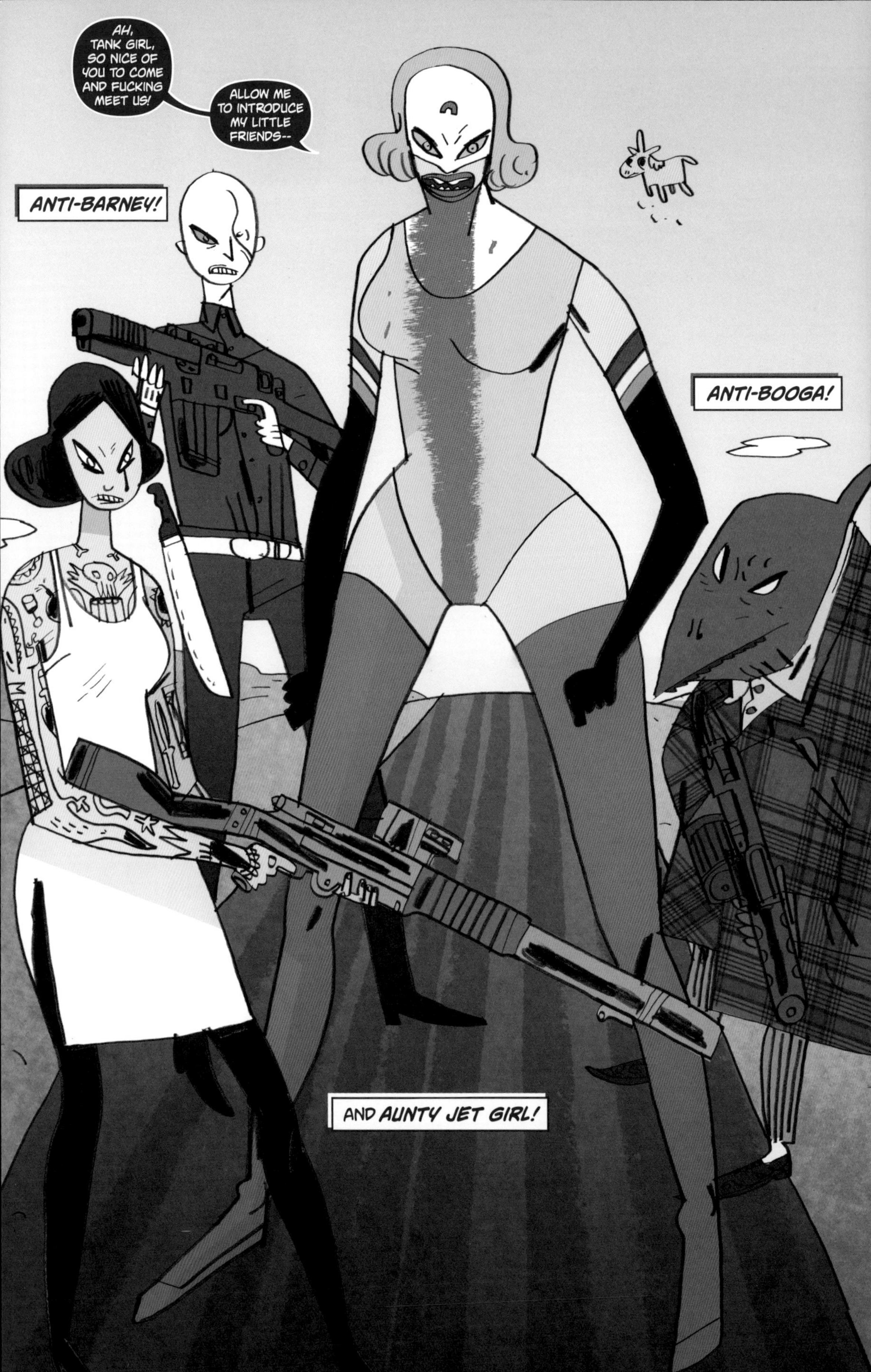
AH, TANK GIRL, SO NICE OF YOU TO COME AND FUCKING MEET US!
ALLOW ME TO INTRODUCE MY LITTLE FRIENDS--
ANTI-BARNEY!
ANTI-BOOGA!
AND AUNTY JET GIRL!

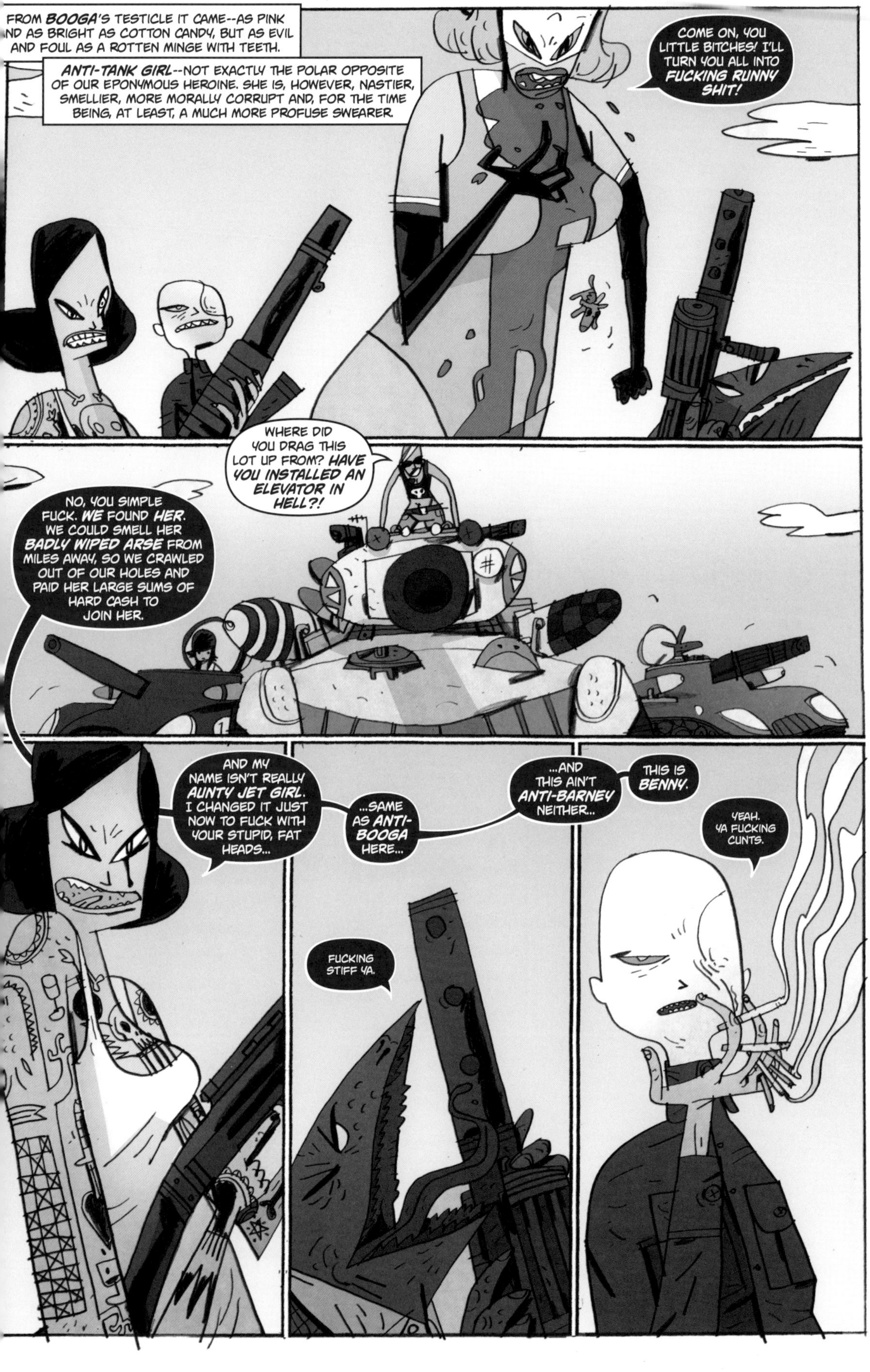
FROM BOOGA'S TESTICLE IT CAME--AS PINK
ND AS BRIGHT AS COTTON CANDY, BUT AS EVIL
AND FOUL AS A ROTTEN MINGE WITH TEETH.
ANTI-TANK GIRL--NOT EXACTLY THE POLAR OPPOSITE OF OUR EPONYMOUS HEROINE. SHE IS, HOWEVER, NASTIER, SMELLIER, MORE MORALLY CORRUPT AND, FOR THE TIME BEING, AT LEAST, A MUCH MORE PROFUSE SWEARER.
COME ON, YOU LITTLE BITCHES! I'LL TURN YOU ALL INTO FUCKING RUNNY SHIT!
WHERE DID YOU DRAG THIS LOT UP FROM? HAVE YOU INSTALLED AN ELEVATOR IN HELL?!
NO, YOU SIMPLE FUCK. WE FOUND HER. WE COULD SMELL HER BADLY WIPED ARSE FROM MILES AWAY, SO WE CRAWLED OUT OF OUR HOLES AND PAID HER LARGE SUMS OF HARD CASH TO JOIN HER.
AND MY NAME ISN'T REALLY AUNTY JET GIRL. I CHANGED IT JUST NOW TO FUCK WITH YOUR STUPID, FAT HEADS...
...SAME AS ANTI-BOOGA HERE...
FUCKING STIFF YA.
...AND THIS AIN'T ANTI-BARNEY NEITHER...
THIS IS BENNY.
YEAH. YA FUCKING CUNTS.

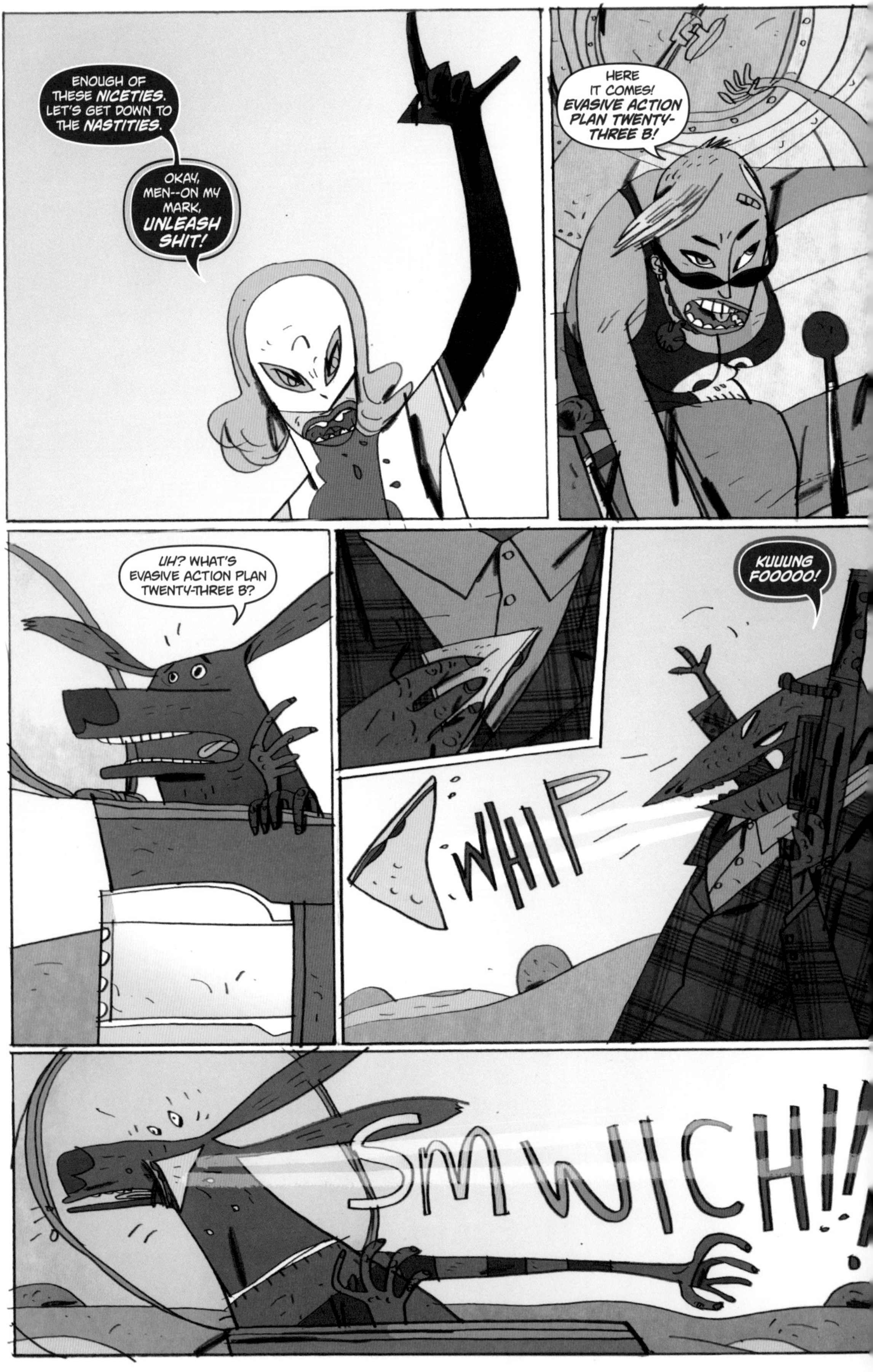
ENOUGH OF THESE NICETIES. LET'S GET DOWN TO THE NASTITIES.
OKAY, MEN--ON MY MARK, UNLEASH SHIT!
HERE IT COMES! EVASIVE ACTION PLAN TWENTY-THREE B!
UH? WHAT'S EVASIVE ACTION PLAN TWENTY-THREE B?
KUUUNG FOOOOO!
WHIP
SMWICH!!

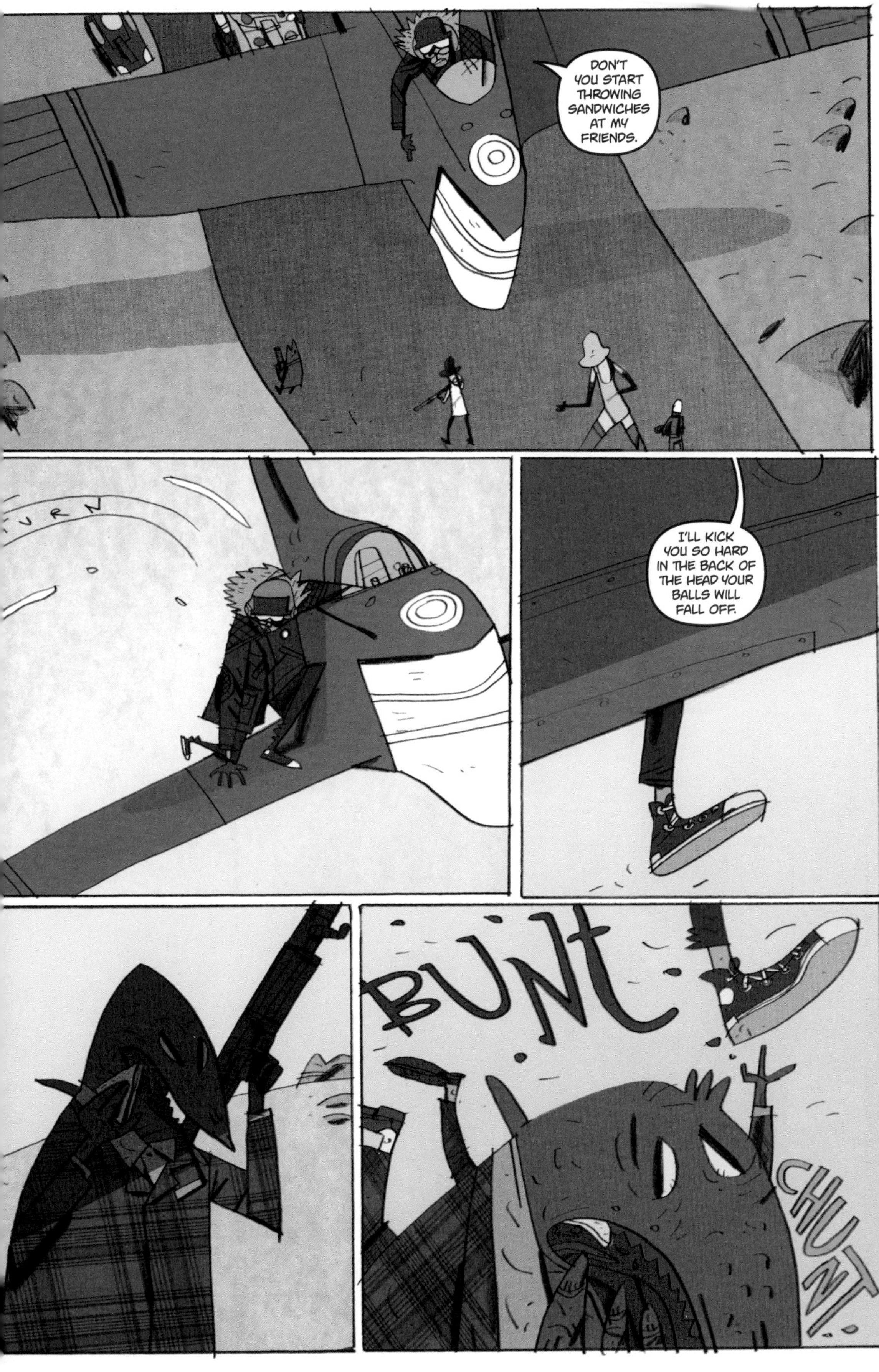
DON'T YOU START THROWING SANDWICHES AT MY FRIENDS.
URN
I'LL KICK YOU SO HARD IN THE BACK OF THE HEAD YOUR BALLS WILL FALL OFF.
BUNT
CHUNT.

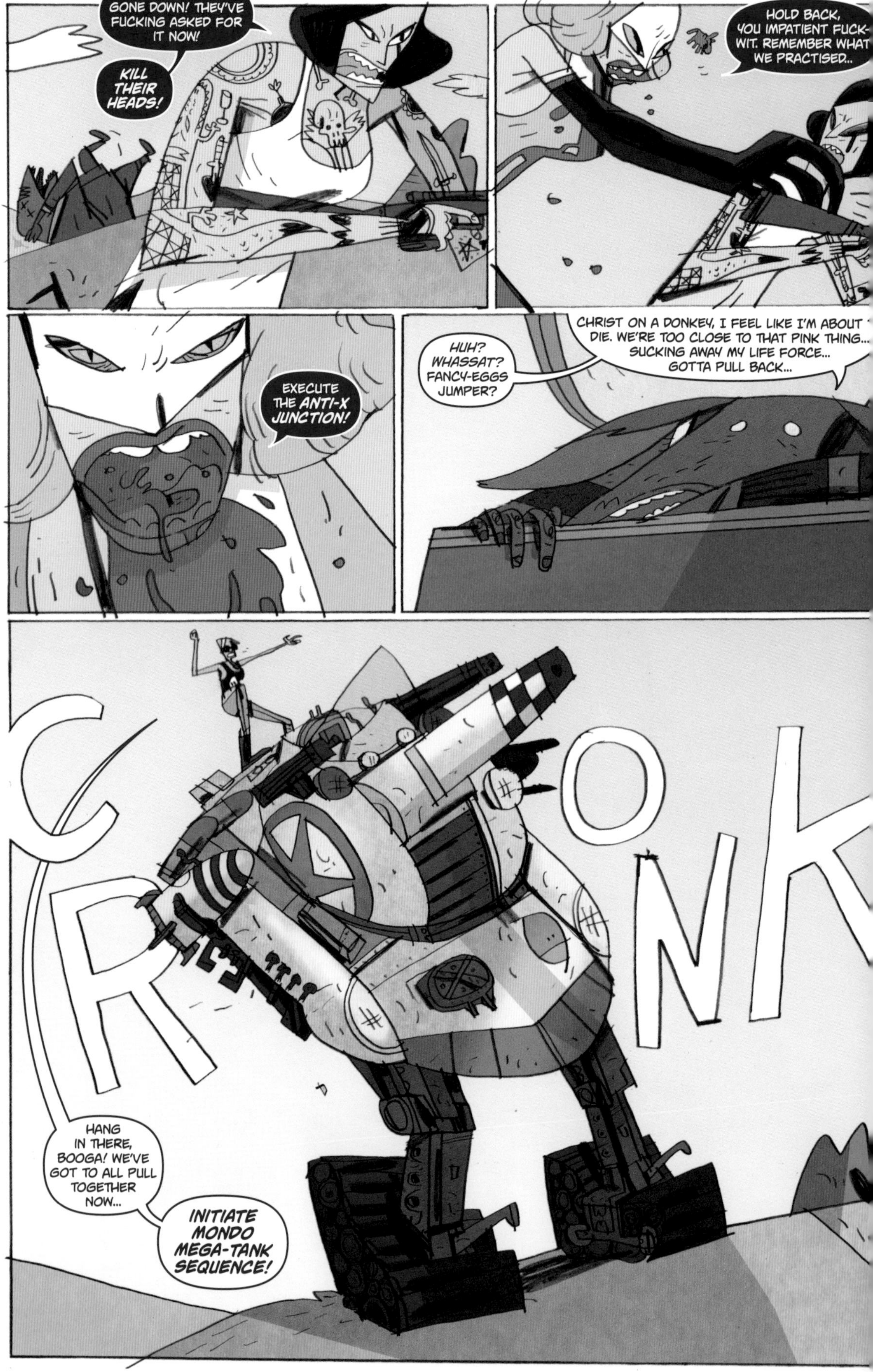
ANTI-BOOGA'S GONE DOWN! THEY'VE FUCKING ASKED FOR IT NOW!
KILL THEIR HEADS!
HOLD BACK, YOU IMPATIENT FUCK-WIT. REMEMBER WHAT WE PRACTISED...
EXECUTE THE ANTI-X JUNCTION!
CHRIST ON A DONKEY, I FEEL LIKE I'M ABOUT TO DIE. WE'RE TOO CLOSE TO THAT PINK THING... SUCKING AWAY MY LIFE FORCE... GOTTA PULL BACK...
HUH? WHASSAT? FANCY-EGGS JUMPER?
CRONK
HANG IN THERE, BOOGA! WE'VE GOT TO ALL PULL TOGETHER NOW...
INITIATE MONDO MEGA-TANK SEQUENCE!

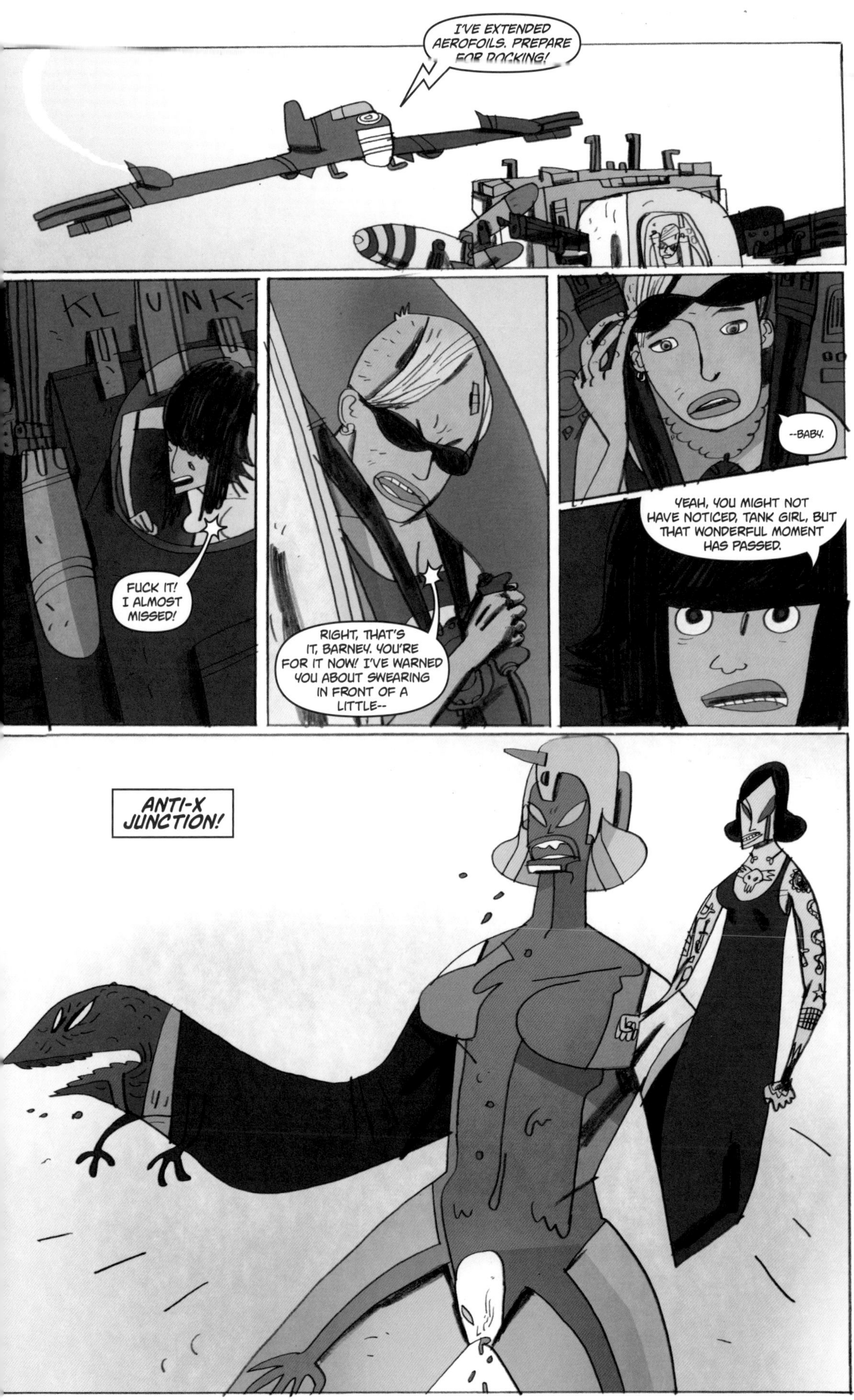
I'VE EXTENDED AEROFOILS. PREPARE FOR DOCKING!
KLUNK
FUCK IT! I ALMOST MISSED!
RIGHT, THAT'S IT, BARNEY. YOU'RE FOR IT NOW! I'VE WARNED YOU ABOUT SWEARING IN FRONT OF A LITTLE--
--BABY.
YEAH, YOU MIGHT NOT HAVE NOTICED, TANK GIRL, BUT THAT WONDERFUL MOMENT HAS PASSED.
ANTI-X JUNCTION!

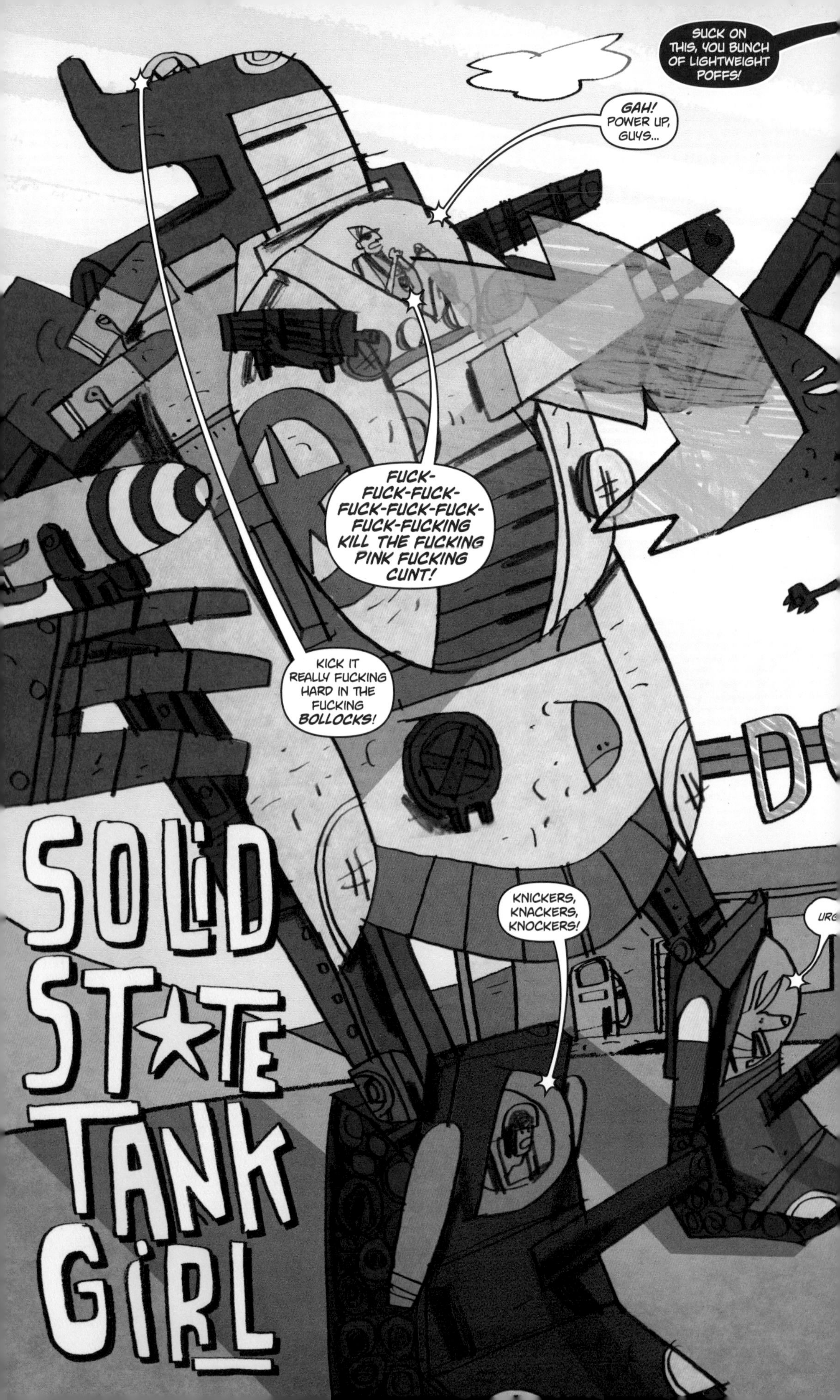
SUCK ON THIS, YOU BUNCH OF LIGHTWEIGHT POFFS!
GAH! POWER UP, GUYS...
FUCK-FUCK-FUCK-FUCK-FUCK-FUCK-FUCK-FUCKING KILL THE FUCKING PINK FUCKING CUNT!
KICK IT REALLY FUCKING HARD IN THE FUCKING BOLLOCKS!
KNICKERS, KNACKERS, KNOCKERS!
URG
SOLID STATE TANK GIRL

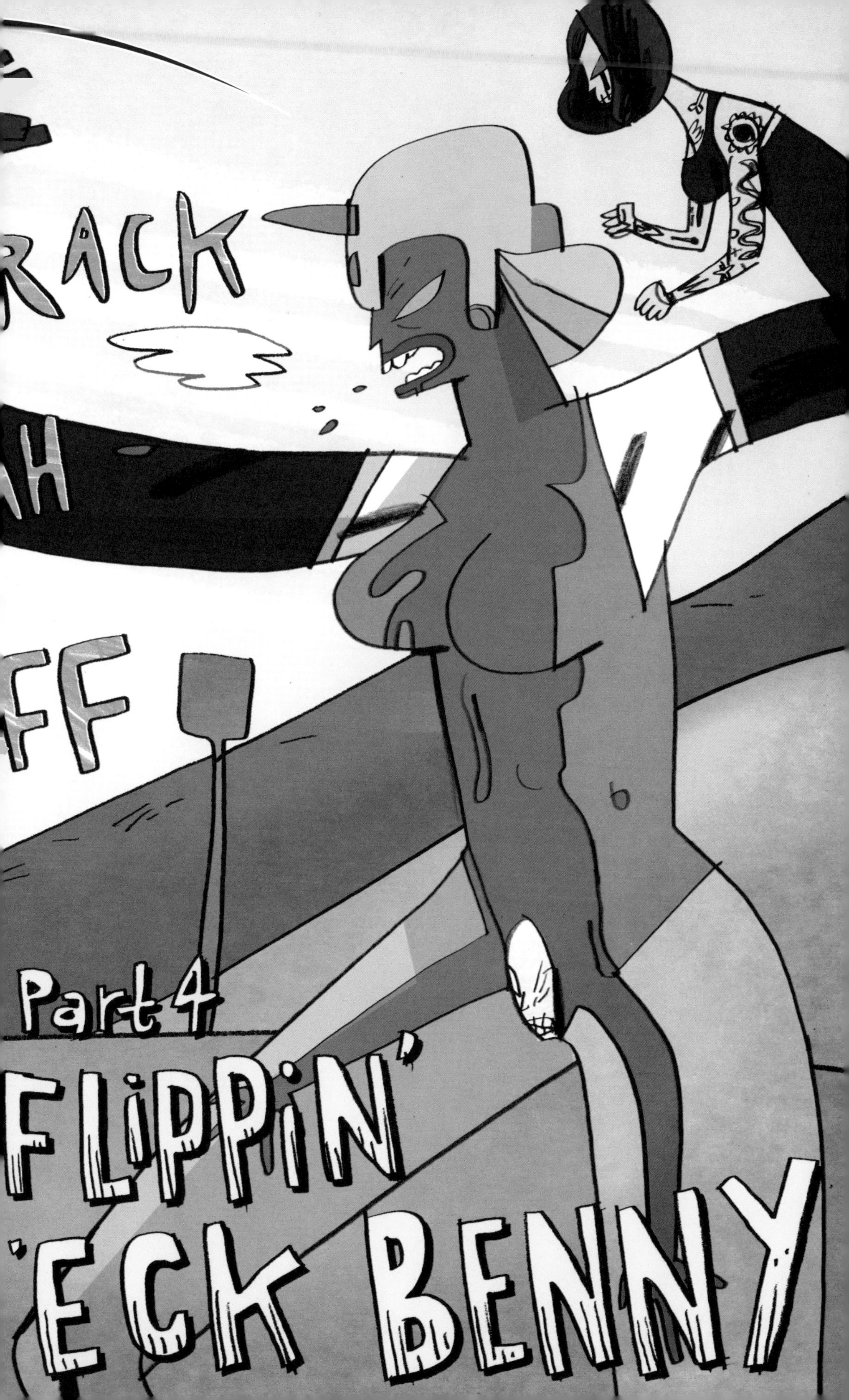
RACK
AH
FF
Part 4
FLIPPIN'
'ECK BENNY

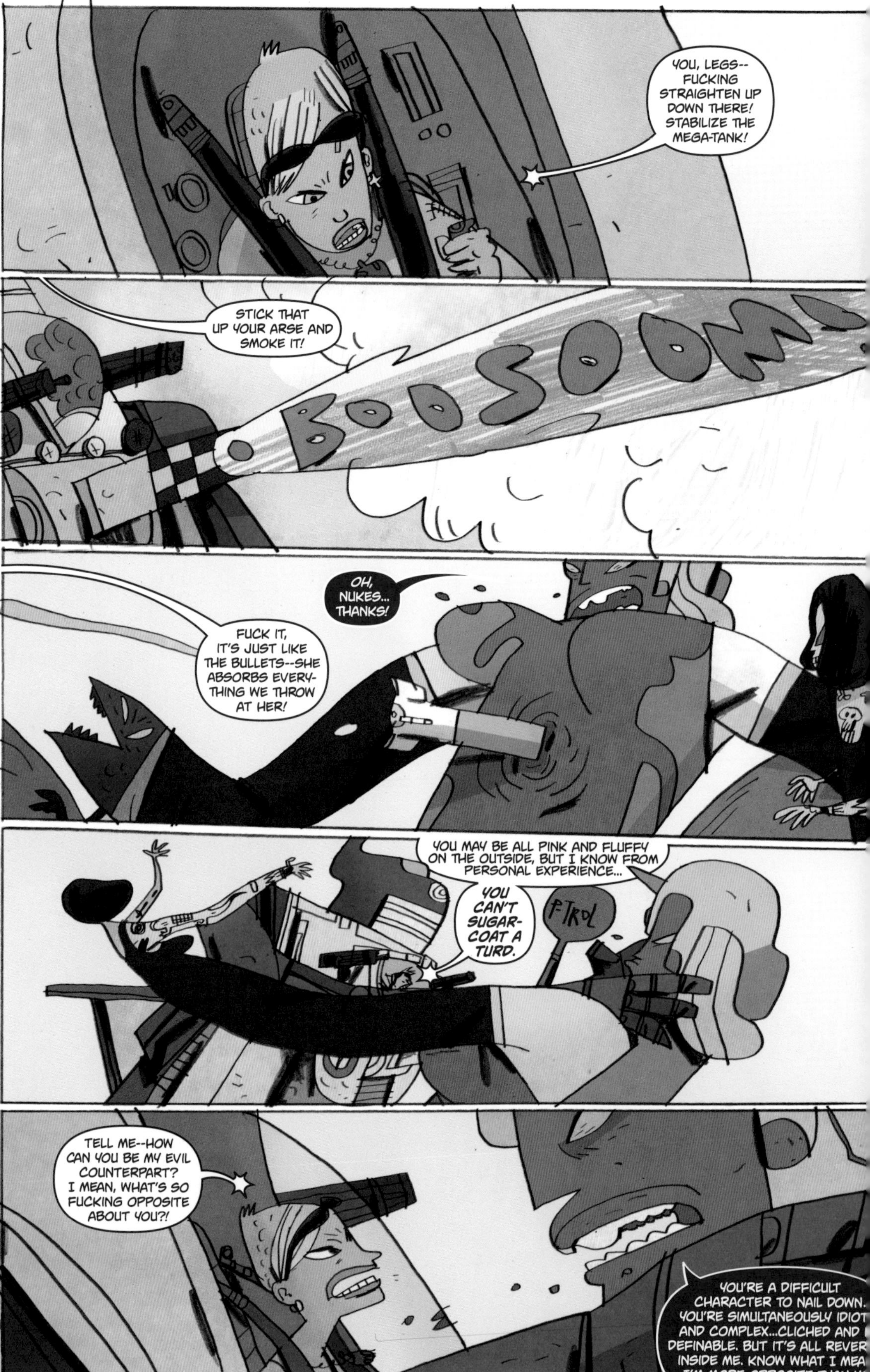
YOU, LEGS-- FUCKING STRAIGHTEN UP DOWN THERE! STABILIZE THE MEGA-TANK!
STICK THAT UP YOUR ARSE AND SMOKE IT!
BOOSOOM!
OH, NUKES... THANKS!
FUCK IT, IT'S JUST LIKE THE BULLETS--SHE ABSORBS EVERY-THING WE THROW AT HER!
YOU MAY BE ALL PINK AND FLUFFY ON THE OUTSIDE, BUT I KNOW FROM PERSONAL EXPERIENCE...
YOU CAN'T SUGAR-COAT A TURD.
P-TROL
TELL ME--HOW CAN YOU BE MY EVIL COUNTERPART? I MEAN, WHAT'S SO FUCKING OPPOSITE ABOUT YOU?!
YOU'RE A DIFFICULT CHARACTER TO NAIL DOWN. YOU'RE SIMULTANEOUSLY IDIOT AND COMPLEX...CLICHED AND DEFINABLE. BUT IT'S ALL REVER INSIDE ME. KNOW WHAT I MEA I'M MORE OPPOSITE THAN YO COULD POSSIBLY IMAGINE!

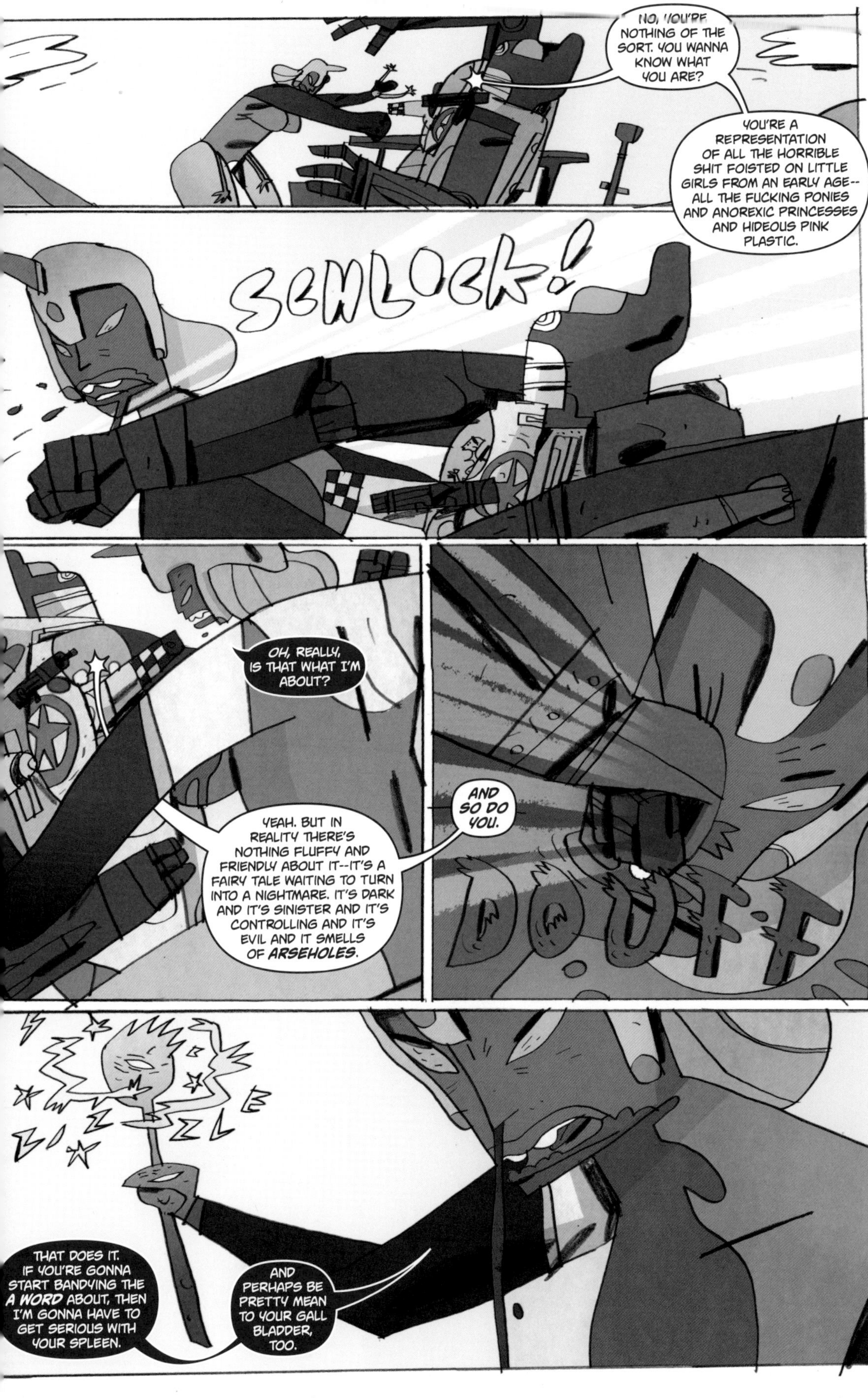
NO, YOU'RE NOTHING OF THE SORT. YOU WANNA KNOW WHAT YOU ARE?
YOU'RE A REPRESENTATION OF ALL THE HORRIBLE SHIT FOISTED ON LITTLE GIRLS FROM AN EARLY AGE-- ALL THE FUCKING PONIES AND ANOREXIC PRINCESSES AND HIDEOUS PINK PLASTIC.
SCHLOCK!
OH, REALLY, IS THAT WHAT I'M ABOUT?
YEAH. BUT IN REALITY THERE'S NOTHING FLUFFY AND FRIENDLY ABOUT IT--IT'S A FAIRY TALE WAITING TO TURN INTO A NIGHTMARE. IT'S DARK AND IT'S SINISTER AND IT'S CONTROLLING AND IT'S EVIL AND IT SMELLS OF ARSEHOLES.
AND SO DO YOU.
DOOFF
BZZZLE
THAT DOES IT. IF YOU'RE GONNA START BANDYING THE A WORD ABOUT, THEN I'M GONNA HAVE TO GET SERIOUS WITH YOUR SPLEEN.
AND PERHAPS BE PRETTY MEAN TO YOUR GALL BLADDER, TOO.

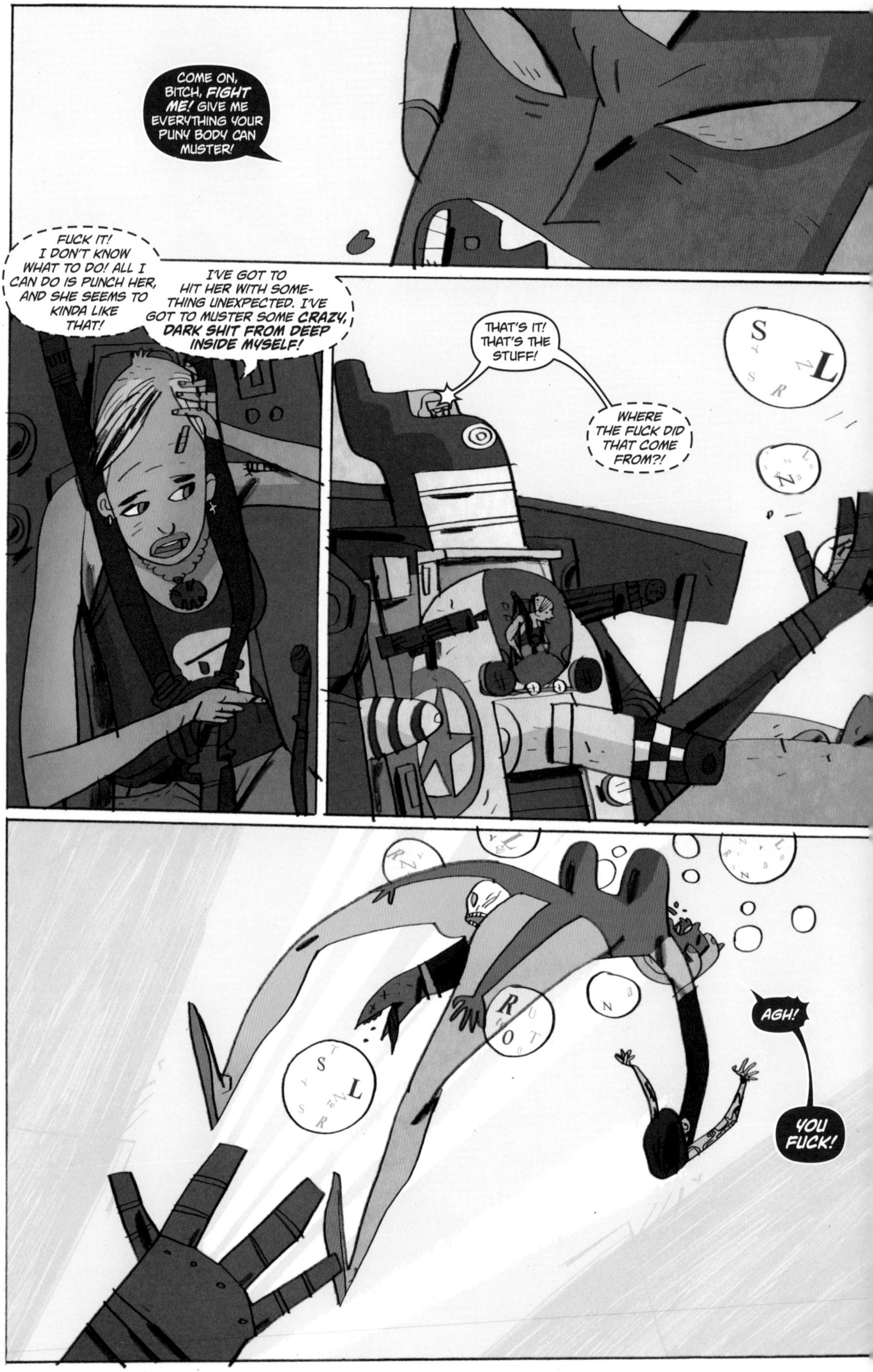
COME ON, BITCH, FIGHT ME! GIVE ME EVERYTHING YOUR PUNY BODY CAN MUSTER!
FUCK IT! I DON'T KNOW WHAT TO DO! ALL I CAN DO IS PUNCH HER, AND SHE SEEMS TO KINDA LIKE THAT!
I'VE GOT TO HIT HER WITH SOMETHING UNEXPECTED. I'VE GOT TO MUSTER SOME CRAZY, DARK SHIT FROM DEEP INSIDE MYSELF!
THAT'S IT! THAT'S THE STUFF!
WHERE THE FUCK DID THAT COME FROM?!
AGH!
YOU FUCK!

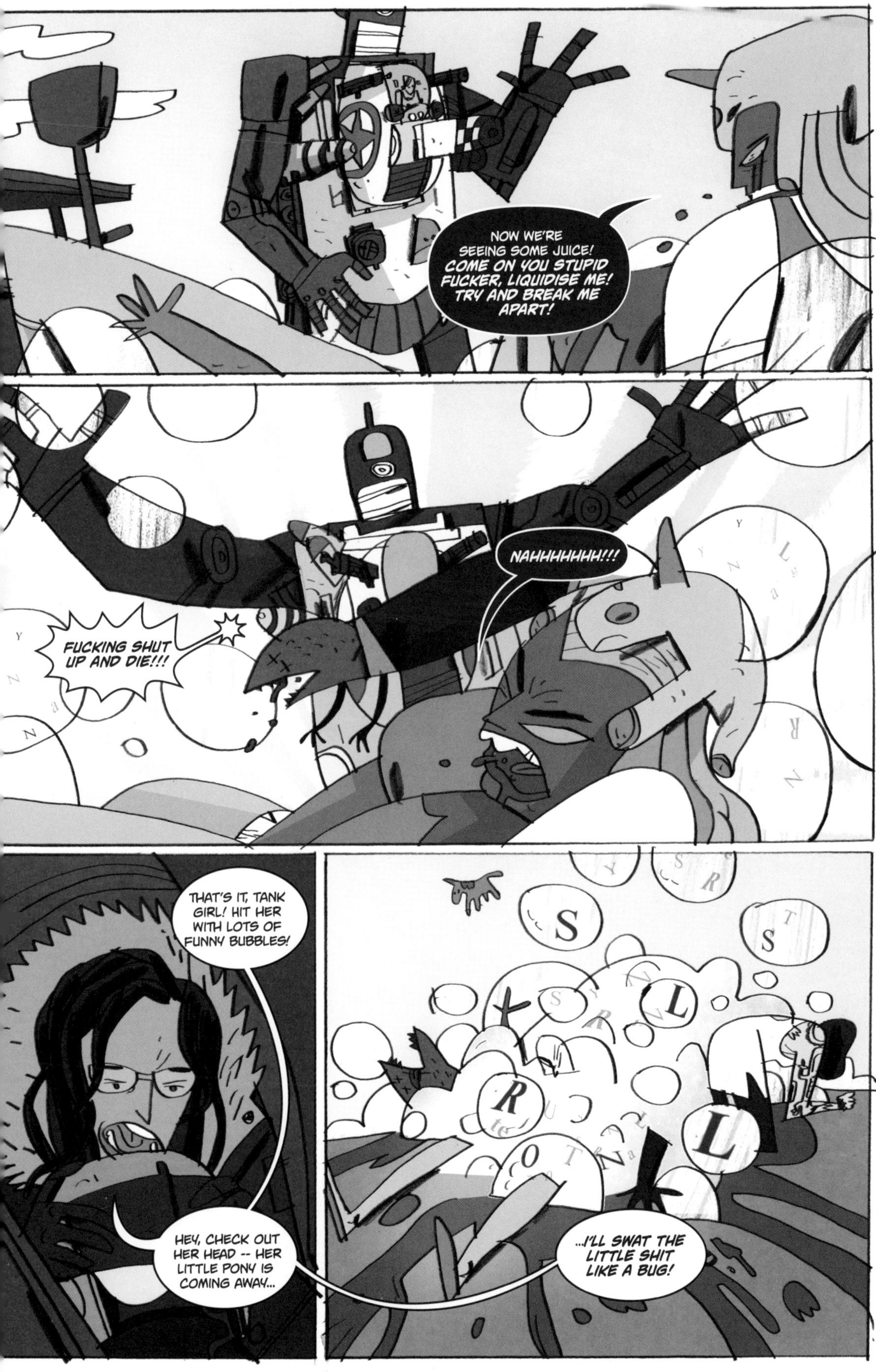
NOW WE'RE SEEING SOME JUICE! COME ON YOU STUPID FUCKER, LIQUIDISE ME! TRY AND BREAK ME APART!
NAHHHHHHH!!!
FUCKING SHUT UP AND DIE!!!
THAT'S IT, TANK GIRL! HIT HER WITH LOTS OF FUNNY BUBBLES!
HEY, CHECK OUT HER HEAD -- HER LITTLE PONY IS COMING AWAY...
...I'LL SWAT THE LITTLE SHIT LIKE A BUG!

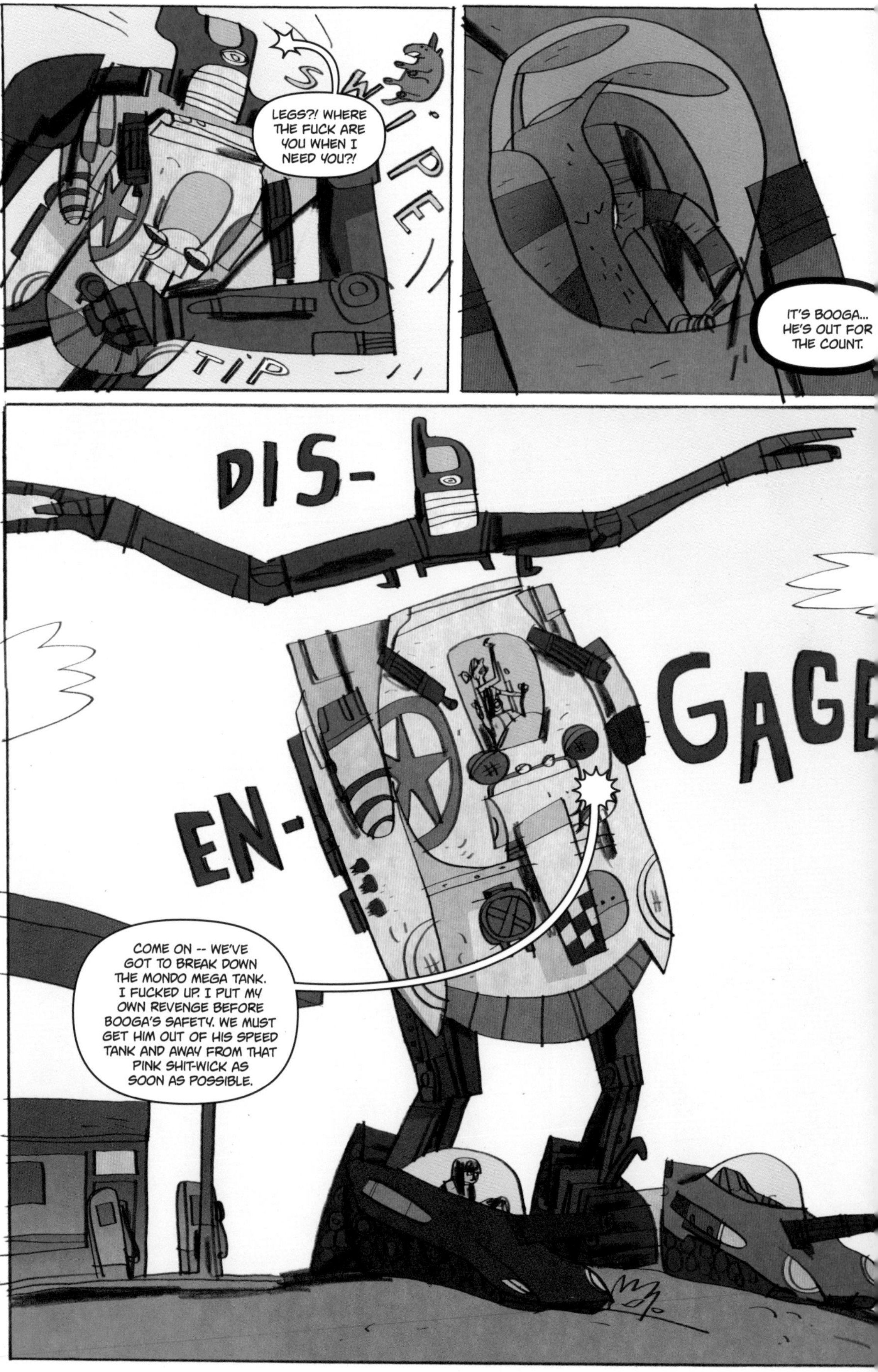

LEGS?! WHERE THE FUCK ARE YOU WHEN I NEED YOU?!
SWIPE
TIP
IT'S BOOGA... HE'S OUT FOR THE COUNT.
DIS-
EN-
GAGE
COME ON -- WE'VE GOT TO BREAK DOWN THE MONDO MEGA TANK. I FUCKED UP. I PUT MY OWN REVENGE BEFORE BOOGA'S SAFETY. WE MUST GET HIM OUT OF HIS SPEED TANK AND AWAY FROM THAT PINK SHIT-WICK AS SOON AS POSSIBLE.

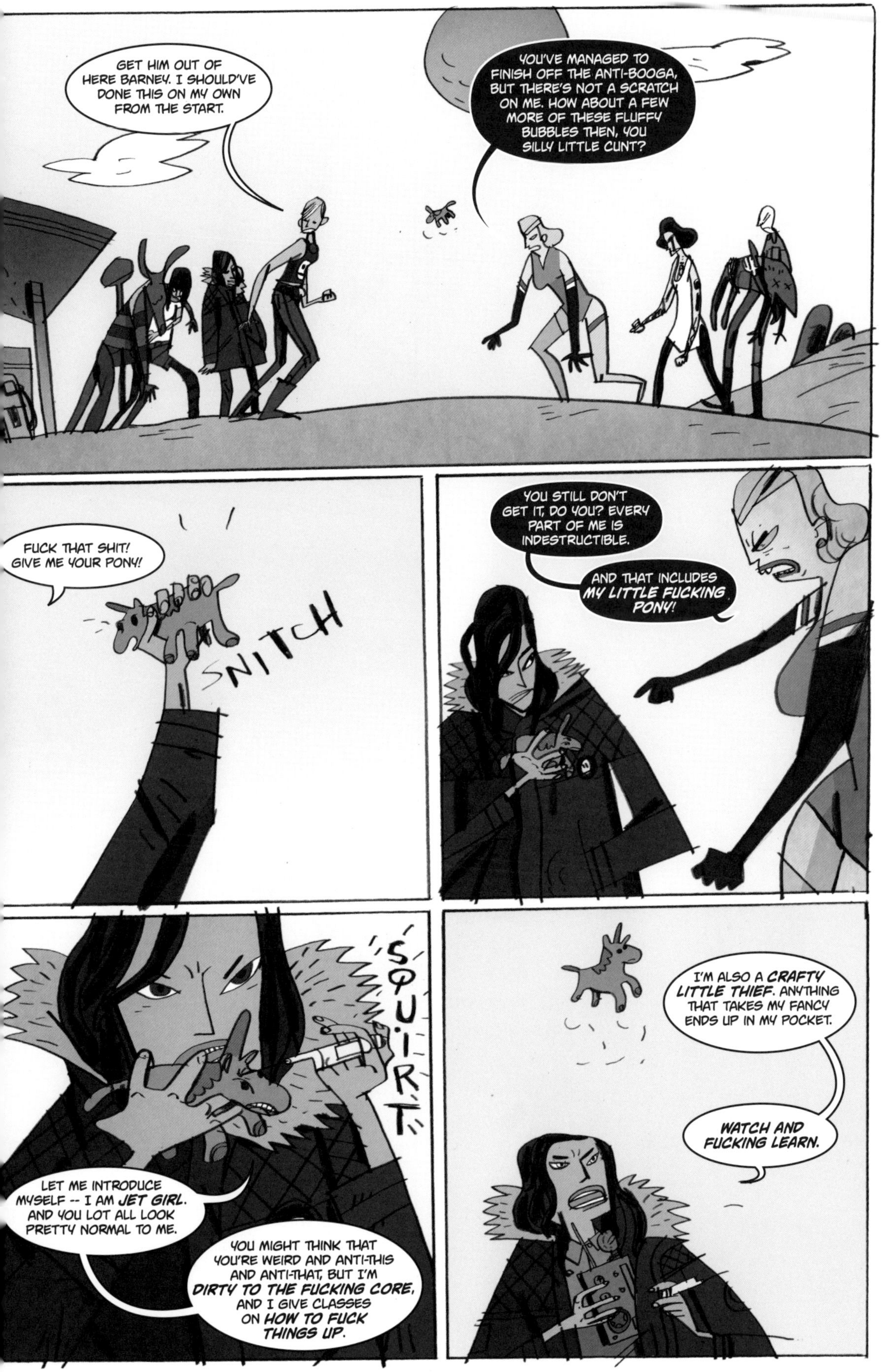
GET HIM OUT OF HERE BARNEY. I SHOULD'VE DONE THIS ON MY OWN FROM THE START.
YOU'VE MANAGED TO FINISH OFF THE ANTI-BOOGA, BUT THERE'S NOT A SCRATCH ON ME. HOW ABOUT A FEW MORE OF THESE FLUFFY BUBBLES THEN, YOU SILLY LITTLE CUNT?
FUCK THAT SHIT! GIVE ME YOUR PONY!
SNITCH
YOU STILL DON'T GET IT, DO YOU? EVERY PART OF ME IS INDESTRUCTIBLE.
AND THAT INCLUDES MY LITTLE FUCKING PONY!
SQUIRT
LET ME INTRODUCE MYSELF -- I AM JET GIRL. AND YOU LOT ALL LOOK PRETTY NORMAL TO ME.
YOU MIGHT THINK THAT YOU'RE WEIRD AND ANTI-THIS AND ANTI-THAT, BUT I'M DIRTY TO THE FUCKING CORE, AND I GIVE CLASSES ON HOW TO FUCK THINGS UP.
I'M ALSO A CRAFTY LITTLE THIEF. ANYTHING THAT TAKES MY FANCY ENDS UP IN MY POCKET.
WATCH AND FUCKING LEARN.

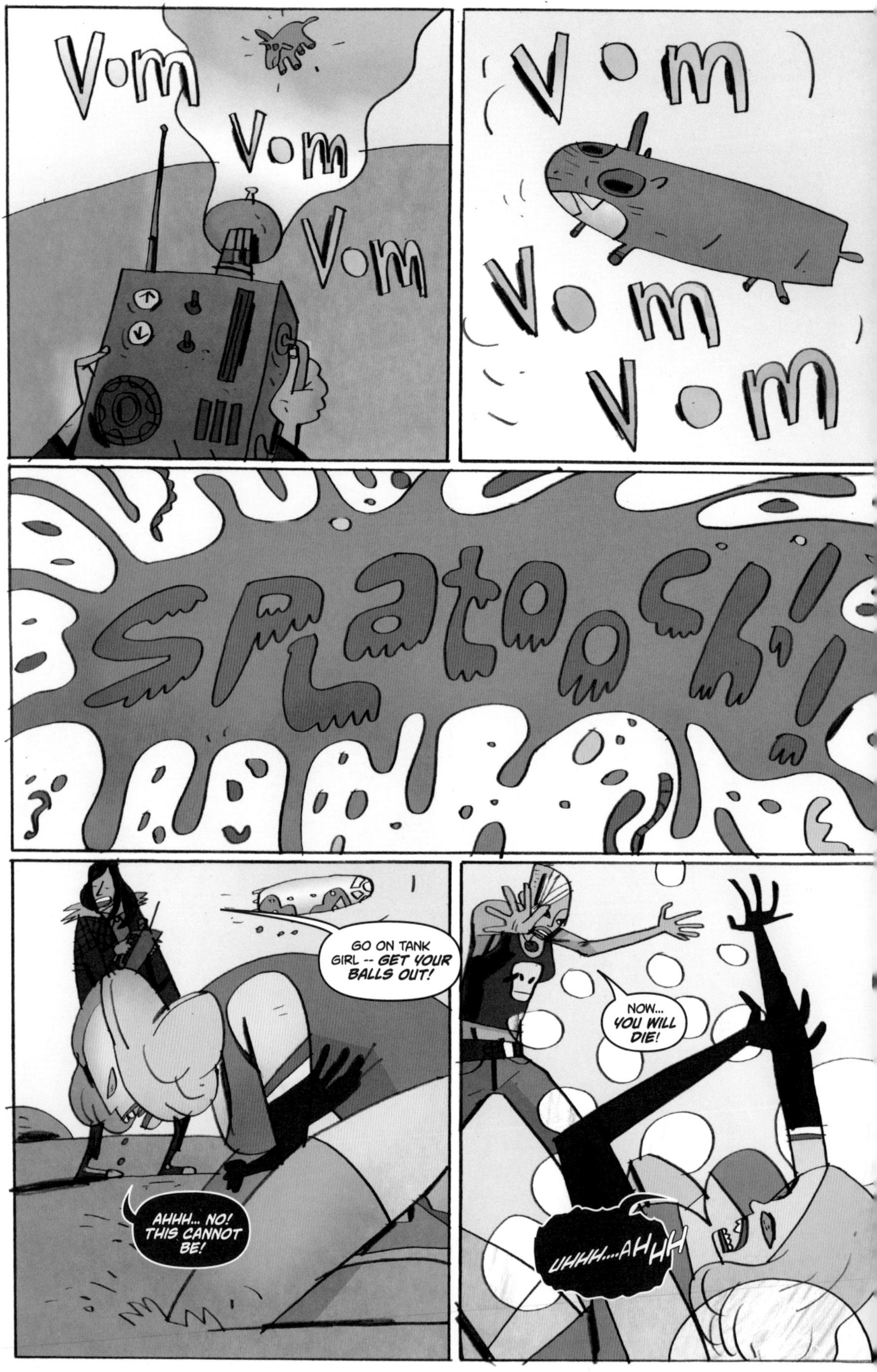

Vom
Vom
Vom
Vom
Vom
Vom
Splatoosh!
GO ON TANK GIRL -- GET YOUR BALLS OUT!
AHHH... NO! THIS CANNOT BE!
NOW... YOU WILL DIE!
UHHH....AHHH

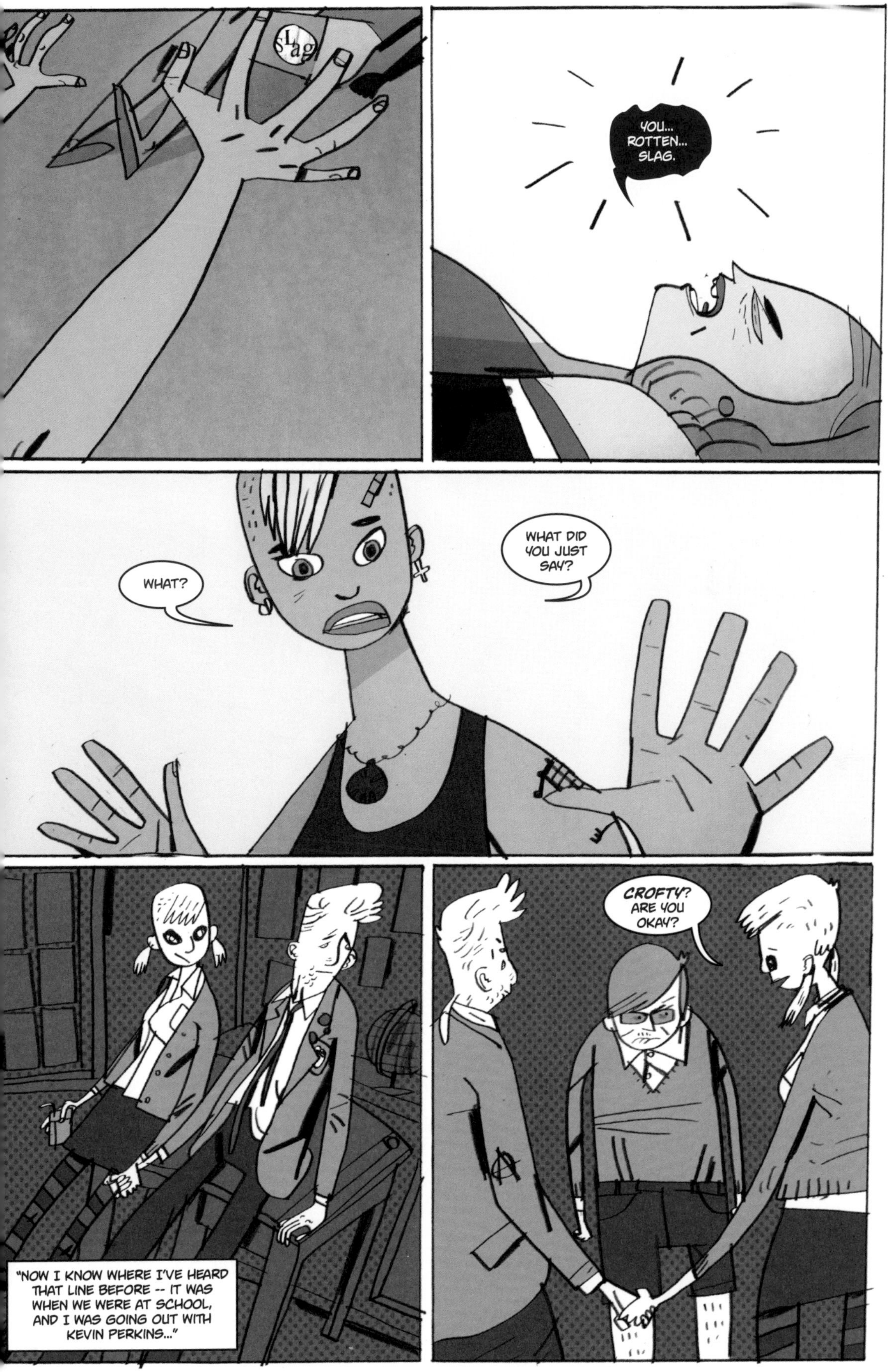
SLAG
YOU... ROTTEN... SLAG.
WHAT?
WHAT DID YOU JUST SAY?
"NOW I KNOW WHERE I'VE HEARD THAT LINE BEFORE -- IT WAS WHEN WE WERE AT SCHOOL, AND I WAS GOING OUT WITH KEVIN PERKINS..."
CROFTY? ARE YOU OKAY?

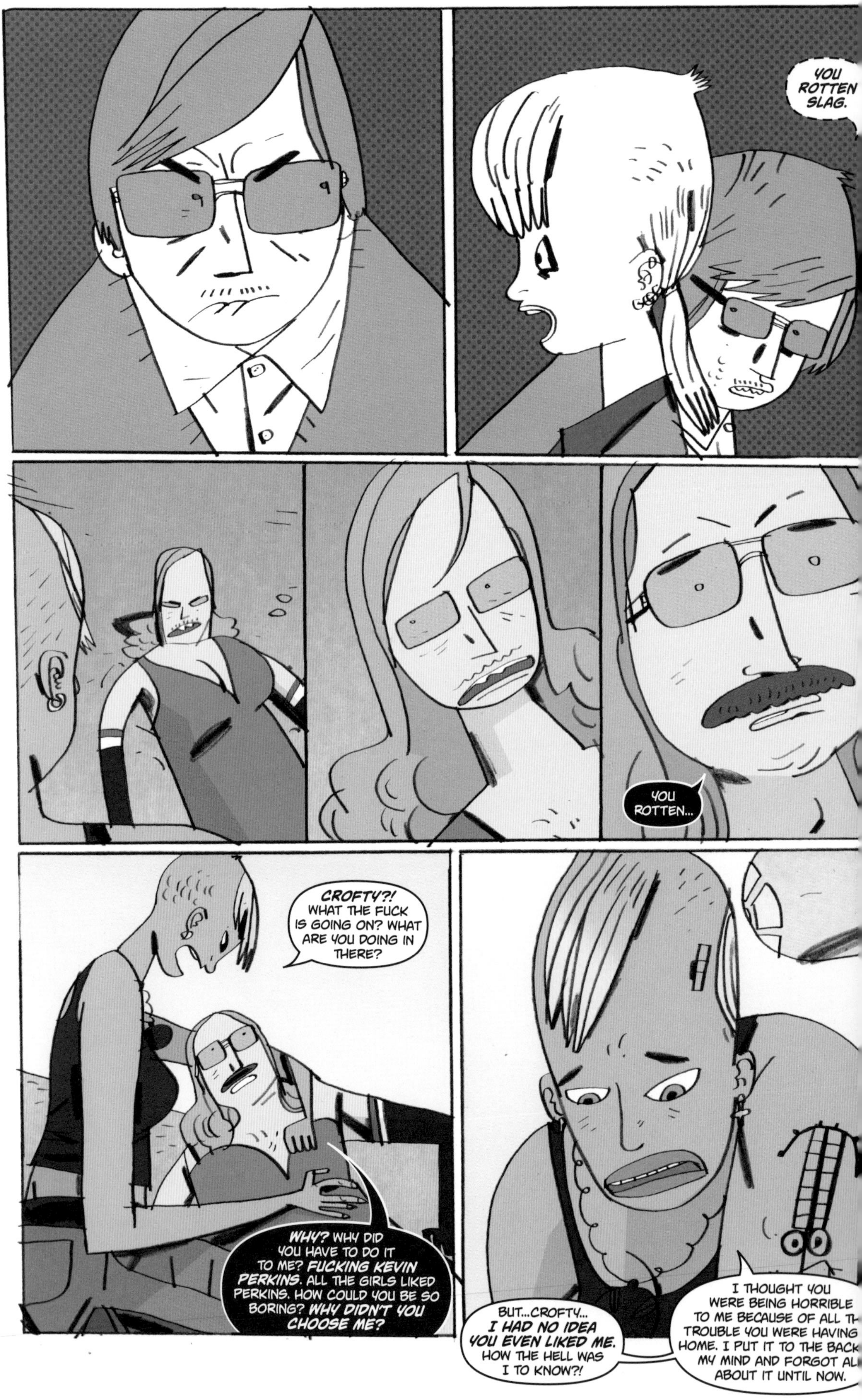
YOU ROTTEN SLAG.
YOU ROTTEN...
CROFTY?! WHAT THE FUCK IS GOING ON? WHAT ARE YOU DOING IN THERE?
WHY? WHY DID YOU HAVE TO DO IT TO ME? FUCKING KEVIN PERKINS. ALL THE GIRLS LIKED PERKINS. HOW COULD YOU BE SO BORING? WHY DIDN'T YOU CHOOSE ME?
BUT...CROFTY... I HAD NO IDEA YOU EVEN LIKED ME. HOW THE HELL WAS I TO KNOW?!
I THOUGHT YOU WERE BEING HORRIBLE TO ME BECAUSE OF ALL TH TROUBLE YOU WERE HAVING HOME. I PUT IT TO THE BACK MY MIND AND FORGOT AL ABOUT IT UNTIL NOW.

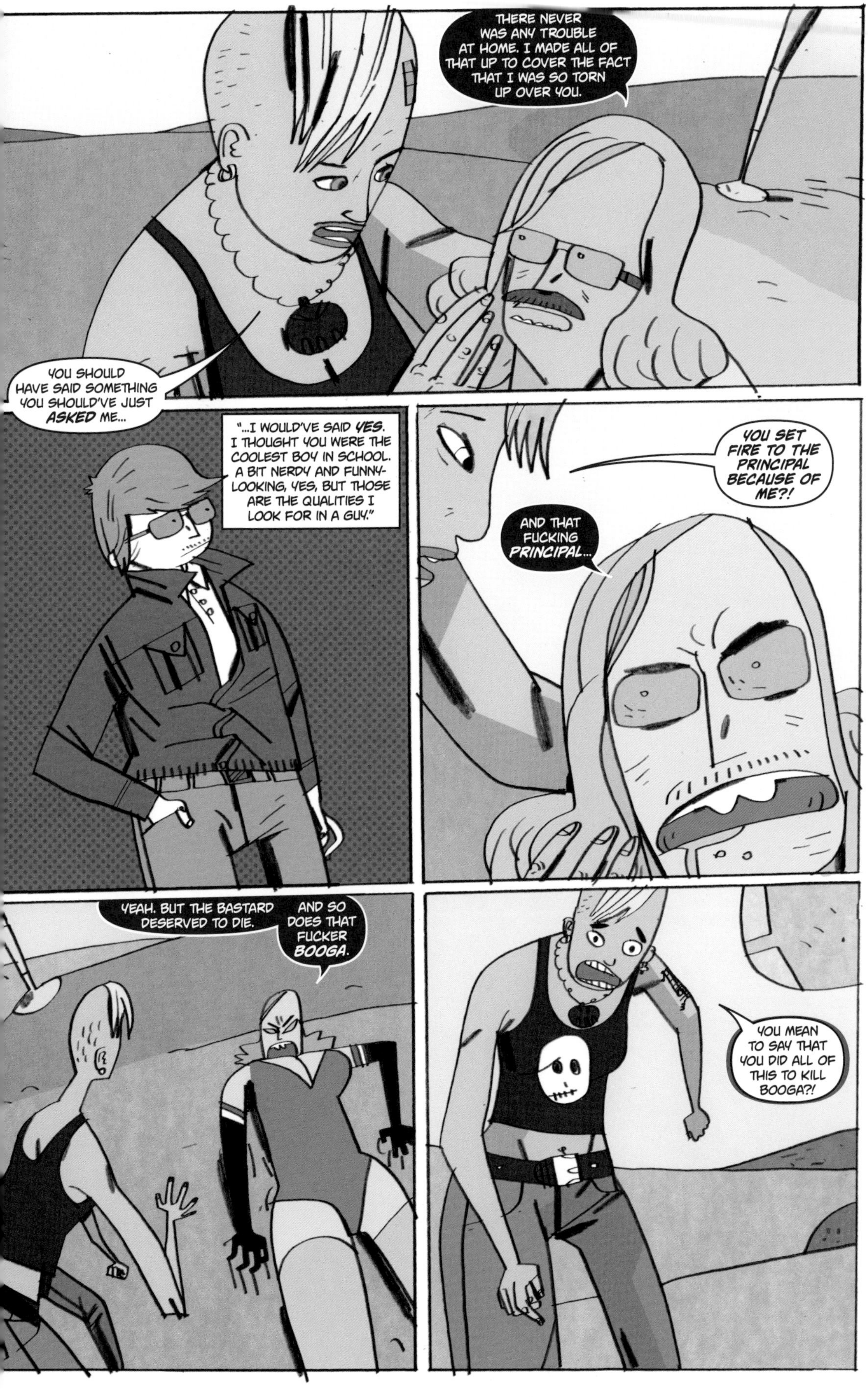

THERE NEVER WAS ANY TROUBLE AT HOME. I MADE ALL OF THAT UP TO COVER THE FACT THAT I WAS SO TORN UP OVER YOU.
YOU SHOULD HAVE SAID SOMETHING YOU SHOULD'VE JUST *ASKED* ME...
"...I WOULD'VE SAID *YES*. I THOUGHT YOU WERE THE COOLEST BOY IN SCHOOL. A BIT NERDY AND FUNNY-LOOKING, YES, BUT THOSE ARE THE QUALITIES I LOOK FOR IN A GUY."
YOU SET FIRE TO THE PRINCIPAL BECAUSE OF ME?!
AND THAT FUCKING *PRINCIPAL*...
YEAH. BUT THE BASTARD DESERVED TO DIE.
AND SO DOES THAT FUCKER *BOOGA*.
YOU MEAN TO SAY THAT YOU DID ALL OF THIS TO KILL BOOGA?!

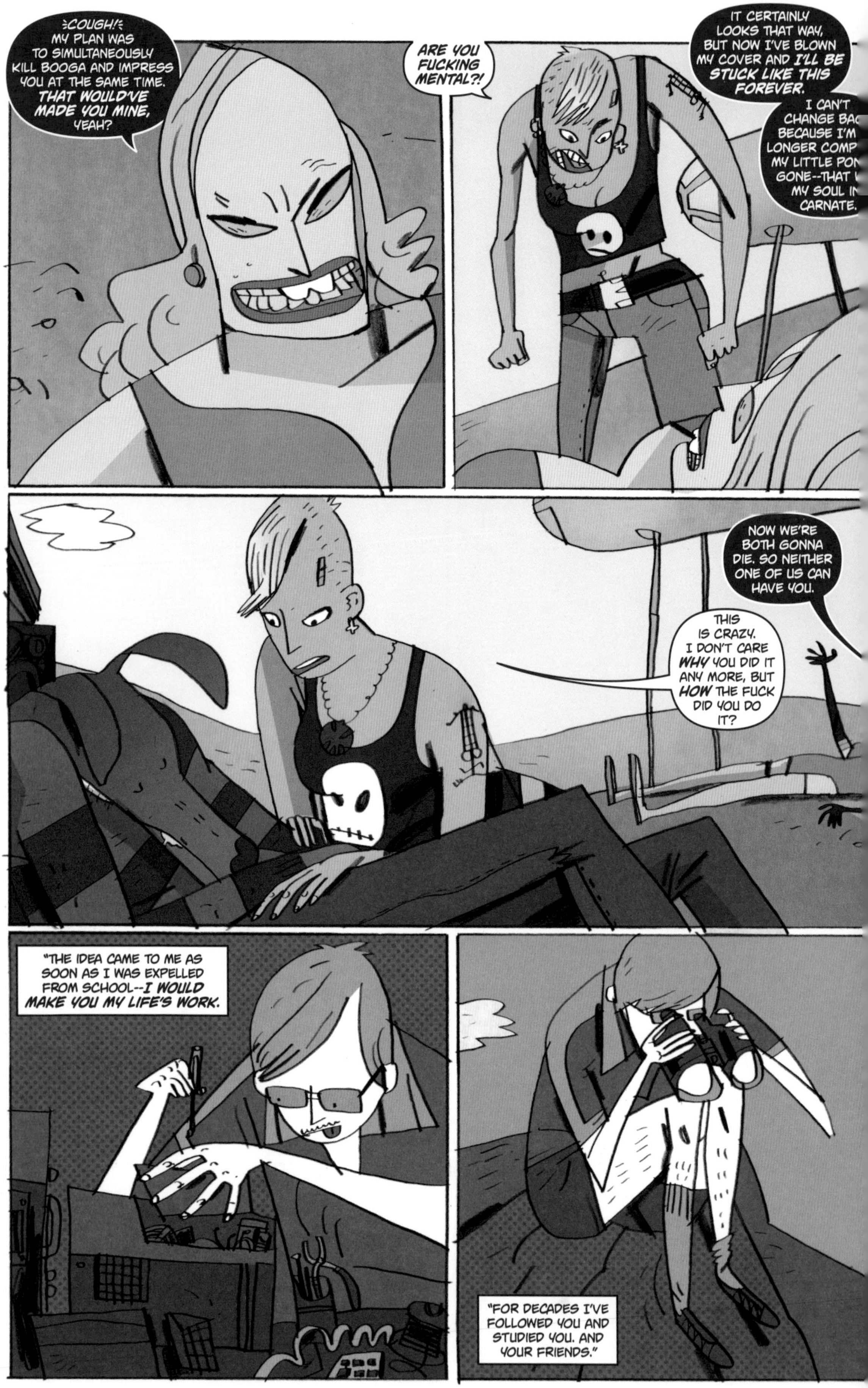

COUGH! MY PLAN WAS TO SIMULTANEOUSLY KILL BOOGA AND IMPRESS YOU AT THE SAME TIME. THAT WOULD'VE MADE YOU MINE, YEAH?
ARE YOU FUCKING MENTAL?!
IT CERTAINLY LOOKS THAT WAY, BUT NOW I'VE BLOWN MY COVER AND I'LL BE STUCK LIKE THIS FOREVER.
I CAN'T CHANGE BAC BECAUSE I'M LONGER COMP MY LITTLE PON GONE--THAT MY SOUL IN CARNATE.
NOW WE'RE BOTH GONNA DIE. SO NEITHER ONE OF US CAN HAVE YOU.
THIS IS CRAZY. I DON'T CARE WHY YOU DID IT ANY MORE, BUT HOW THE FUCK DID YOU DO IT?
"THE IDEA CAME TO ME AS SOON AS I WAS EXPELLED FROM SCHOOL--I WOULD MAKE YOU MY LIFE'S WORK.
"FOR DECADES I'VE FOLLOWED YOU AND STUDIED YOU. AND YOUR FRIENDS."

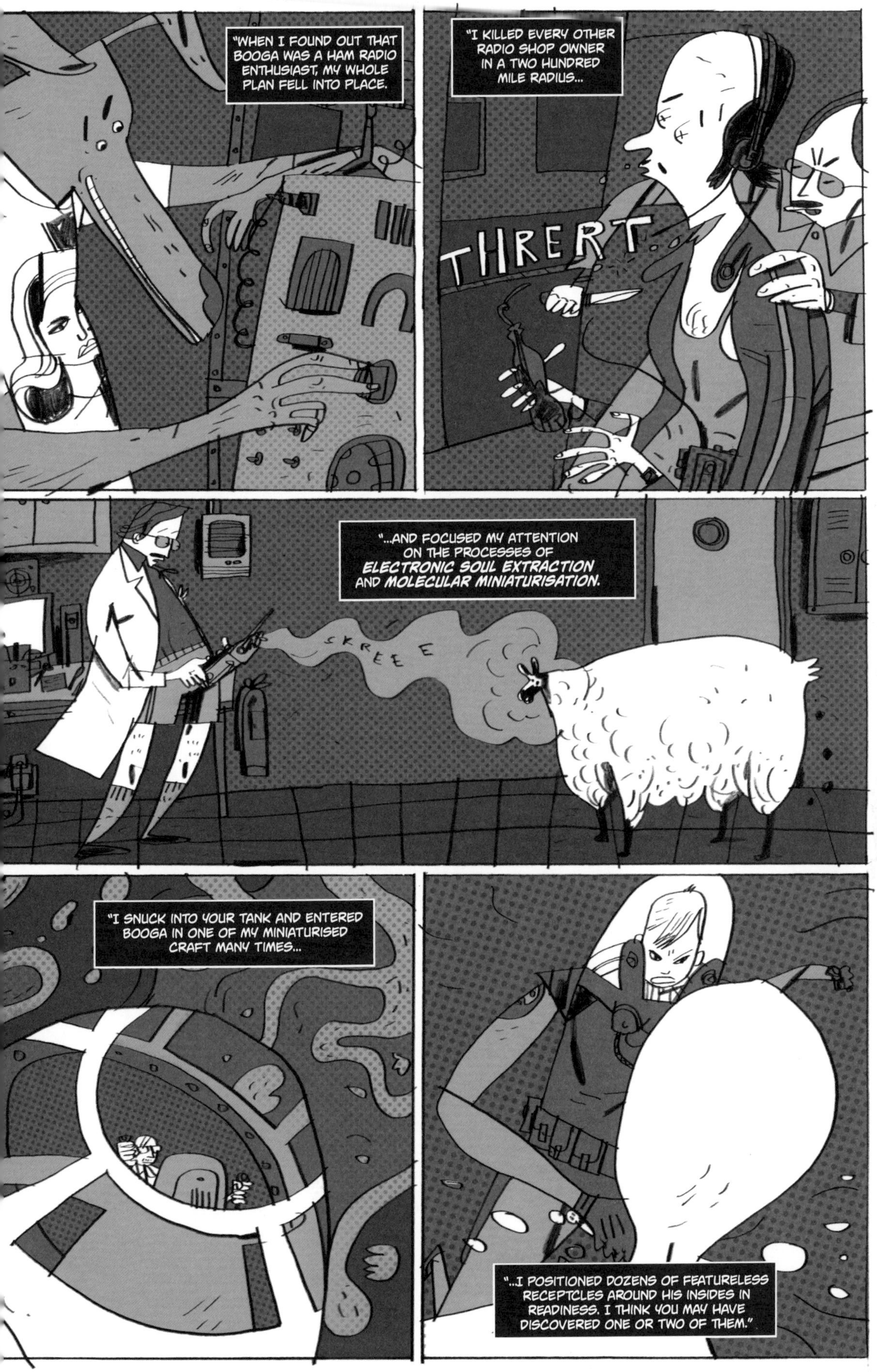
"WHEN I FOUND OUT THAT BOOGA WAS A HAM RADIO ENTHUSIAST, MY WHOLE PLAN FELL INTO PLACE.
"I KILLED EVERY OTHER RADIO SHOP OWNER IN A TWO HUNDRED MILE RADIUS...
THRERT
"...AND FOCUSED MY ATTENTION ON THE PROCESSES OF *ELECTRONIC SOUL EXTRACTION* AND *MOLECULAR MINIATURISATION.*
SKREEE
"I SNUCK INTO YOUR TANK AND ENTERED BOOGA IN ONE OF MY MINIATURISED CRAFT MANY TIMES...
"...I POSITIONED DOZENS OF FEATURELESS RECEPTCLES AROUND HIS INSIDES IN READINESS. I THINK YOU MAY HAVE DISCOVERED ONE OR TWO OF THEM."

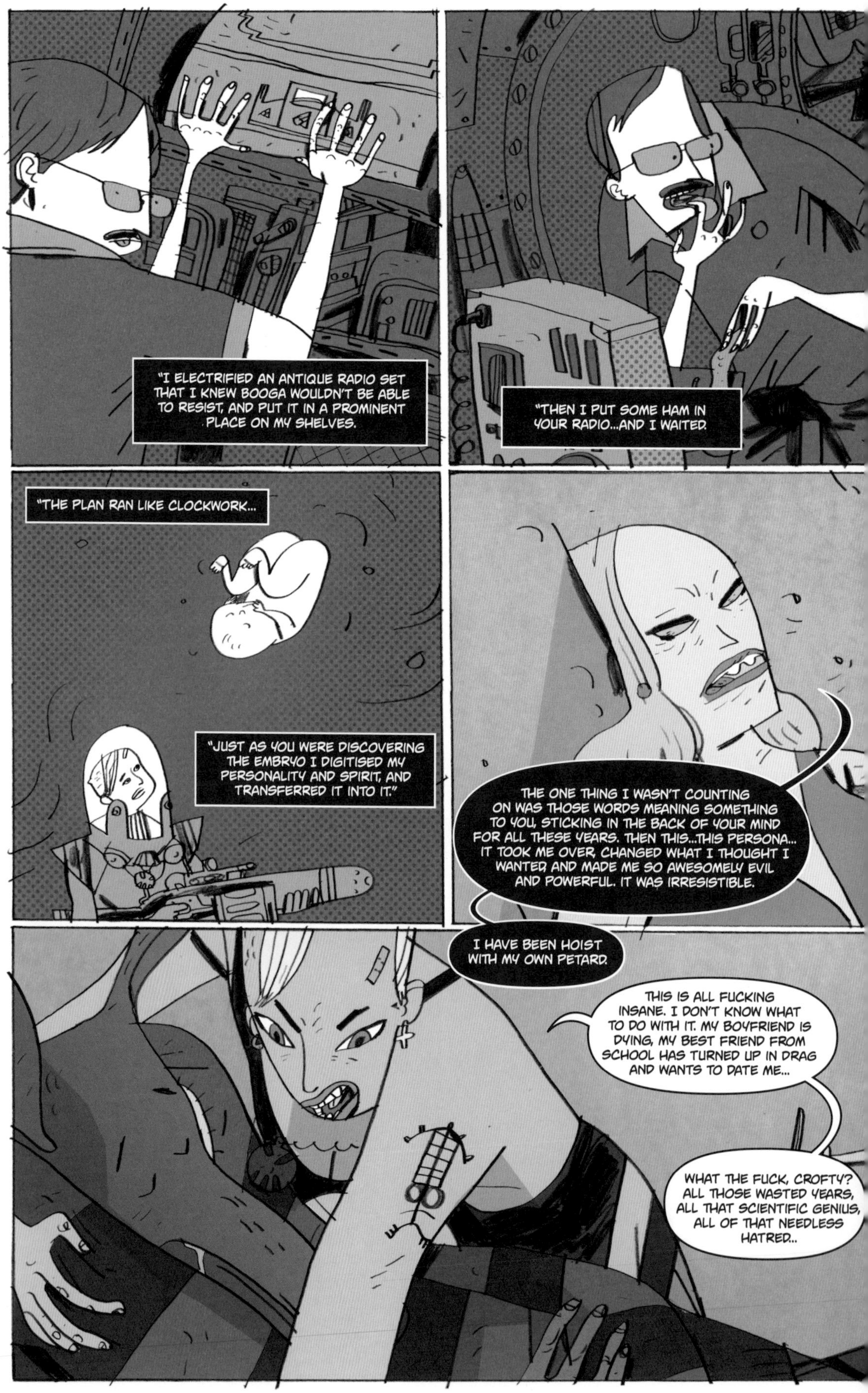
"I ELECTRIFIED AN ANTIQUE RADIO SET THAT I KNEW BOOGA WOULDN'T BE ABLE TO RESIST, AND PUT IT IN A PROMINENT PLACE ON MY SHELVES.
"THEN I PUT SOME HAM IN YOUR RADIO...AND I WAITED.
"THE PLAN RAN LIKE CLOCKWORK...
"JUST AS YOU WERE DISCOVERING THE EMBRYO I DIGITISED MY PERSONALITY AND SPIRIT, AND TRANSFERRED IT INTO IT."
THE ONE THING I WASN'T COUNTING ON WAS THOSE WORDS MEANING SOMETHING TO YOU, STICKING IN THE BACK OF YOUR MIND FOR ALL THESE YEARS. THEN THIS...THIS PERSONA... IT TOOK ME OVER, CHANGED WHAT I THOUGHT I WANTED AND MADE ME SO AWESOMELY EVIL AND POWERFUL. IT WAS IRRESISTIBLE.
I HAVE BEEN HOIST WITH MY OWN PETARD.
THIS IS ALL FUCKING INSANE. I DON'T KNOW WHAT TO DO WITH IT. MY BOYFRIEND IS DYING, MY BEST FRIEND FROM SCHOOL HAS TURNED UP IN DRAG AND WANTS TO DATE ME...
WHAT THE FUCK, CROFTY? ALL THOSE WASTED YEARS, ALL THAT SCIENTIFIC GENIUS, ALL OF THAT NEEDLESS HATRED...

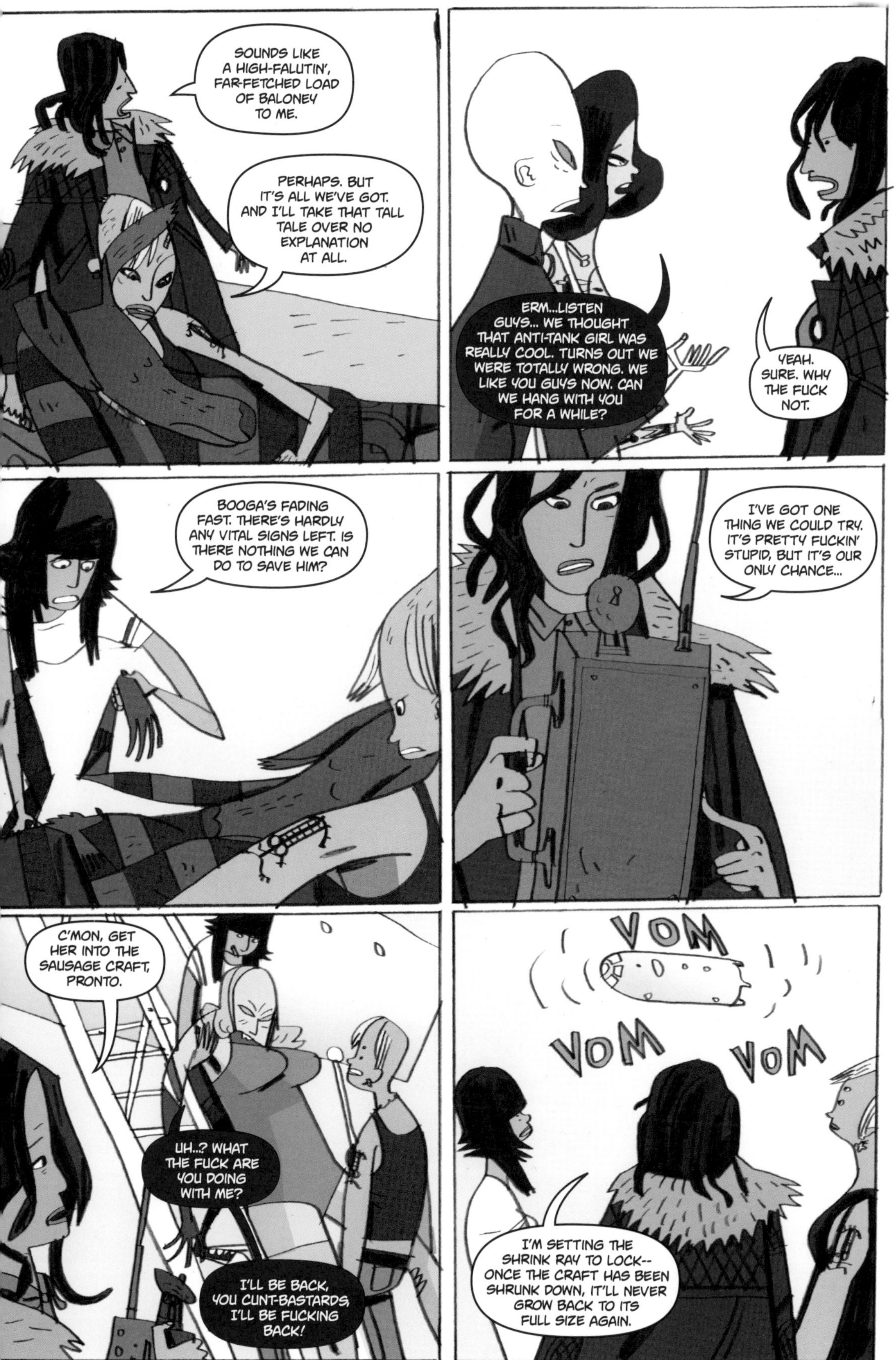
SOUNDS LIKE A HIGH-FALUTIN', FAR-FETCHED LOAD OF BALONEY TO ME.
PERHAPS. BUT IT'S ALL WE'VE GOT. AND I'LL TAKE THAT TALL TALE OVER NO EXPLANATION AT ALL.
ERM...LISTEN GUYS... WE THOUGHT THAT ANTI-TANK GIRL WAS REALLY COOL. TURNS OUT WE WERE TOTALLY WRONG. WE LIKE YOU GUYS NOW. CAN WE HANG WITH YOU FOR A WHILE?
YEAH. SURE. WHY THE FUCK NOT.
BOOGA'S FADING FAST. THERE'S HARDLY ANY VITAL SIGNS LEFT. IS THERE NOTHING WE CAN DO TO SAVE HIM?
I'VE GOT ONE THING WE COULD TRY. IT'S PRETTY FUCKIN' STUPID, BUT IT'S OUR ONLY CHANCE...
C'MON, GET HER INTO THE SAUSAGE CRAFT, PRONTO.
UH..? WHAT THE FUCK ARE YOU DOING WITH ME?
I'LL BE BACK, YOU CUNT-BASTARDS, I'LL BE FUCKING BACK!
VOM
VOM
VOM
I'M SETTING THE SHRINK RAY TO LOCK-- ONCE THE CRAFT HAS BEEN SHRUNK DOWN, IT'LL NEVER GROW BACK TO ITS FULL SIZE AGAIN.

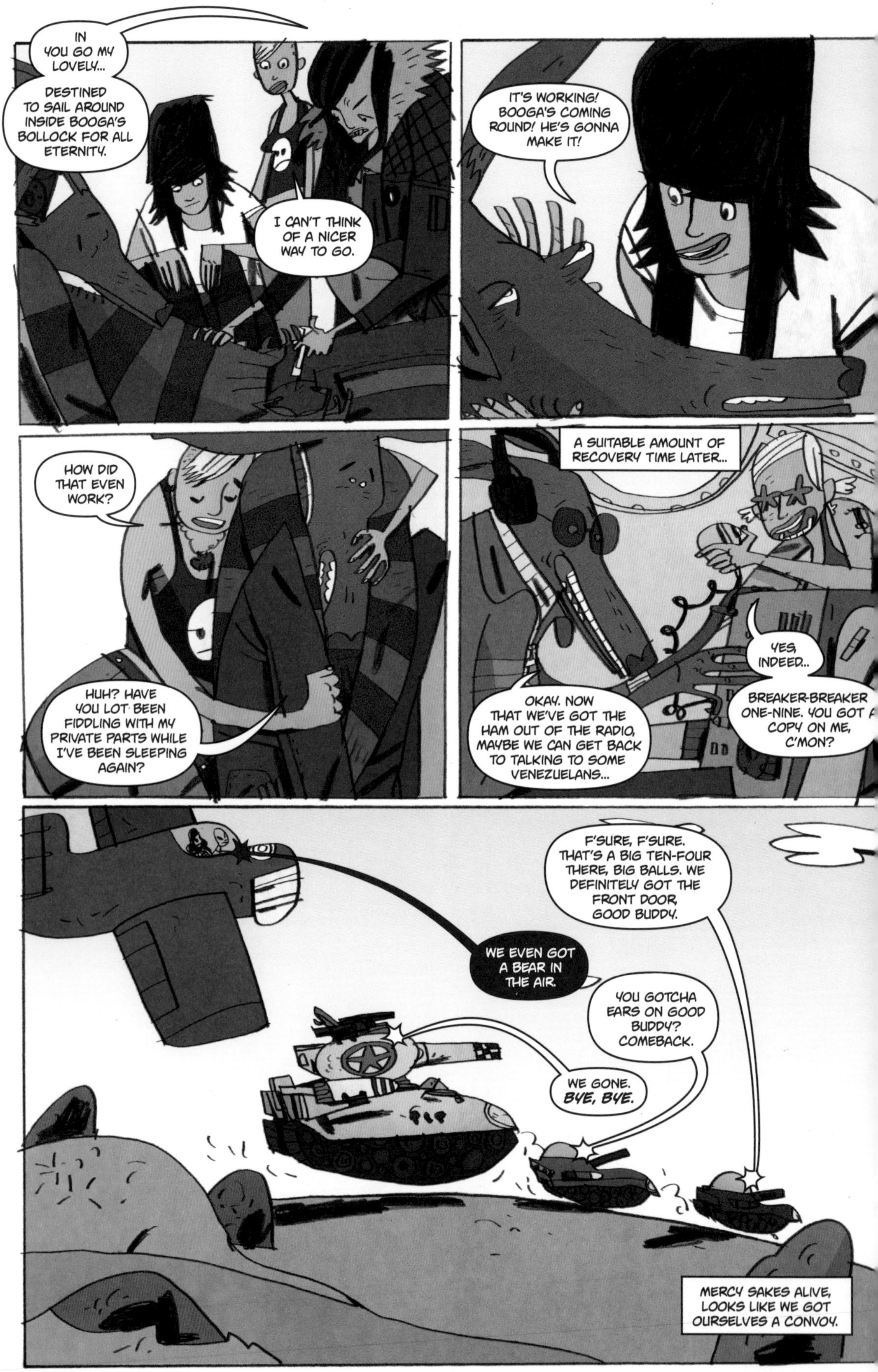
IN YOU GO MY LOVELY...
DESTINED TO SAIL AROUND INSIDE BOOGA'S BOLLOCK FOR ALL ETERNITY.
I CAN'T THINK OF A NICER WAY TO GO.
IT'S WORKING! BOOGA'S COMING ROUND! HE'S GONNA MAKE IT!
HOW DID THAT EVEN WORK?
HUH? HAVE YOU LOT BEEN FIDDLING WITH MY PRIVATE PARTS WHILE I'VE BEEN SLEEPING AGAIN?
A SUITABLE AMOUNT OF RECOVERY TIME LATER...
OKAY. NOW THAT WE'VE GOT THE HAM OUT OF THE RADIO, MAYBE WE CAN GET BACK TO TALKING TO SOME VENEZUELANS...
YES, INDEED...
BREAKER-BREAKER ONE-NINE. YOU GOT A COPY ON ME, C'MON?
F'SURE, F'SURE. THAT'S A BIG TEN-FOUR THERE, BIG BALLS. WE DEFINITELY GOT THE FRONT DOOR, GOOD BUDDY.
WE EVEN GOT A BEAR IN THE AIR.
YOU GOTCHA EARS ON GOOD BUDDY? COMEBACK.
WE GONE. BYE, BYE.
MERCY SAKES ALIVE, LOOKS LIKE WE GOT OURSELVES A CONVOY.

THE END.

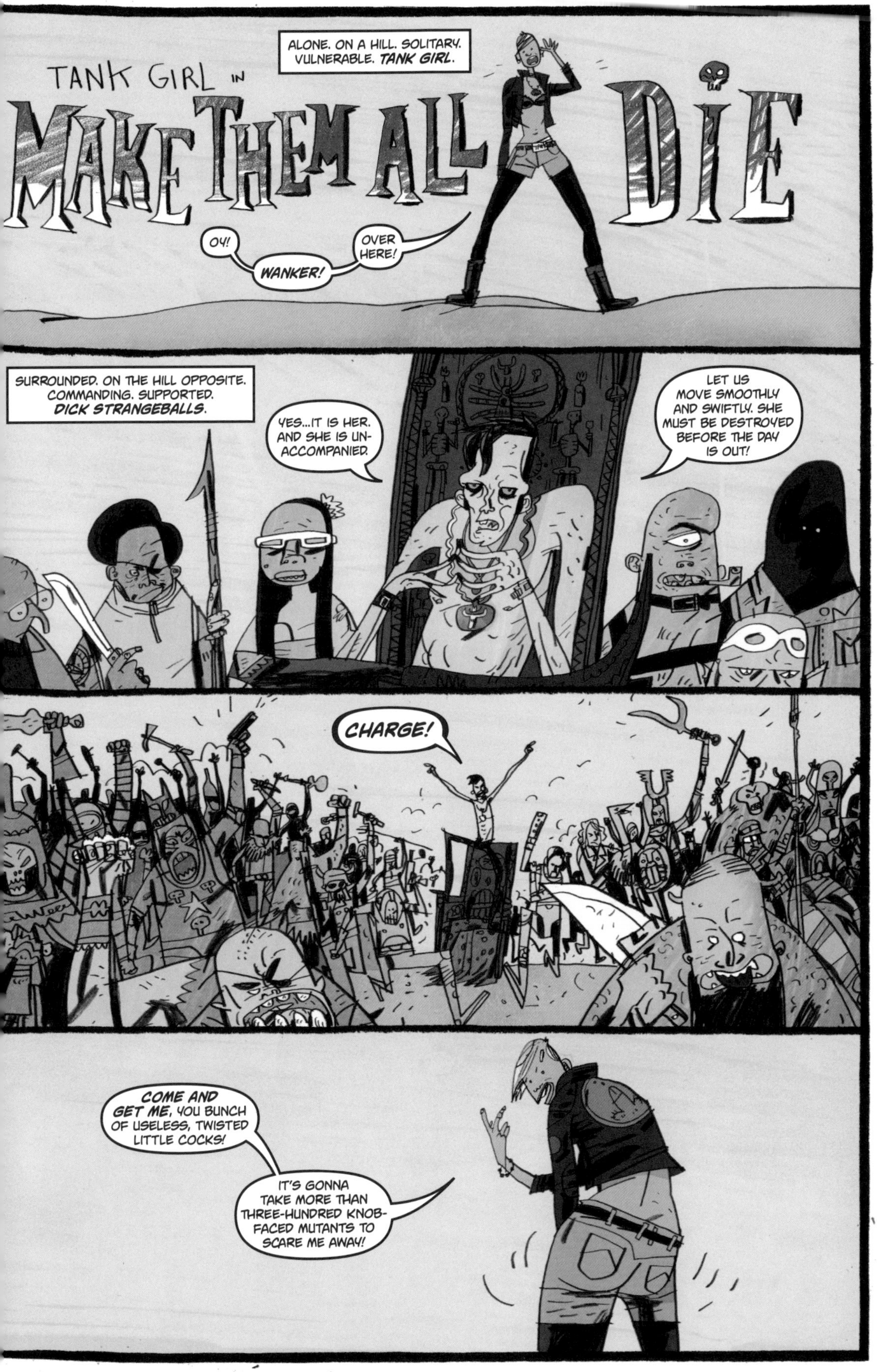
ALONE. ON A HILL. SOLITARY. VULNERABLE. TANK GIRL.
TANK GIRL IN
MAKE THEM ALL DIE
OY!
WANKER!
OVER HERE!
SURROUNDED. ON THE HILL OPPOSITE. COMMANDING. SUPPORTED. DICK STRANGEBALLS.
YES...IT IS HER. AND SHE IS UN-ACCOMPANIED.
LET US MOVE SMOOTHLY AND SWIFTLY. SHE MUST BE DESTROYED BEFORE THE DAY IS OUT!
CHARGE!
COME AND GET ME, YOU BUNCH OF USELESS, TWISTED LITTLE COCKS!
IT'S GONNA TAKE MORE THAN THREE-HUNDRED KNOB-FACED MUTANTS TO SCARE ME AWAY!

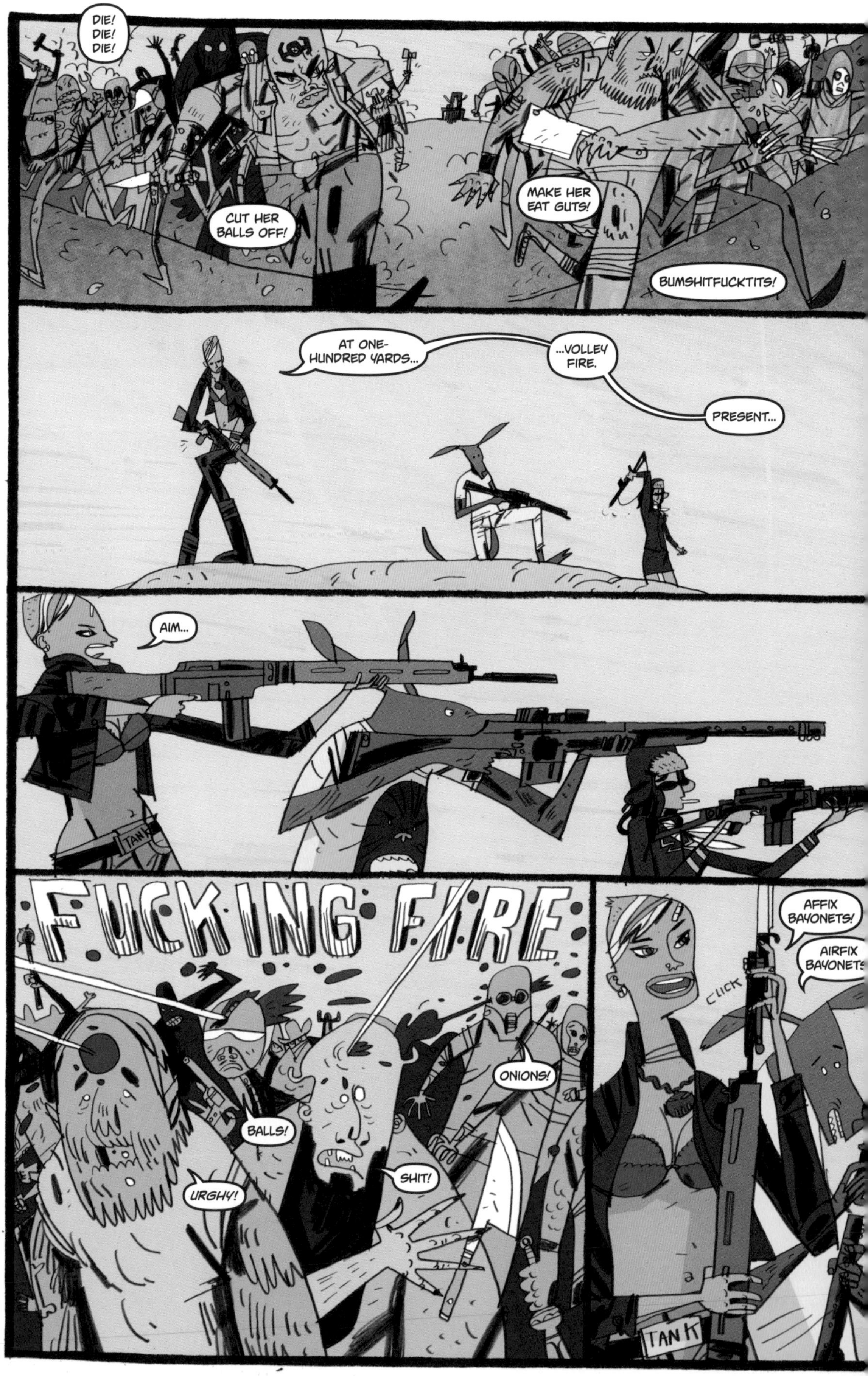
DIE! DIE! DIE!
CUT HER BALLS OFF!
MAKE HER EAT GUTS!
BUMSHITFUCKTITS!
AT ONE-HUNDRED YARDS...
...VOLLEY FIRE.
PRESENT...
AIM...
TANK
FUCKING FIRE
BALLS!
URGHY!
SHIT!
ONIONS!
AFFIX BAYONETS!
AIRFIX BAYONETS
CLICK
TANK

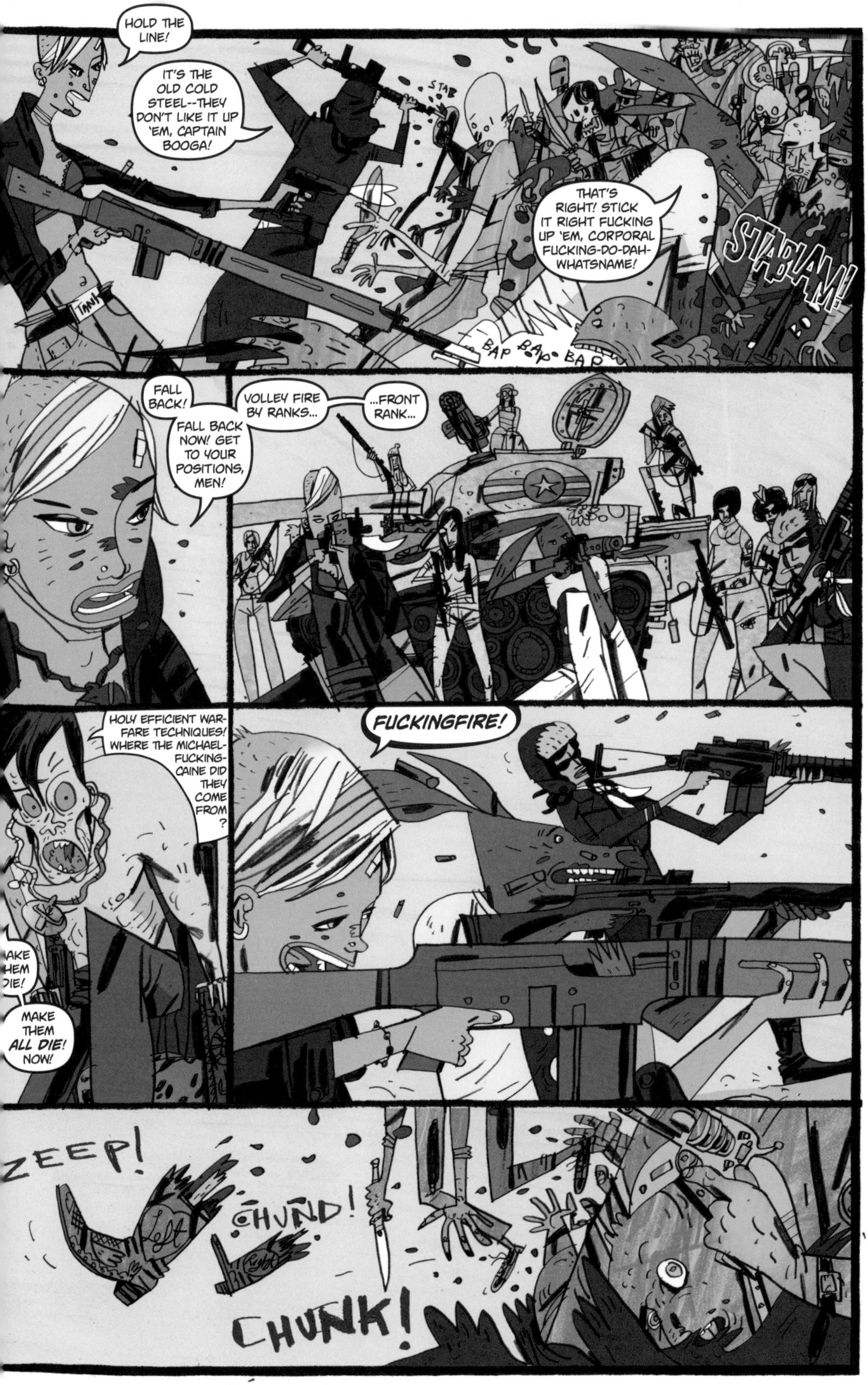

HOLD THE LINE!
IT'S THE OLD COLD STEEL--THEY DON'T LIKE IT UP 'EM, CAPTAIN BOOGA!
STAB
THAT'S RIGHT! STICK IT RIGHT FUCKING UP 'EM, CORPORAL FUCKING-DO-DAH-WHATSNAME!
STABLAM!
BAP BAP BAP
FALL BACK!
FALL BACK NOW! GET TO YOUR POSITIONS, MEN!
VOLLEY FIRE BY RANKS...
...FRONT RANK...
HOLY EFFICIENT WARFARE TECHNIQUES! WHERE THE MICHAEL-FUCKING-CAINE DID THEY COME FROM?
FUCKINGFIRE!
MAKE THEM DIE!
MAKE THEM ALL DIE! NOW!
ZEEP!
CHUND!
CHUNK!

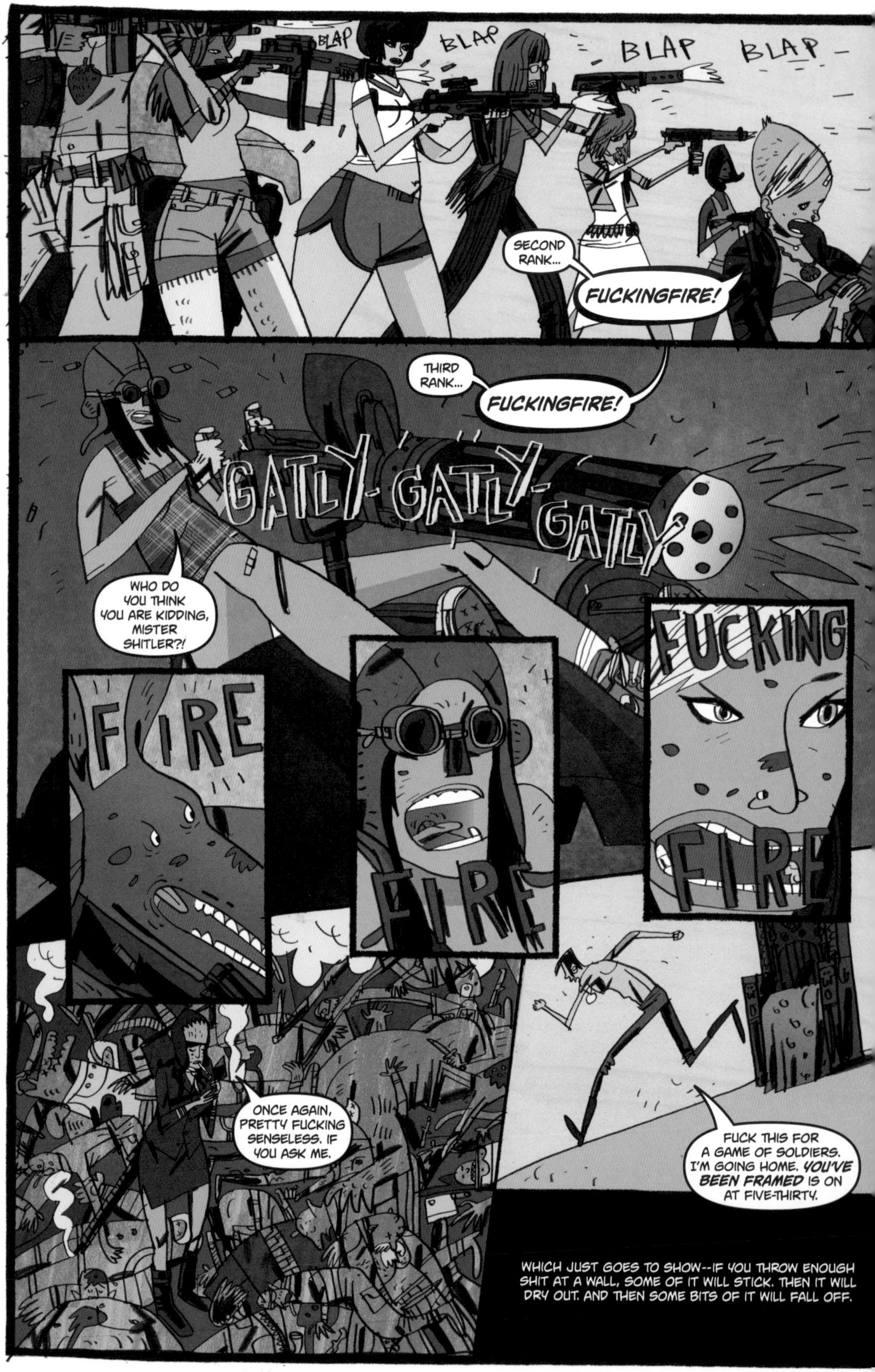
BLAP
BLAP
BLAP
BLAP
SECOND RANK...
FUCKINGFIRE!
THIRD RANK...
FUCKINGFIRE!
GATLY-GATLY-GATLY
WHO DO YOU THINK YOU ARE KIDDING, MISTER SHITLER?!
FIRE
FIRE
FUCKING
FIRE
ONCE AGAIN, PRETTY FUCKING SENSELESS. IF YOU ASK ME.
FUCK THIS FOR A GAME OF SOLDIERS. I'M GOING HOME. *YOU'VE BEEN FRAMED* IS ON AT FIVE-THIRTY.
WHICH JUST GOES TO SHOW--IF YOU THROW ENOUGH SHIT AT A WALL, SOME OF IT WILL STICK. THEN IT WILL DRY OUT. AND THEN SOME BITS OF IT WILL FALL OFF.

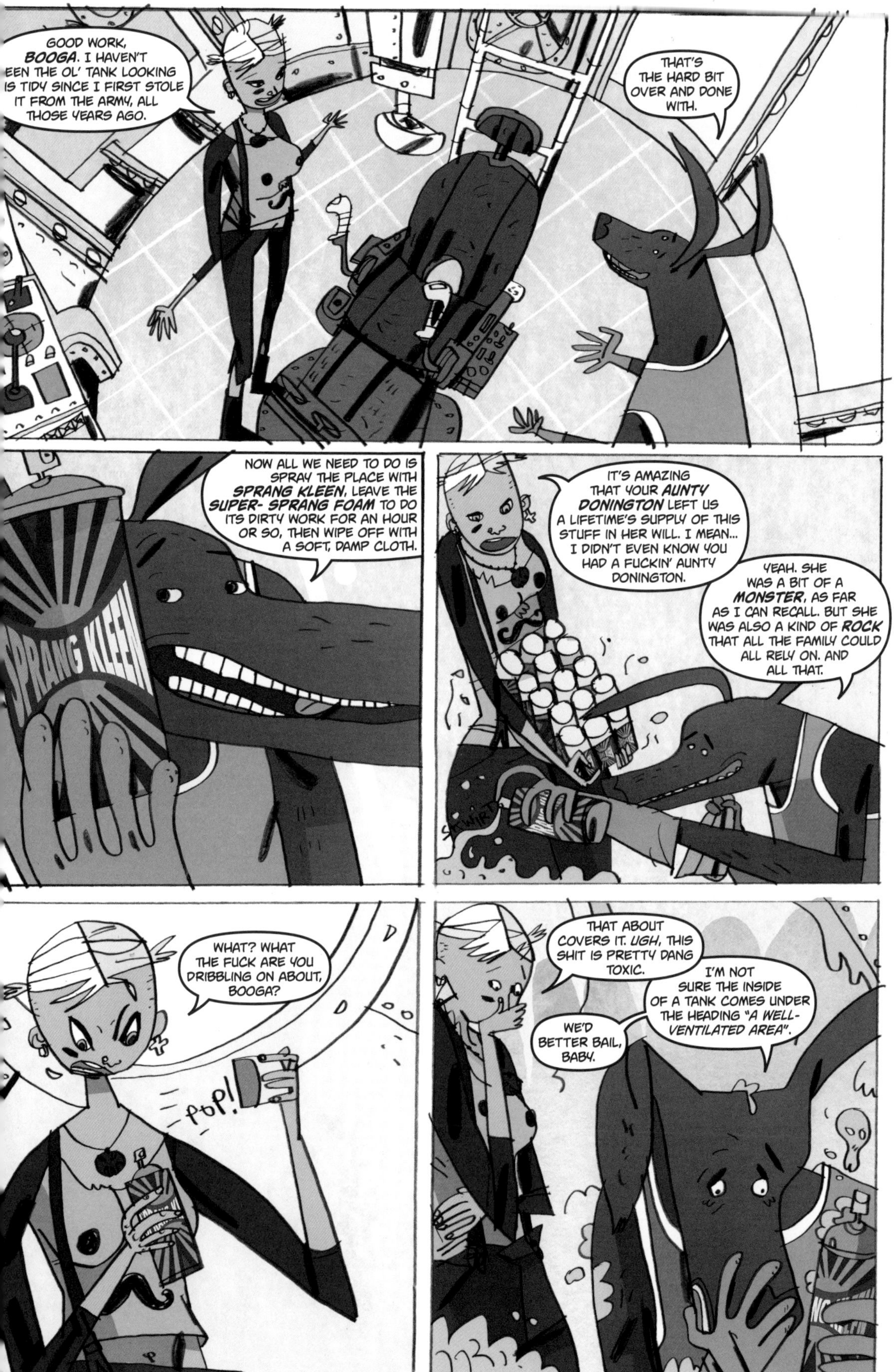
GOOD WORK, BOOGA. I HAVEN'T EEN THE OL' TANK LOOKING IS TIDY SINCE I FIRST STOLE IT FROM THE ARMY, ALL THOSE YEARS AGO.
THAT'S THE HARD BIT OVER AND DONE WITH.
NOW ALL WE NEED TO DO IS SPRAY THE PLACE WITH SPRANG KLEEN, LEAVE THE SUPER- SPRANG FOAM TO DO ITS DIRTY WORK FOR AN HOUR OR SO, THEN WIPE OFF WITH A SOFT, DAMP CLOTH.
SPRANG KLEEN
IT'S AMAZING THAT YOUR AUNTY DONINGTON LEFT US A LIFETIME'S SUPPLY OF THIS STUFF IN HER WILL. I MEAN... I DIDN'T EVEN KNOW YOU HAD A FUCKIN' AUNTY DONINGTON.
YEAH. SHE WAS A BIT OF A MONSTER, AS FAR AS I CAN RECALL. BUT SHE WAS ALSO A KIND OF ROCK THAT ALL THE FAMILY COULD ALL RELY ON. AND ALL THAT.
SKWIRT
WHAT? WHAT THE FUCK ARE YOU DRIBBLING ON ABOUT, BOOGA?
POP!
THAT ABOUT COVERS IT. UGH, THIS SHIT IS PRETTY DANG TOXIC.
I'M NOT SURE THE INSIDE OF A TANK COMES UNDER THE HEADING "A WELL-VENTILATED AREA".
WE'D BETTER BAIL, BABY.

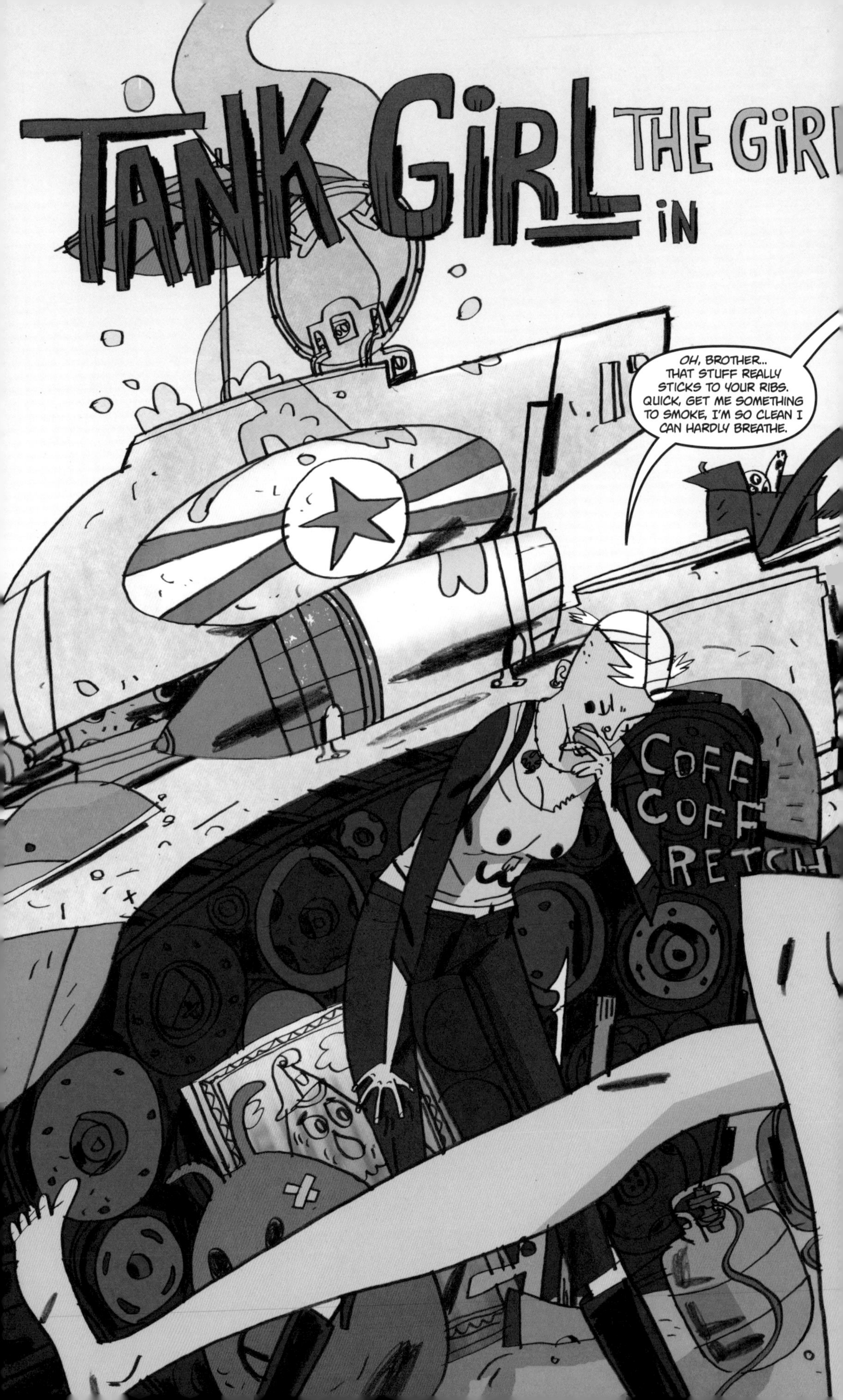
TANK GIRL in
THE GIRL
OH, BROTHER... THAT STUFF REALLY STICKS TO YOUR RIBS. QUICK, GET ME SOMETHING TO SMOKE, I'M SO CLEAN I CAN HARDLY BREATHE.
COFF COFF RETCH

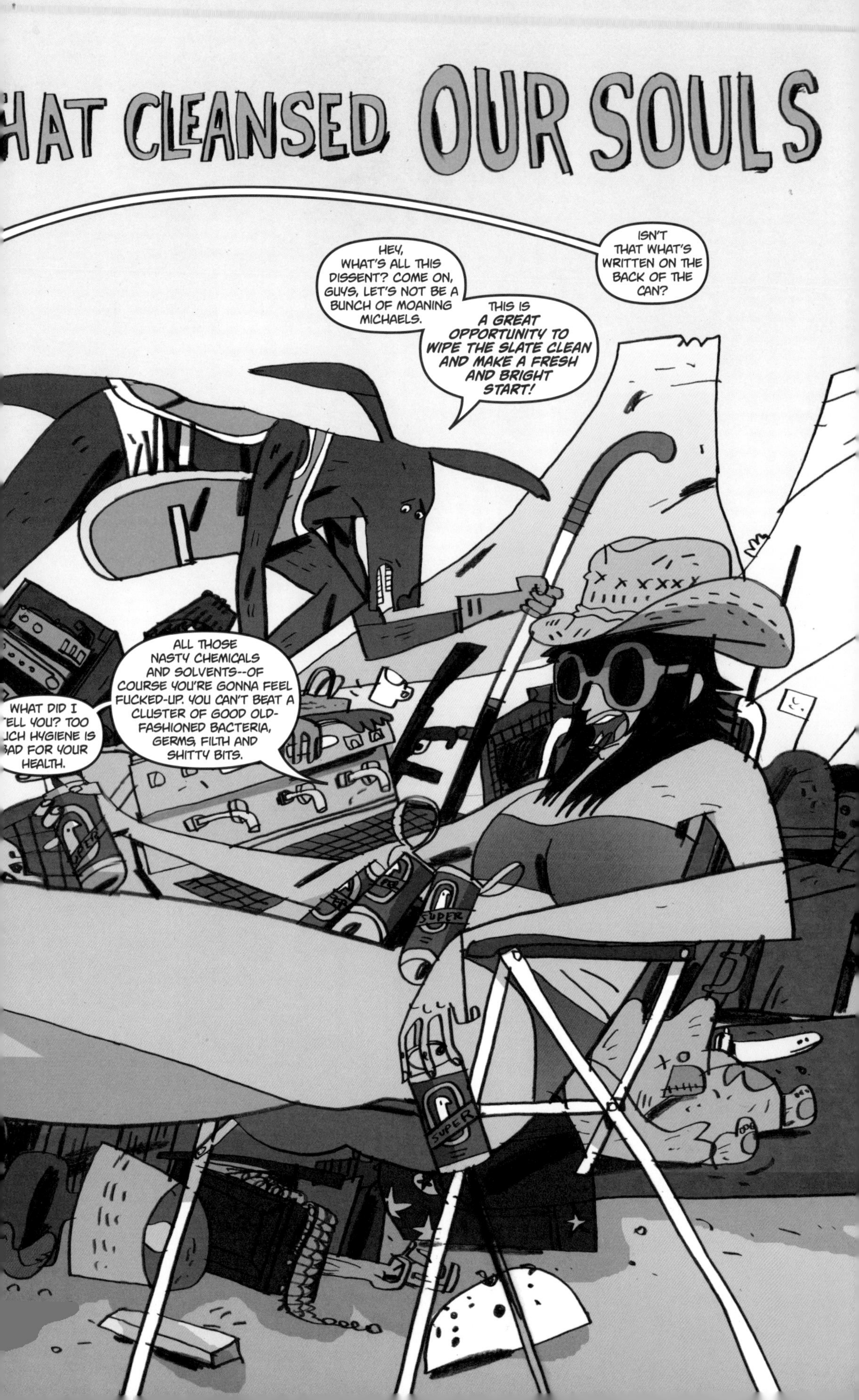

HAT CLEANSED OUR SOULS
HEY, WHAT'S ALL THIS DISSENT? COME ON, GUYS, LET'S NOT BE A BUNCH OF MOANING MICHAELS.
THIS IS A GREAT OPPORTUNITY TO WIPE THE SLATE CLEAN AND MAKE A FRESH AND BRIGHT START!
ISN'T THAT WHAT'S WRITTEN ON THE BACK OF THE CAN?
WHAT DID I TELL YOU? TOO UCH HYGIENE IS BAD FOR YOUR HEALTH.
ALL THOSE NASTY CHEMICALS AND SOLVENTS--OF COURSE YOU'RE GONNA FEEL FUCKED-UP. YOU CAN'T BEAT A CLUSTER OF GOOD OLD-FASHIONED BACTERIA, GERMS, FILTH AND SHITTY BITS.
SUPER
SUPER
SUPER

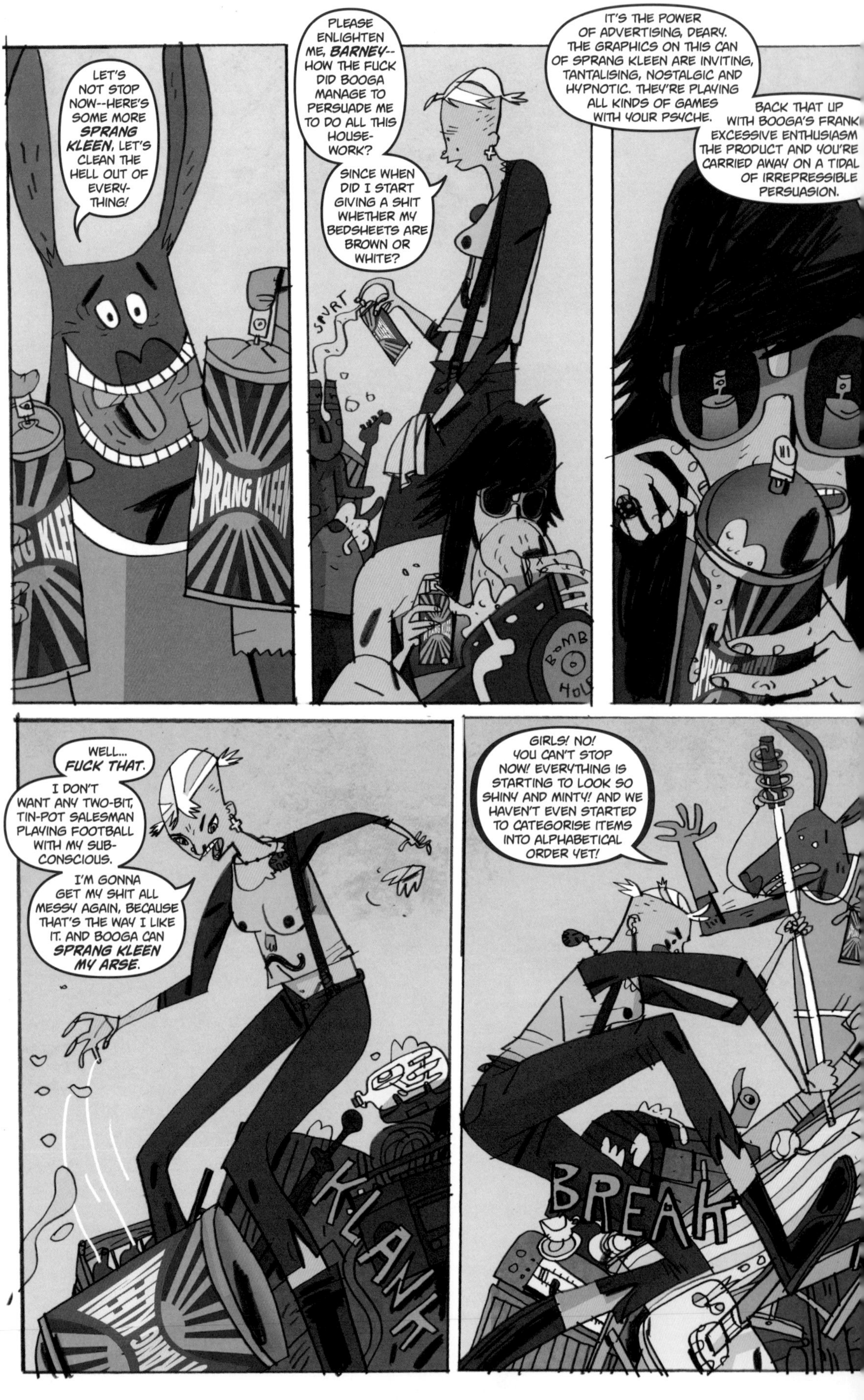

LET'S NOT STOP NOW--HERE'S SOME MORE SPRANG KLEEN, LET'S CLEAN THE HELL OUT OF EVERY-THING!
SPRANG KLEEN
PLEASE ENLIGHTEN ME, BARNEY-- HOW THE FUCK DID BOOGA MANAGE TO PERSUADE ME TO DO ALL THIS HOUSE-WORK?
SINCE WHEN DID I START GIVING A SHIT WHETHER MY BEDSHEETS ARE BROWN OR WHITE?
SPURT
IT'S THE POWER OF ADVERTISING, DEARY. THE GRAPHICS ON THIS CAN OF SPRANG KLEEN ARE INVITING, TANTALISING, NOSTALGIC AND HYPNOTIC. THEY'RE PLAYING ALL KINDS OF GAMES WITH YOUR PSYCHE.
BACK THAT UP WITH BOOGA'S FRANK EXCESSIVE ENTHUSIASM THE PRODUCT AND YOU'RE CARRIED AWAY ON A TIDAL OF IRREPRESSIBLE PERSUASION.
WELL... FUCK THAT.
I DON'T WANT ANY TWO-BIT, TIN-POT SALESMAN PLAYING FOOTBALL WITH MY SUB-CONSCIOUS.
I'M GONNA GET MY SHIT ALL MESSY AGAIN, BECAUSE THAT'S THE WAY I LIKE IT. AND BOOGA CAN SPRANG KLEEN MY ARSE.
KLANK
GIRLS! NO! YOU CAN'T STOP NOW! EVERYTHING IS STARTING TO LOOK SO SHINY AND MINTY! AND WE HAVEN'T EVEN STARTED TO CATEGORISE ITEMS INTO ALPHABETICAL ORDER YET!
BREAK

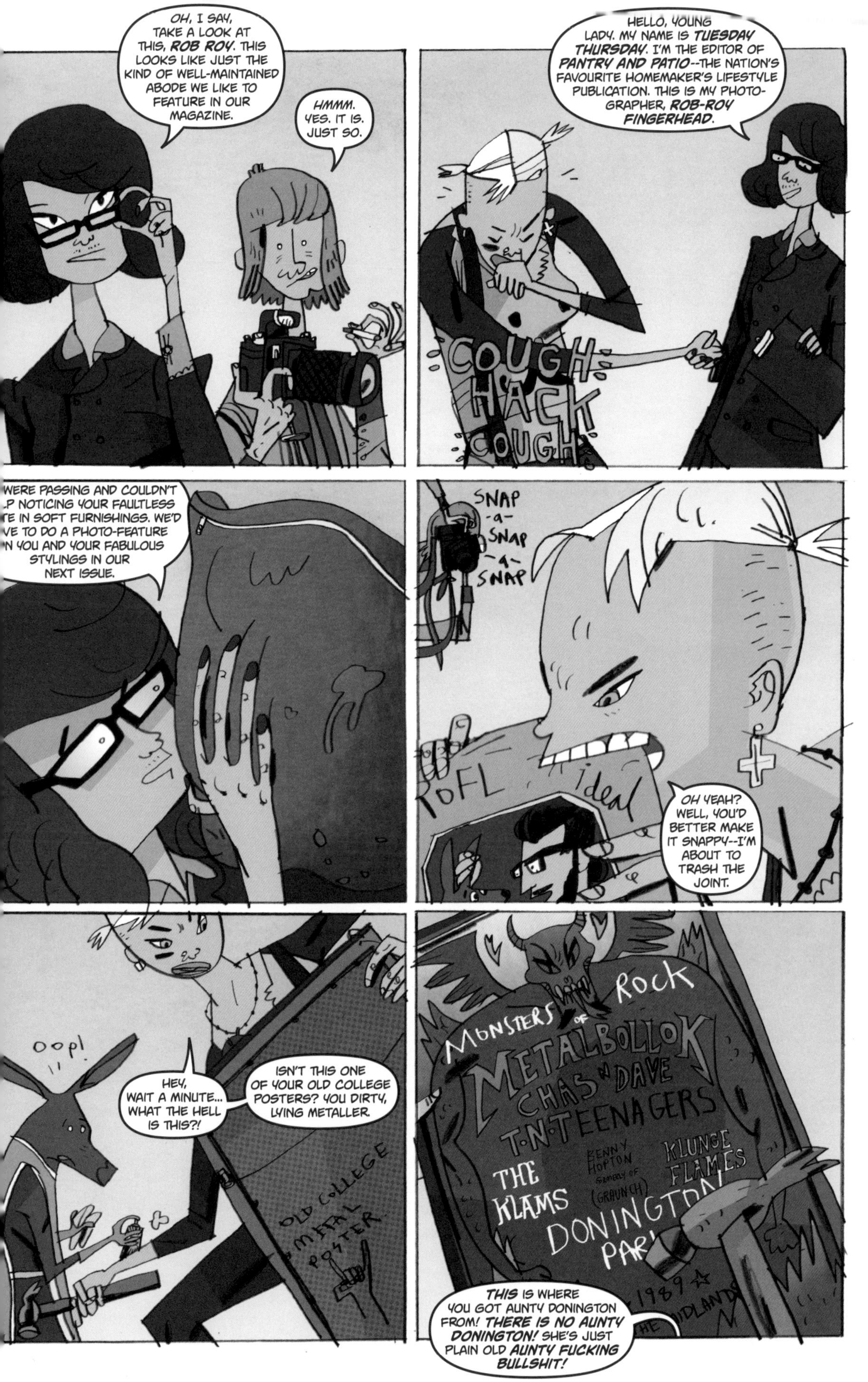
OH, I SAY, TAKE A LOOK AT THIS, ROB ROY. THIS LOOKS LIKE JUST THE KIND OF WELL-MAINTAINED ABODE WE LIKE TO FEATURE IN OUR MAGAZINE.
HMMM. YES. IT IS. JUST SO.
HELLO, YOUNG LADY. MY NAME IS TUESDAY THURSDAY. I'M THE EDITOR OF PANTRY AND PATIO--THE NATION'S FAVOURITE HOMEMAKER'S LIFESTYLE PUBLICATION. THIS IS MY PHOTOGRAPHER, ROB-ROY FINGERHEAD.
COUGH HACK COUGH!
WERE PASSING AND COULDN'T .P NOTICING YOUR FAULTLESS TE IN SOFT FURNISHINGS. WE'D VE TO DO A PHOTO-FEATURE N YOU AND YOUR FABULOUS STYLINGS IN OUR NEXT ISSUE.
SNAP -a- SNAP -a- SNAP
OH YEAH? WELL, YOU'D BETTER MAKE IT SNAPPY--I'M ABOUT TO TRASH THE JOINT.
OOP!
HEY, WAIT A MINUTE... WHAT THE HELL IS THIS?!
ISN'T THIS ONE OF YOUR OLD COLLEGE POSTERS? YOU DIRTY, LYING METALLER.
OLD COLLEGE METAL POSTER
MONSTERS OF ROCK
METALBOLLOK
CHAS N DAVE
T.N.TEENAGERS
BENNY HOPTON
THE KLAMS
KLUNGE FLAMES
DONINGTON PARK
1989
THIS IS WHERE YOU GOT AUNTY DONINGTON FROM! THERE IS NO AUNTY DONINGTON! SHE'S JUST PLAIN OLD AUNTY FUCKING BULLSHIT!

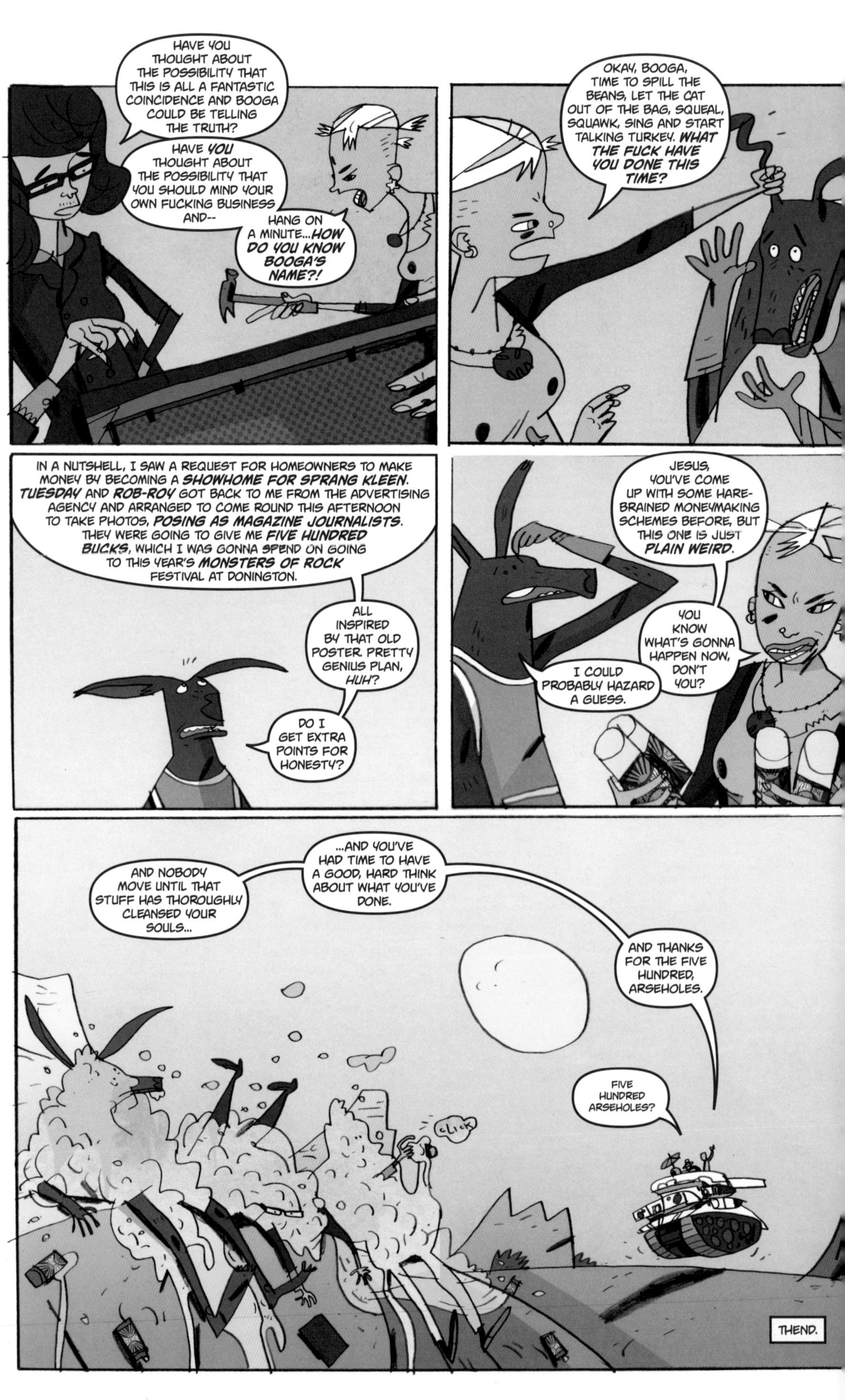
HAVE YOU THOUGHT ABOUT THE POSSIBILITY THAT THIS IS ALL A FANTASTIC COINCIDENCE AND BOOGA COULD BE TELLING THE TRUTH?
HAVE YOU THOUGHT ABOUT THE POSSIBILITY THAT YOU SHOULD MIND YOUR OWN FUCKING BUSINESS AND--
HANG ON A MINUTE...HOW DO YOU KNOW BOOGA'S NAME?!
OKAY, BOOGA, TIME TO SPILL THE BEANS, LET THE CAT OUT OF THE BAG, SQUEAL, SQUAWK, SING AND START TALKING TURKEY. WHAT THE FUCK HAVE YOU DONE THIS TIME?
IN A NUTSHELL, I SAW A REQUEST FOR HOMEOWNERS TO MAKE MONEY BY BECOMING A SHOWHOME FOR SPRANG KLEEN. TUESDAY AND ROB-ROY GOT BACK TO ME FROM THE ADVERTISING AGENCY AND ARRANGED TO COME ROUND THIS AFTERNOON TO TAKE PHOTOS, POSING AS MAGAZINE JOURNALISTS. THEY WERE GOING TO GIVE ME FIVE HUNDRED BUCKS, WHICH I WAS GONNA SPEND ON GOING TO THIS YEAR'S MONSTERS OF ROCK FESTIVAL AT DONINGTON.
ALL INSPIRED BY THAT OLD POSTER. PRETTY GENIUS PLAN, HUH?
DO I GET EXTRA POINTS FOR HONESTY?
JESUS, YOU'VE COME UP WITH SOME HARE-BRAINED MONEYMAKING SCHEMES BEFORE, BUT THIS ONE IS JUST PLAIN WEIRD.
YOU KNOW WHAT'S GONNA HAPPEN NOW, DON'T YOU?
I COULD PROBABLY HAZARD A GUESS.
AND NOBODY MOVE UNTIL THAT STUFF HAS THOROUGHLY CLEANSED YOUR SOULS...
...AND YOU'VE HAD TIME TO HAVE A GOOD, HARD THINK ABOUT WHAT YOU'VE DONE.
AND THANKS FOR THE FIVE HUNDRED, ARSEHOLES.
FIVE HUNDRED ARSEHOLES?
CLICK
THEND.

The Nutbag Ranger and Bonto say

"WE ARE NOT AFRAID OF YOUR SHIT"

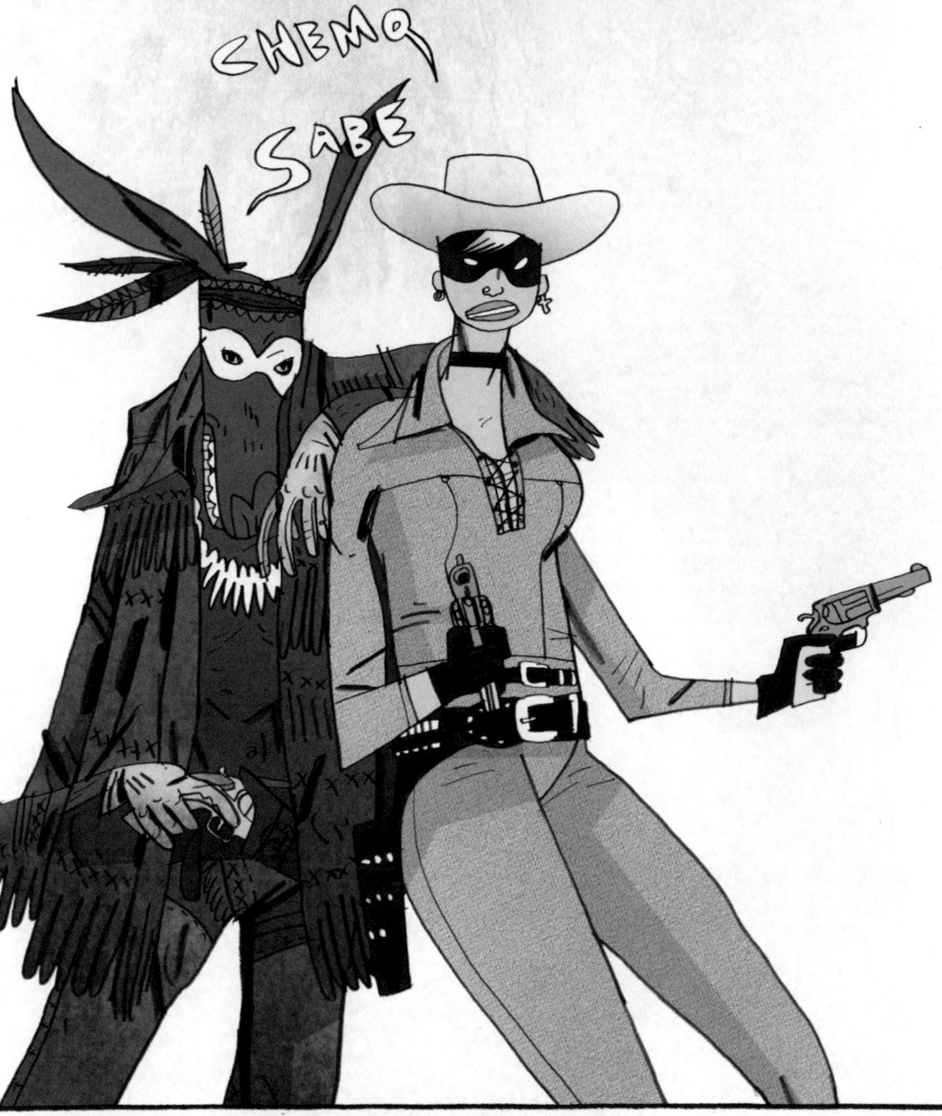
CHEMO
SABE

WHAT HAVE YOU GOT?
LAY IT ALL OUT ON THE TABLE. ALL OF IT. THE TERROR, THE PARANOIA, THE DUPES, THE CONSPIRACY THEORIES, THE NUKES, THE CHEMICALS, THE ENDLESS BAREFACED TWISTED LIES, THE TINY SPYING ROBOTS THAT ARE INVISIBLE TO THE NAKED EYE. ALL OF THIS. EVERYTHING YOU'VE GOT. SHOW US EVERYTHING.

BECAUSE WE ARE NOT AFRAID OF YOUR FUCKING SHIT.

It's 1969
I'm three years old
I'm sat in front of the black and white T.V
with my lemon curd sandwich
And my glass of Nesquick

And Davy Jones is dead

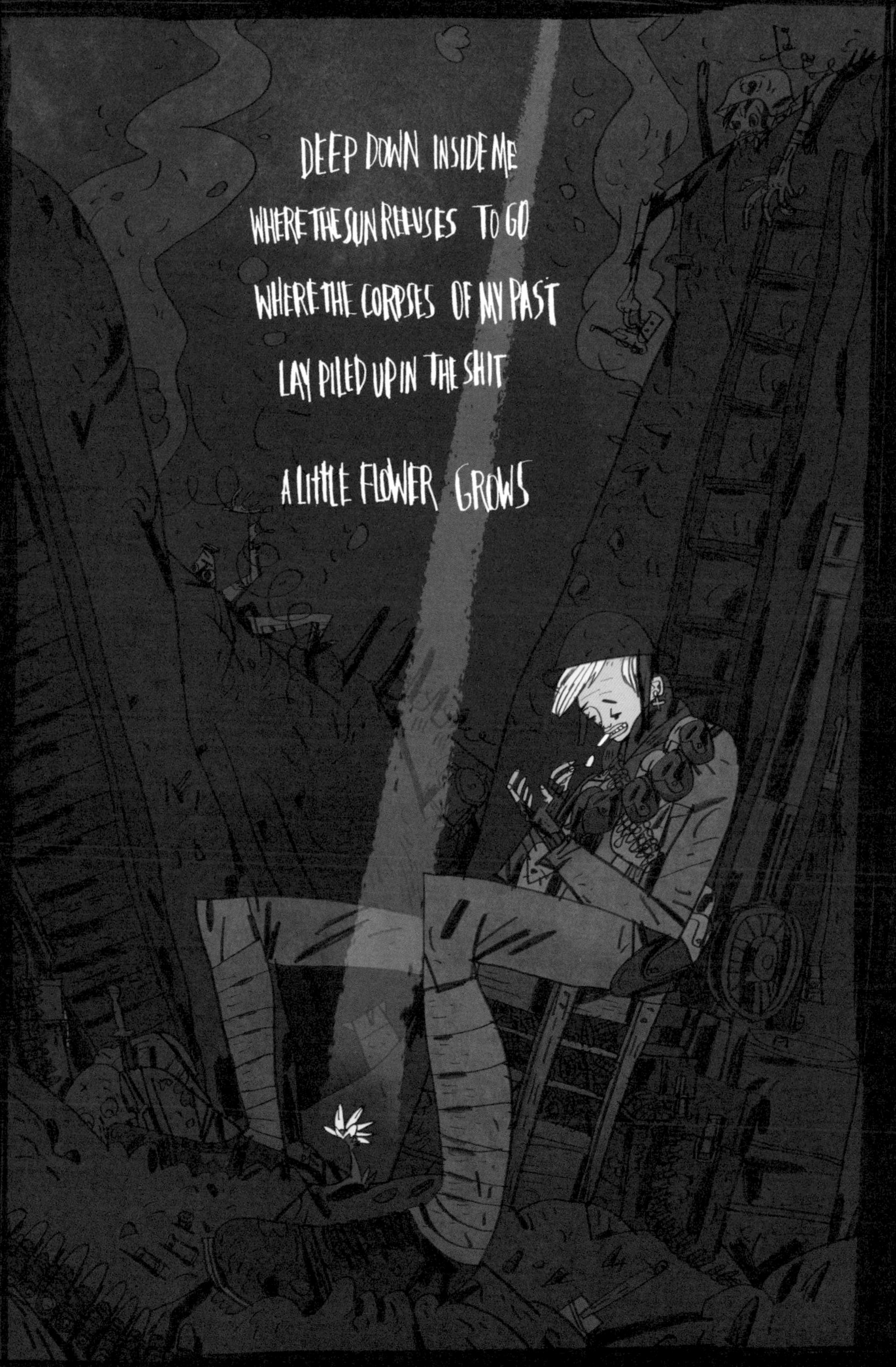
DEEP DOWN INSIDE ME
WHERE THE SUN REFUSES TO GO
WHERE THE CORPSES OF MY PAST
LAY PILED UP IN THE SHIT
A LITTLE FLOWER GROWS

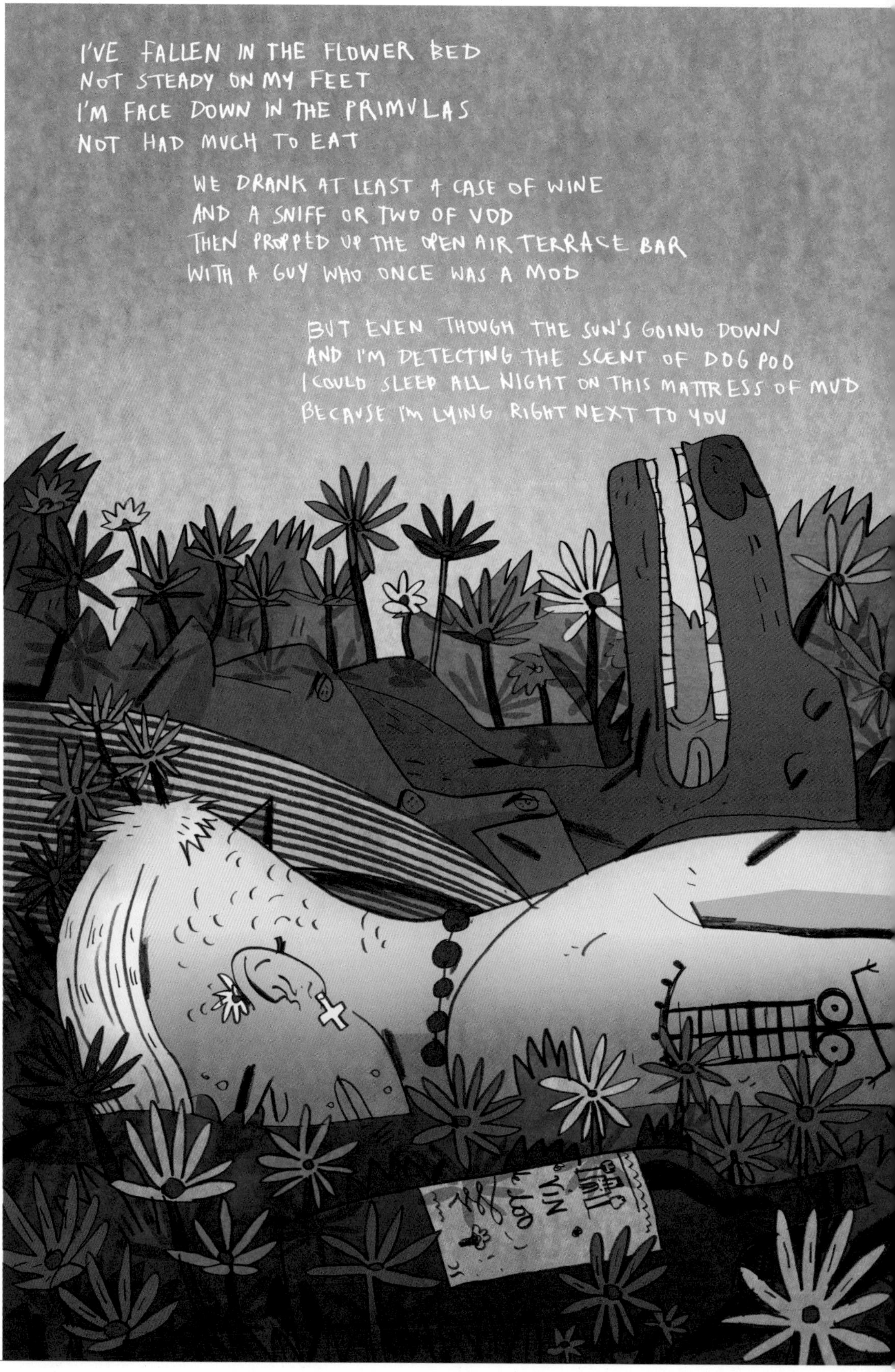
I'VE FALLEN IN THE FLOWER BED
NOT STEADY ON MY FEET
I'M FACE DOWN IN THE PRIMULAS
NOT HAD MUCH TO EAT
WE DRANK AT LEAST A CASE OF WINE
AND A SNIFF OR TWO OF VOD
THEN PROPPED UP THE OPEN AIR TERRACE BAR
WITH A GUY WHO ONCE WAS A MOD
BUT EVEN THOUGH THE SUN'S GOING DOWN
AND I'M DETECTING THE SCENT OF DOG POO
I COULD SLEEP ALL NIGHT ON THIS MATTRESS OF MUD
BECAUSE I'M LYING RIGHT NEXT TO YOU

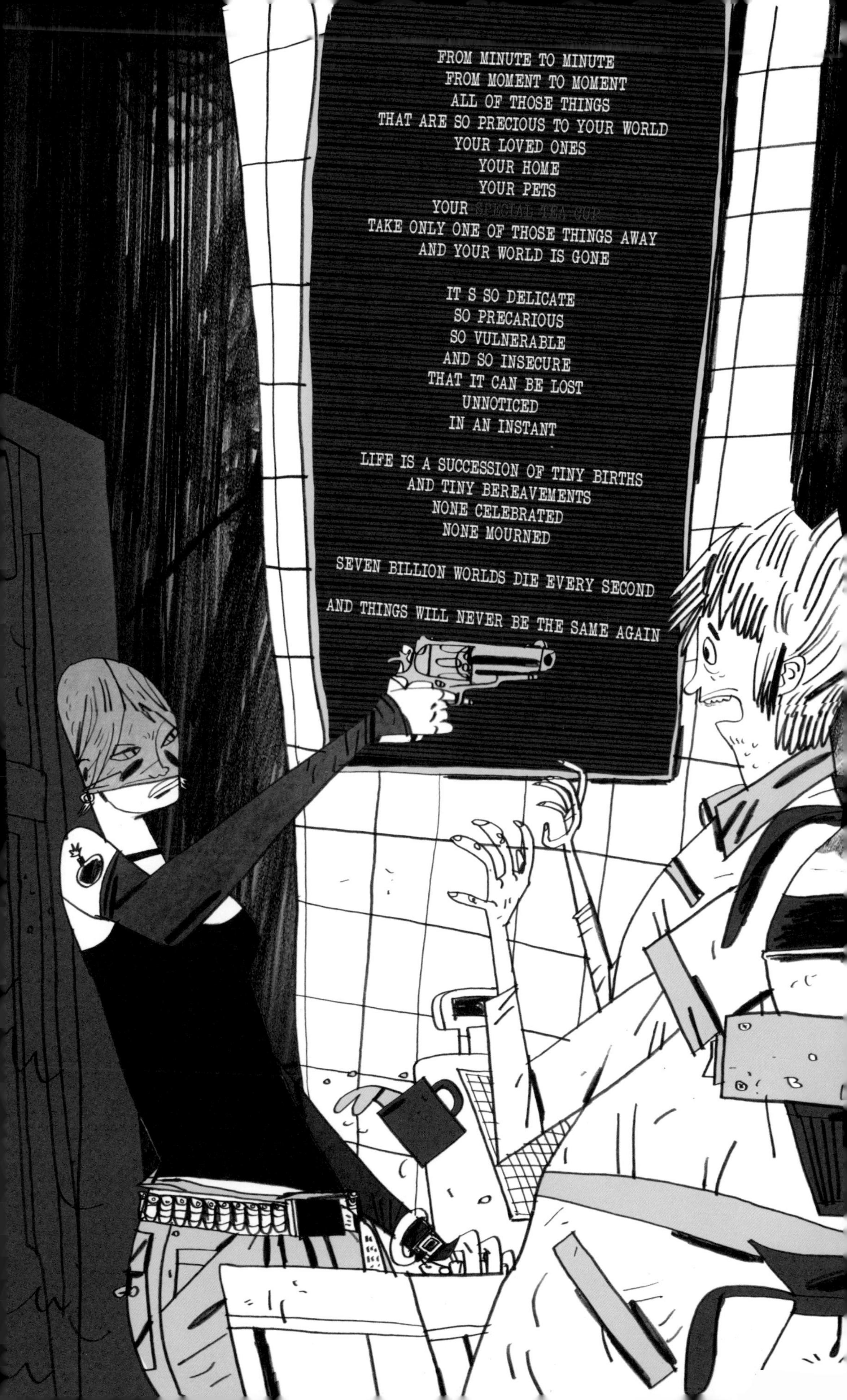
FROM MINUTE TO MINUTE
FROM MOMENT TO MOMENT
ALL OF THOSE THINGS
THAT ARE SO PRECIOUS TO YOUR WORLD
YOUR LOVED ONES
YOUR HOME
YOUR PETS
YOUR SPECIAL TEA CUP
TAKE ONLY ONE OF THOSE THINGS AWAY
AND YOUR WORLD IS GONE
IT S SO DELICATE
SO PRECARIOUS
SO VULNERABLE
AND SO INSECURE
THAT IT CAN BE LOST
UNNOTICED
IN AN INSTANT
LIFE IS A SUCCESSION OF TINY BIRTHS
AND TINY BEREAVEMENTS
NONE CELEBRATED
NONE MOURNED
SEVEN BILLION WORLDS DIE EVERY SECOND
AND THINGS WILL NEVER BE THE SAME AGAIN

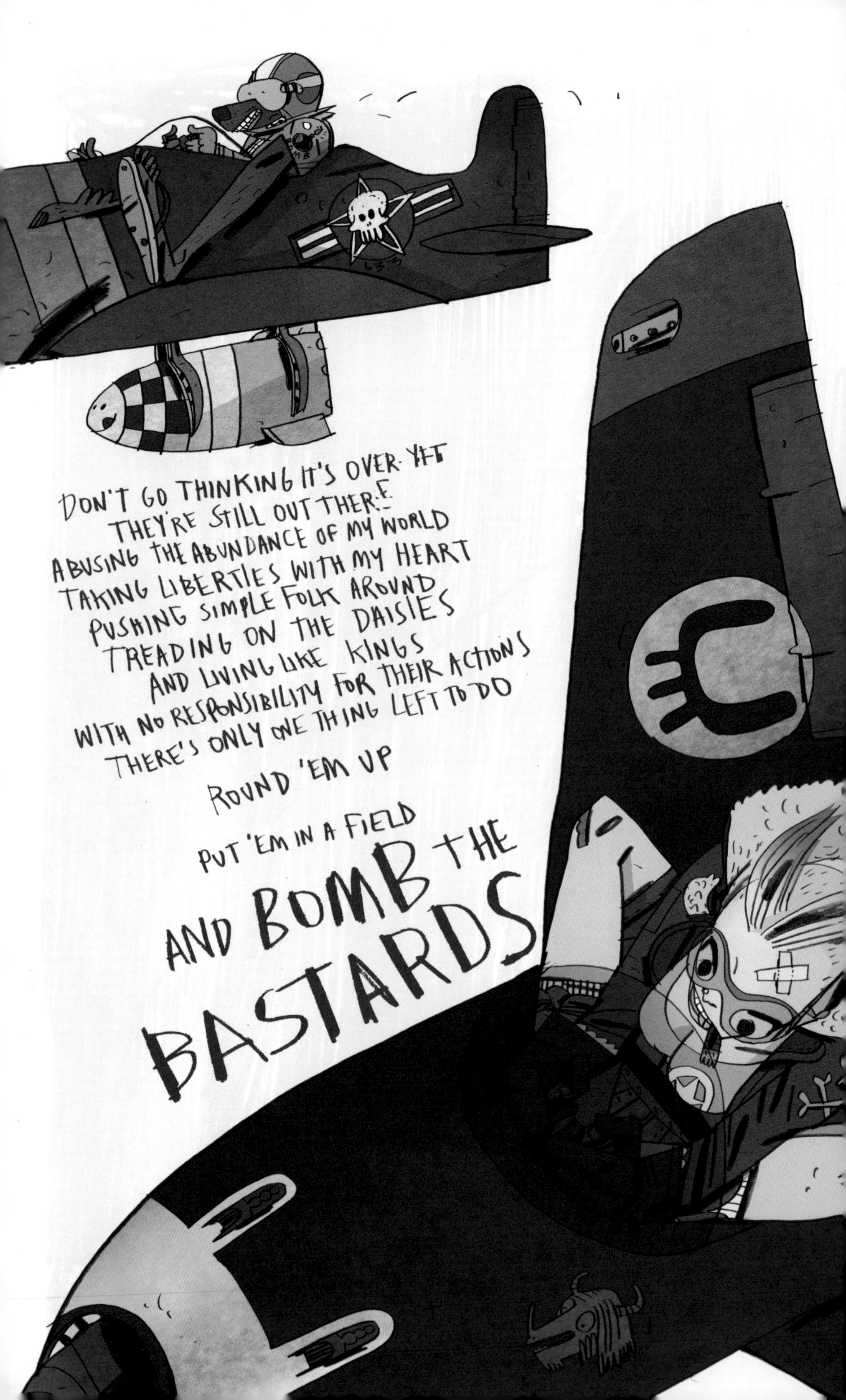
DON'T GO THINKING IT'S OVER YET
THEY'RE STILL OUT THERE
ABUSING THE ABUNDANCE OF MY WORLD
TAKING LIBERTIES WITH MY HEART
PUSHING SIMPLE FOLK AROUND
TREADING ON THE DAISIES
AND LIVING LIKE KINGS
WITH NO RESPONSIBILITY FOR THEIR ACTIONS
THERE'S ONLY ONE THING LEFT TO DO
ROUND 'EM UP
PUT 'EM IN A FIELD
AND BOMB THE
BASTARDS

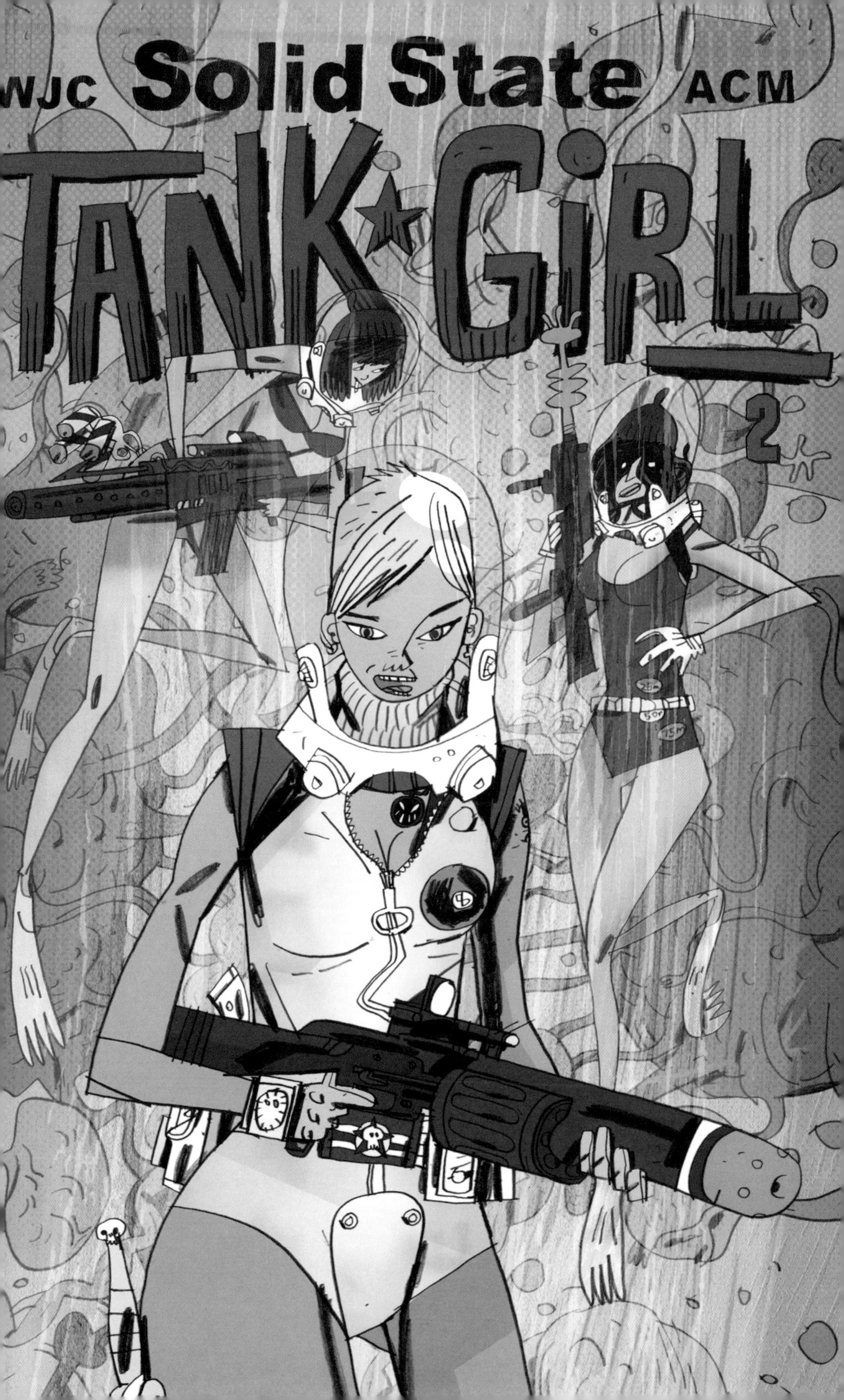
WJC
Solid State
ACM
TANK GIRL
2

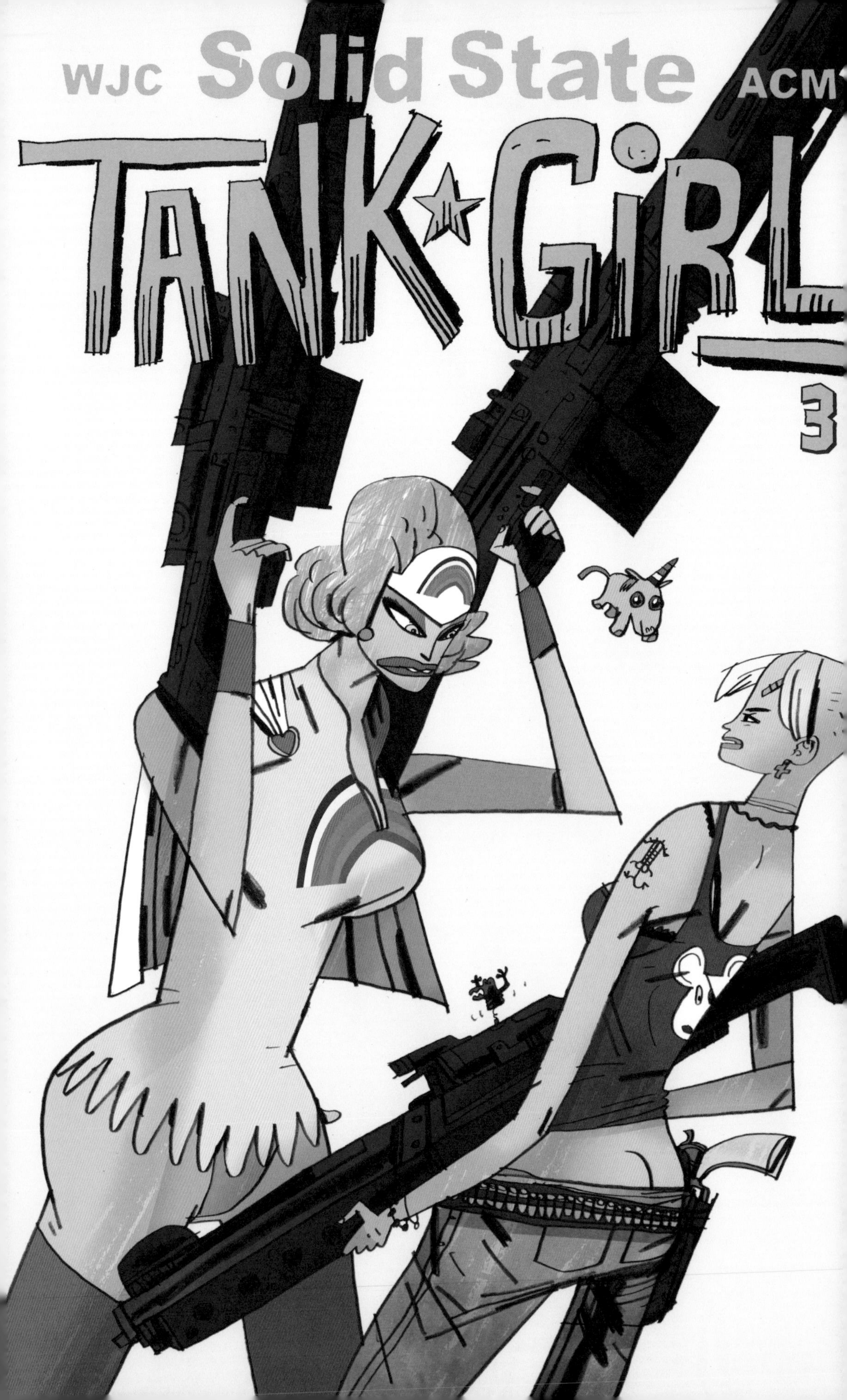
WJC
Solid State
ACM
TANK GIRL
3

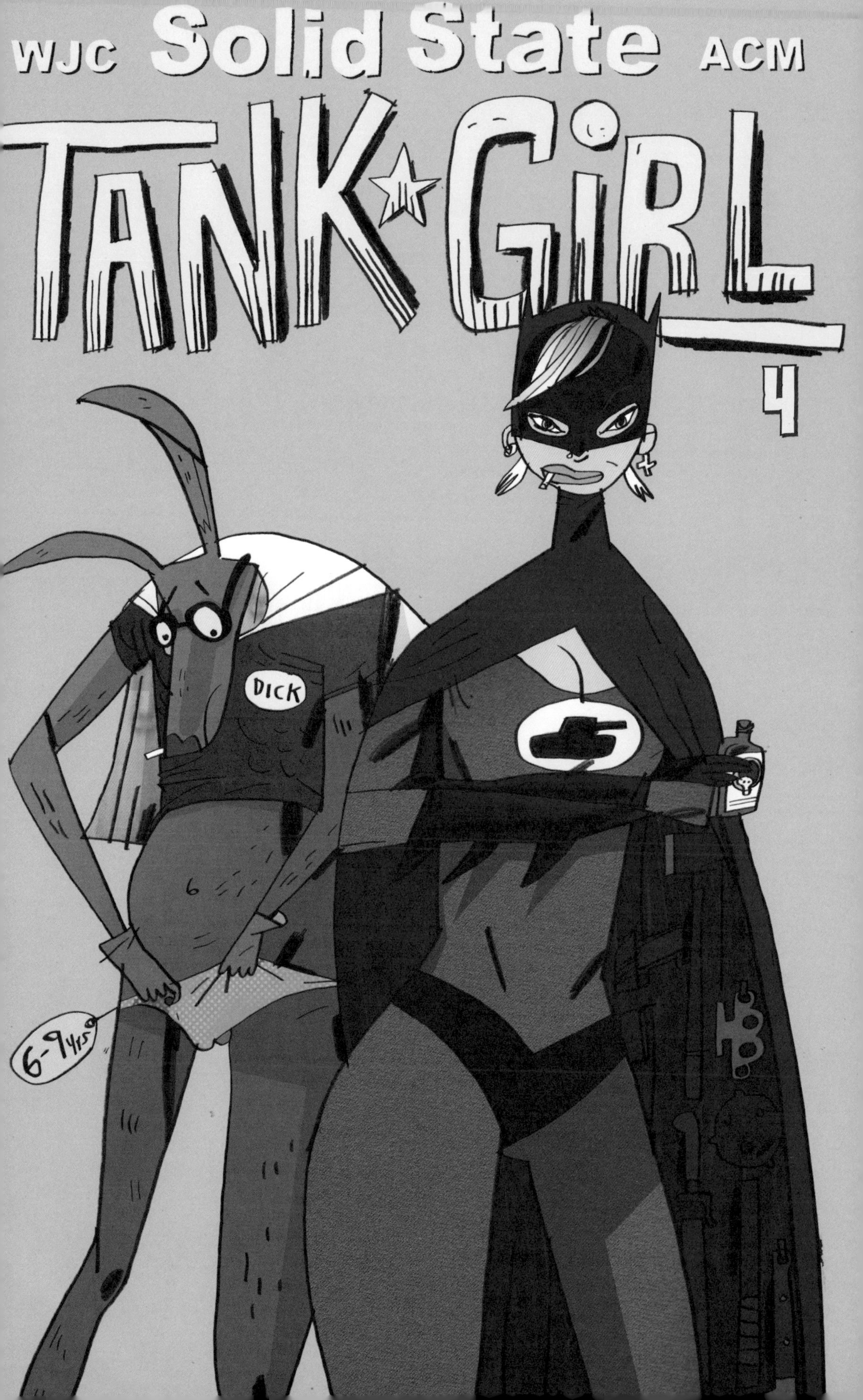
WJC Solid State ACM
TANK GIRL
4
DICK

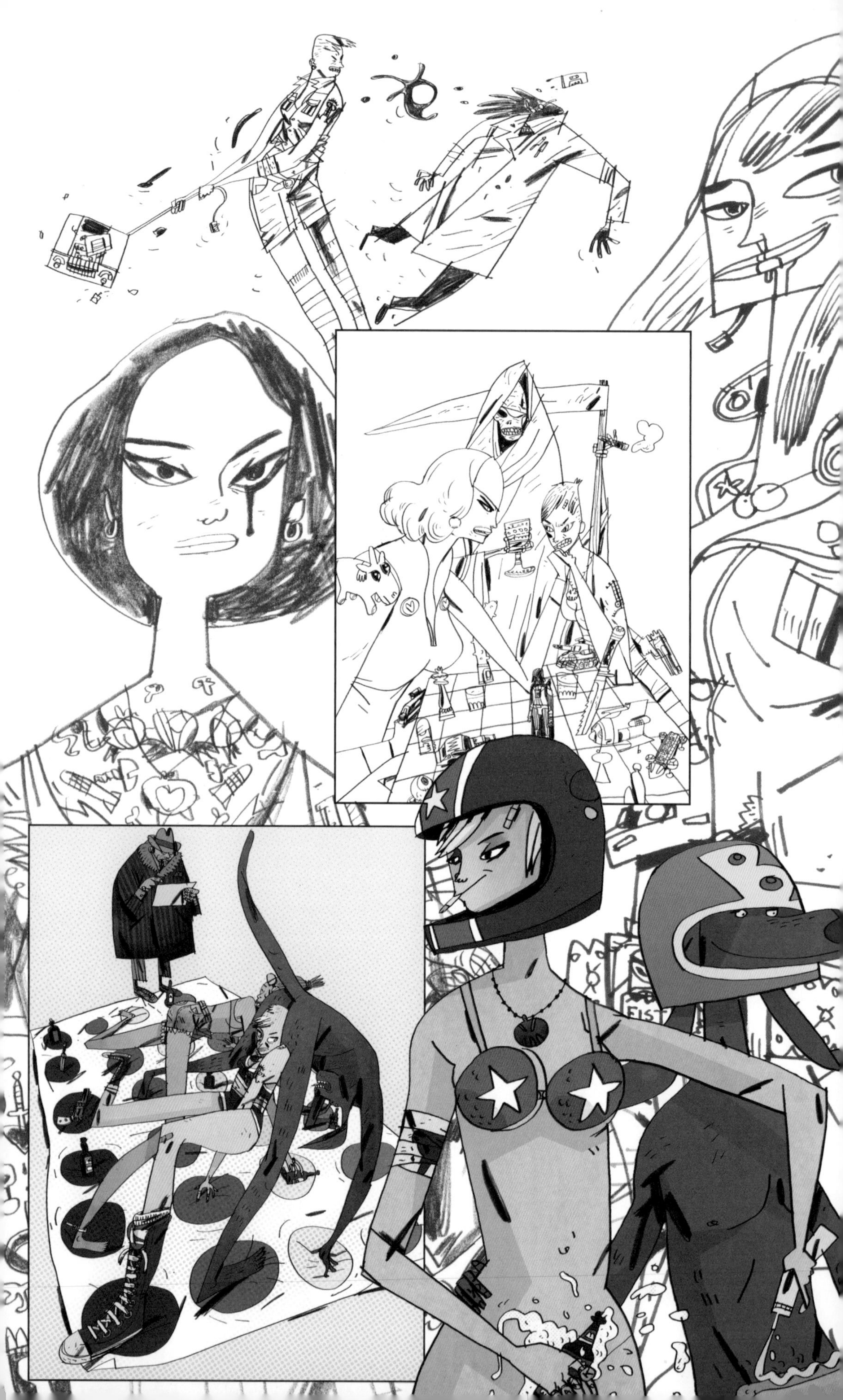
FIST

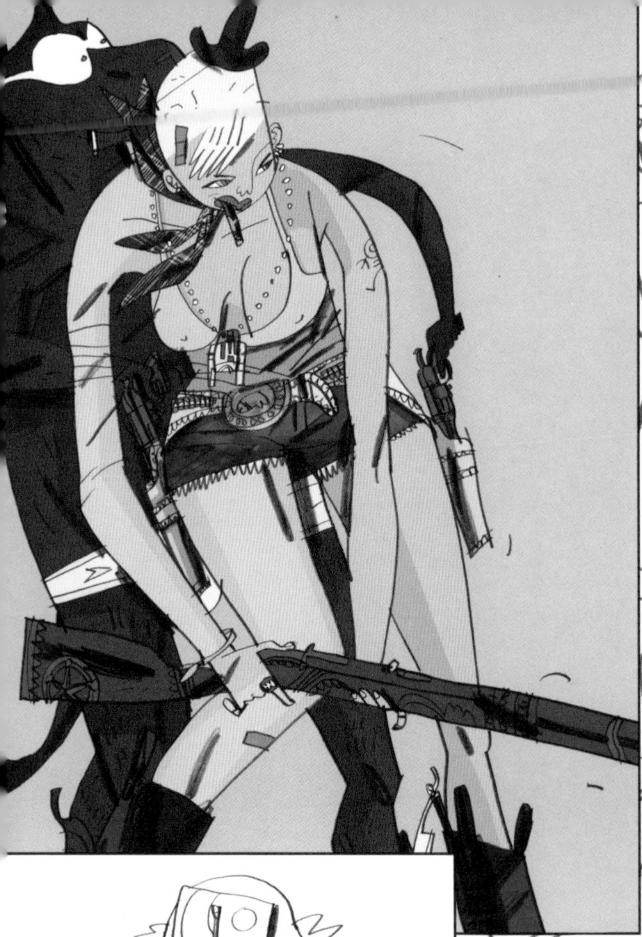

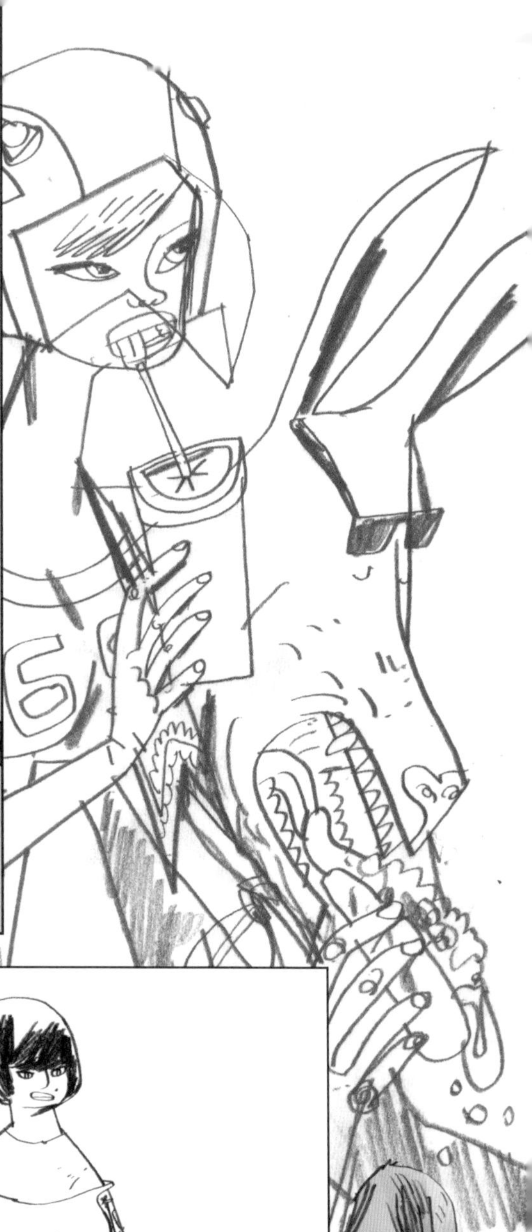

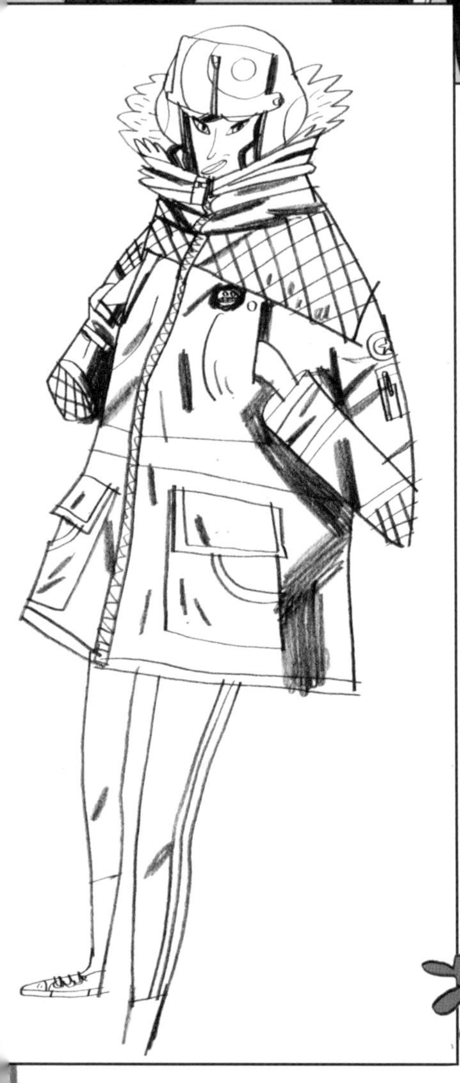

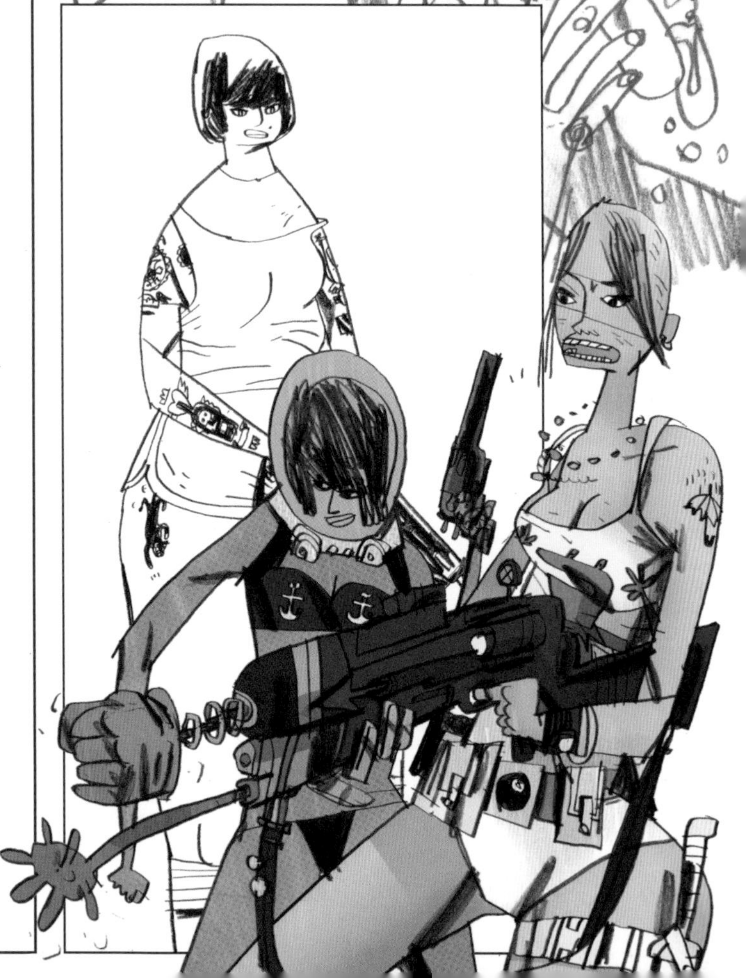

The basic premise of this story started of as a hum-drum, run-of-the-mill comic book standard - hero meets nemesis, both are almost destroyed, revelations about protagonist ensue. But, as soon as I put pen to paper, things started to mutate. Similarly, the nemesis herself found it hard to stay true to my original plan for her character, which was drawn from the anti-tank guns and missiles of World War Two, and the brutal machinery of war.

As soon as Warwick was on board I couldn't resist fucking things up to see what he would do with them. Warwick's style strikes me as almost cubist - upsetting, exciting, revelatory, and unnerving - I twisted my story as hard as I could to see how it would gel. So anti-tank guns turned into Transformers, a trip into a jungle turned into a journey to the centre of a testicle, and a battle between good and evil became a tale of unrequited love.

I'm very pleased with the results, it's as crazy-arsed as Tank Girl has ever been and, reading back through it now as we put this collection together, is still full of shocks and surprises even for me.

We hope you'll enjoy the story and the extra material in this book. It was hard-won for us; we know we make it look like we are super-professional, and it's a piece of cake to produce such a book, but there is blood in these pages, real blood, and magick in the story, real, scary magick. This book will change you forever.

Take extreme care

Ten-Ten 'til we do it again

The Anti-Alan
Splashpoint
Worthing
August 2013

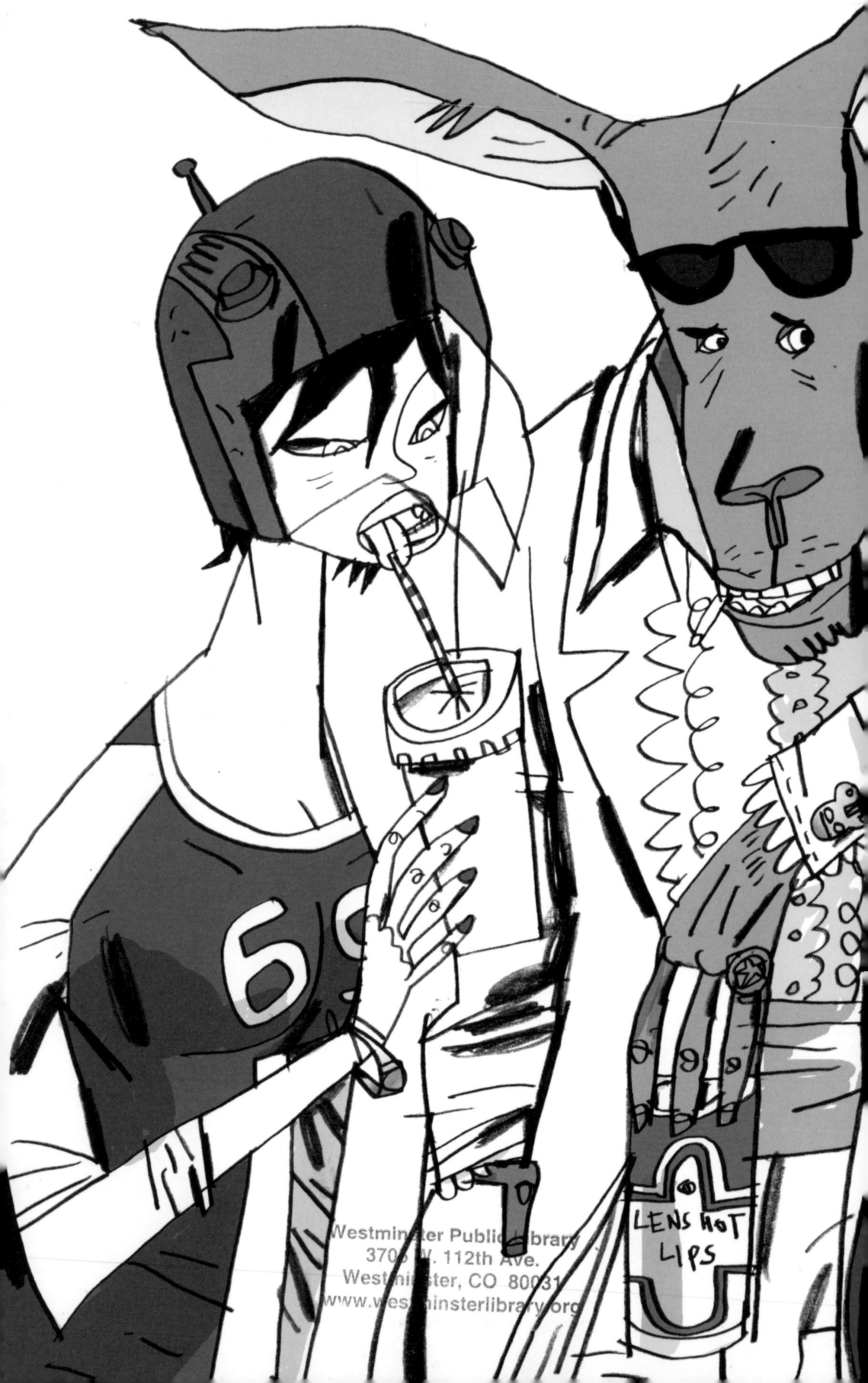
LENS HOT
LIPS